Java™ Message Service

THE
JAVA™
SERIES

Also from O'Reilly

Java™ Message Service

Richard Monson-Haefel & David A. Chappell

O'REILLY®

Beijing · Cambridge · Farnham · Köln · Paris · Sebastopol · Taipei · Tokyo

Java™ Message Service
by Richard Monson-Haefel and David A. Chappell

Copyright © 2001 O'Reilly & Associates, Inc. All rights reserved.
Printed in the United States of America.

Published by O'Reilly & Associates, Inc., 101 Morris Street, Sebastopol, CA 95472.

Editor: Mike Loukides

Production Editor: Colleen Gorman

Cover Designer: Hanna Dyer

Printing History:

January 2001:   First Edition.

Library of Congress Cataloging-in-Publication Data

Monson-Haefel, Richard.
    Java message service / Richard Monson-Haefel & David Chappell. p. cm.
    ISBN 0-596-00068-5
    1. Java (Computer program language) 2. Telecommunication–Message processing.
      I. Chappell, David (David A.) II. Title.

QA76.73.J38 M655 2000
005.7'12762–dc21   00-053024

ISBN: 0-596-00068-5
[M]   [9/01]

*To my brother, Kurt, whose spirit and courage
are an inspiration.*
—Richard Monson-Haefel

*To my wife Wendy, and our children Dave, Amy,
and Chris, for their love and support.*
—David A. Chappell

Table of Contents

Preface

What Is the Java Message Service?

When Java™ was first introduced, most of the IT industry focused on its graphical user interface characteristics and the competitive advantage it offered in terms of distribution and platform independence. Today, the focus has broadened considerably: Java has been recognized as an excellent platform for creating enterprise solutions, specifically for developing distributed server-side applications. This shift has much to do with Java's emerging role as a universal language for producing implementation-independent abstractions for common enterprise technologies. The JDBC™ API is the first and most familiar example. JDBC provides a vendor-independent Java interface for accessing SQL relational databases. This abstraction has been so successful that it's difficult to find a relational database vendor that doesn't support JDBC. Java abstractions for enterprise technologies have expanded considerably to include JNDI (Java Naming and Directory Interface™) for abstracting directory services, JMX (Java Management Extensions) for abstracting access to computer devices on a network, and JMS™ (Java Message Service) for abstracting access to different Message-Oriented Middleware products.

JMS has quickly become a de facto industry standard. In its second version, most enterprise messaging vendors now support the JMS specification, making for a large selection of JMS providers to choose from.

The Java Message Service is a Java API implemented by enterprise messaging vendors to provide Java applications with a common and elegant programming model that is portable across messaging systems. Enterprise messaging systems are used to send notification of events and data between software applications. There are two common programming models supported by the JMS API: publish-and-subscribe and point-to-point. Each model provides benefits and either or both may be implemented by JMS providers.

JMS and enterprise messaging systems provide Java developers with an asynchronous messaging system that allows systems to interact without requiring them to be tightly coupled. Messages can be delivered to systems that are not currently running and processed when it's convenient. The decoupled, asynchronous characteristics of enterprise messaging make JMS an extremely powerful and critical enterprise API. JMS is used by Java developers in Enterprise Application Integration, Business-to-Business (B2B) projects, and distributed computing in general.

As JMS quickly moves into the forefront as one of the most important J2EE technologies, understanding how JMS works and when to use it will become the hallmark of the most successful distributed computing professionals. Choosing to read this book to learn about JMS may be one of the smartest career moves you ever make.

Who Should Read This Book?

This book explains and demonstrates the fundamentals of the the Java Message Service. This book provides a straightforward, no-nonsense explanation of the underlying technology, Java classes and interfaces, programming models, and various implemenations of the JMS specification.

Although this book focuses on the fundamentals, it's no "dummy's" book. While the JMS API is easy to learn, the API abstracts fairly complex enterprise technology. Before reading this book, you should be fluent with the Java language and have some practical experience developing business solutions. Experience with messaging systems is not required, but you must have a working knowledge of the Java language. If you are unfamiliar with the Java language, we recommend that you pick up a copy of *Learning Java™* by Patrick Neimeyer and Jonathan Knudsen (O'Reilly). If you need a stronger background in distributed computing, we recommend *Java™ Distributed Computing* by Jim Farley (O'Reilly).

Organization

Here's how the book is structured. The first chapter explains messaging systems, centralized and distributed architectures, and how and why JMS is important. Chapters 2 through 5 go into detail about developing JMS clients using the two messaging models, publish-and-subscribe and point-to-point. Chapters 6 and 7 should be considered "advanced topics," covering deployment and administration of messaging systems. Chapter 8 is an overview of the Java™ 2, Enterprise Edition (J2EE) with regard to JMS, including coverage of the new message-driven bean in

Enterprise JavaBeans 2.0. Finally, Chapter 9 provides a summary of several JMS vendors and their products.

Chapter 1, Understanding the Messaging Paradigm
Defines enterprise messaging and common architectures used by messaging vendors. JMS is defined and explained, as are its two programming models, publish-and-subscribe and point-to-point.

Chapter 2, Developing a Simple Example
Walks the reader through the development of a simple publish-and-subscribe JMS client.

Chapter 3, Anatomy of a JMS Message
Provides a detailed examination of the JMS message, the most important part of the JMS API.

Chapter 4, Publish-and-Subscribe Messaging
Examines the publish-and-subscribe programming model through the development of a B2B JMS application.

Chapter 5, Point-to-Point Messaging
Examines the point-to-point programming models through the enhancement of the B2B JMS application developed in Chapter 4.

Chapter 6, Guaranteed Messaging, Transactions, Acknowledgments, and Failures
Provides an in-depth explanation of advanced topics, including guaranteed messaging, transactions, acknowledgments, and failures.

Chapter 7, Deployment Considerations
Provides an in-depth examination of features and issues that should be considered when choosing vendors and deploying JMS applications.

Chapter 8, J2EE, EJB, and JMS
Provides an overview of the Java™ 2, Enterprise Edition (J2EE) with regard to JMS, and also includes coverage of the new JMS-based bean in Enterprise JavaBeans 2.0.

Chapter 9, JMS Providers
Provides a summary of several JMS vendors and their products, including: IBM's MQSeries, Progress' SonicMQ, Fiorano's FioranoMQ, Softwired's iBus, Sun's JMQ, BEA's WebLogic, and Exolab's OpenJMS.

Appendix A, The Java Message Service API
Provides a quick reference to the classes and interfaces defined in the JMS package.

Appendix B, Message Headers
Provides detailed information about message headers.

Appendix C, Message Properties
> Provides detailed information about message properties.

Appendix D, Message Selectors
> Provides detailed information about message selectors.

Software and Versions

This book covers the Java Message Service Version 1.0.2. It uses Java language features from the Java 1.1 platform. Because the focus of this book is to develop vendor-independent JMS clients and applications, we have stayed away from proprietary extensions and vendor-dependent idioms. Any JMS-compliant provider can be used with this book; you should be familiar with that provider's specific installation, deployment, and runtime management procedures to work with the examples. To find out the details of installing and running JMS clients for a specific JMS provider, consult your JMS vendor's documentation; these details aren't covered by the JMS specification.

Examples developed in this book are available from *http://www.oreilly.com/catalog/javmesser/examples/index.html*. The examples are organized by chapter. Special source code modified for specific vendors is also provided. These vendor-specific examples include a *readme.txt* file that points to documentation for downloading and installing the JMS provider, as well as specific instructions on setting up the provider for each example.

Conventions

Italic is used for filenames, pathnames, hostnames, domain names, URLs, email addresses, and new terms where they are defined.

`Constant width` is used for code examples and fragments, class, variable, and method names, Java keywords used within the text, SQL commands, table names, column names, and XML elements and tags.

`Constant width bold` is used for emphasis in some code examples.

`Constant width italic` is used to indicate text that is replaceable.

The term "JMS provider" is used to refer to a vendor that implements the JMS API to provide connectivity to their enterprise messaging service. The term "JMS client" refers to Java components or applications that use the JMS API and a JMS provider to send and receive messages. "JMS application" refers to any combination of JMS clients that work together to provide a software solution.

Comments and Questions

We have tested and verified the information in this book to the best of our ability, but you may find that features have changed (or even that we have made mistakes!). Please let us know about any errors you find, as well as your suggestions for future editions, by writing to:

> O'Reilly & Associates, Inc.
> 101 Morris Street
> Sebastopol, CA 95472
> (800) 998-9938 (in the United States or Canada)
> (707) 829-0515 (international or local)
> (707) 829-0104 (fax)

We have a web page for this book, where we list errata, examples, or any additional information. You can access this page at:

> *http://www.oreilly.com/catalog/javmesser/*

To comment or ask technical questions about this book, send email to:

> *bookquestions@oreilly.com*

For more information about our books, conferences, software, Resource Centers, and the O'Reilly Network, see our web site at:

> *http://www.oreilly.com*

Richard Monson-Haefel maintains a web site for the discussion of JMS and related distributed computing technologies (*http://www.jMiddleware.com*). *jMiddleware. com* provides news about this book as well as code tips, articles, and an extensive list of links to JMS resources.

David Chappell hosts a similar site, the SonicMQ Developers Exchange, which can be found at *http://www.sonicmq.com/developers/*.

Acknowledgments

While there are only two names on the cover of this book, the credit for its development and delivery is shared by many individuals. Michael Loukides, our editor, was pivotal to the success of this book. Without his experience, craft, and guidance, this book would not have been possible.

Many expert technical reviewers helped ensure that the material was technically accurate and true to the spirit of the Java Message Service. Of special note are

Joseph Fialli, Anne Thomas Manes, and Chris Kasso of Sun Microsystems, Andrew Neumann and Giovanni Boschi of Progress, Thomas Haas of Softwired, Mikhail Rizkin of International Systems Group, and Jim Alateras of ExoLab. The contributions of these technical experts are critical to the technical and conceptual accuracy of this book. They brought a combination of industry and real-world experience to bear, and helped to make this the best book on JMS published today.

Thanks also to Mark Hapner of Sun Microsystems, the primary architect of Java 2, Enterprise Edition, who answered several of our most complex questions. Thanks to all the participants in the JMS-INTEREST mailing list hosted by Sun Microsystems for their interesting and informative postings.

Special appreciation goes to George St. Maurice of the SonicMQ tech writing team for his participation in organizing the examples for the O'Reilly web site.

Finally, the most sincere gratitude must be extended to our families. Richard Monson-Haefel thanks his wife, Hollie, for supporting and assisting him through yet another book. Her love makes everything possible. David Chappell thanks his wife, Wendy, and their children Dave, Amy, and Chris, for putting up with him during this endeavor.

David Chappell would also like to thank some of the members of the Progress SonicMQ team—Bill Wood, Andy Neumann, Giovanni Boschi, Christine Semeniuk, David Grigglestone, Bill Cullen, Perry Yin, Kathy Guo, Mitchell Horowitz, Greg O'Connor, Mike Theroux, Ron Rudis, Charlie Nuzzolo, Jeanne Abmayr, Oriana Merlo, George St. Maurice—for helping to ensure that the appropriate topics were addressed, and addressed accurately. And special thanks to George Chappell for helping him with "split infinitives."

1

Understanding the Messaging Paradigm

Computers and people can communicate by using messaging systems to exchange messages over electronic networks. The most ubiquitous messaging system today is email, which facilitates communication among people. While email is an important human-to-human messaging system, this book is not about email. Instead, this book is concerned with messaging systems that allow different software applications to communicate with each other. These application-to-application messaging systems, when used in business systems, are generically referred to as enterprise messaging systems, or Message-Oriented Middleware (MOM).

Enterprise messaging systems allow two or more applications to exchange information in the form of messages. A message, in this case, is a self-contained package of business data and network routing headers. The business data contained in a message can be anything—depending on the business scenario—and usually contains information about some business transaction. In enterprise messaging systems, messages inform an application of some event or occurrence in another system.

Using Message-Oriented Middleware, messages are transmitted from one application to another across a network. MOM products ensure that messages are properly distributed among applications. In addition, MOMs usually provide fault tolerance, load balancing, scalability, and transactional support for enterprises that need to reliably exchange large quantities of messages.

MOM vendors use different message formats and network protocols for exchanging messages, but the basic semantics are the same. An API is used to create a message, give it a payload (application data), assign it routing information, and then send the message. The same API is used to receive messages produced by other applications.

In all modern enterprise messaging systems, applications exchange messages through virtual channels called *destinations*. When a message is sent, it's addressed to a destination, not a specific application. Any application that subscribes or registers an interest in that destination may receive that message. In this way, the applications that receive messages and those that send messages are decoupled. Senders and receivers are not bound to each other in any way and may send and receive messages as they see fit.

All MOM vendors provide application developers with an API for sending and receiving messages. While a MOM vendor implements its own networking protocols, routing, and administration facilities, the basic semantics of the developer API provided by different MOMs are the same. This similarity in APIs makes the Java Message Service possible.

The Java Message Service (JMS) is a vendor-agnostic Java API that can be used with many different MOM vendors. JMS is analogous to JDBC in that application developers reuse the same API to access many different systems. If a vendor provides a compliant service provider for JMS, then the JMS API can be used to send and receive messages to that vendor. For example, you can use the same JMS API to send messages using Progress' SonicMQ as you do IBM's MQSeries. It is the purpose of this book to explain how enterprise messaging systems work and in particular how the Java Message Service is used with these systems. This book focuses on JMS 1.0.2, the most recent version of the specification, which was introduced in November 1999.

The rest of this chapter explores enterprise messaging and JMS in more detail, so that you have a solid foundation with which to learn about the JMS API and messaging concepts in the rest of this book. We assume that you are already familiar with the Java programming language—other than that, everything is explained.

Enterprise Messaging

Enterprise messaging is not a new concept. Messaging products such as IBM MQSeries, Microsoft MSMQ, TIBCO Rendevous, Open Horizon Ambrosia, and Modulus InterAgent have been in existence for many years. Newer messaging products such as Progress SonicMQ, Softwired iBus, and FioranoMQ have been built from the ground up, based on the need for doing reliable Business-to-Business communications over the Internet.

A key concept of enterprise messaging is messages are delivered *asynchronously* from one system to others over a network. To deliver a message asynchronously means the sender is not required to wait for the message to be received or handled by the recipient; it is free to send the message and continue processing. Asynchronous messages are treated as autonomous units—each message is self-contained and carries all of the data and state needed by the business logic that processes it.

In asynchronous messaging, applications use a simple API to construct a message, then hand it off to the Message-Oriented Middleware for delivery to one or more intended recipients (Figure 1-1). A message is a package of business data that is sent from one application to another over the network. The message should be self-describing in that it should contain all the necessary context to allow the recipients to carry out their work independently.

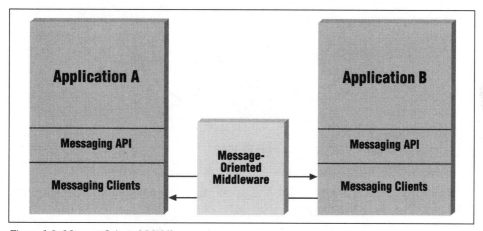

Figure 1-1. Message-Oriented Middleware

Message-Oriented Middleware architectures of today vary in their implementation. The spectrum ranges from a centralized architecture that depends on a message server to perform routing, to a decentralized architecture that distributes the "server" processing out to the client machines. A varied array of protocols including TCP/IP, HTTP, SSL, and IP multicast are employed at the network transport layer. Some messaging products use a hybrid of both approaches, depending on the usage model.

Before we discuss the different architectures, it is important to explain what we mean by the term client. Messaging systems are composed of *messaging clients* and some kind of MOM. The clients send messages to the MOM, which then distributes those messages to other clients. The client is a business application or component that is using the messaging API (in our case JMS).

Centralized Architectures

Enterprise messaging systems that use a centralized architecture rely on a *message server*. A message server, also called a message router or broker, is responsible for delivering messages from one messaging client to other messaging clients. The message server decouples a sending client from other receiving clients. Clients only see the messaging server, not other clients, which allows clients to be added and removed without impacting the system as a whole.

Typically, a centralized architecture uses a hub-and-spoke topology. In a simple case, there is a centralized message server and all clients connect to it. As shown in Figure 1-2, the hub-and-spoke architecture lends itself to a minimal amount of network connections while still allowing any part of the system to communicate with any other part of the system.

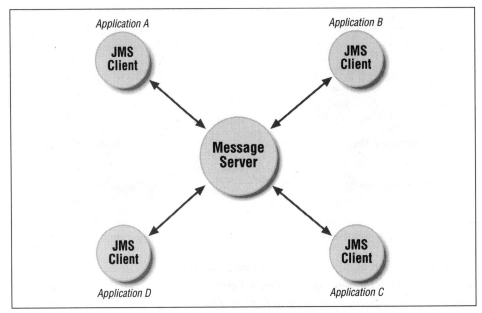

Figure 1-2. Centralized hub-and-spoke architecture

In practice, the centralized message server may be a cluster of distributed servers operating as a logical unit.

Decentralized Architectures

All decentralized architectures currently use IP multicast at the network level. A messaging system based on multicasting has no centralized server. Some of the server functionality (persistence, transactions, security) is embedded as a local part of the client, while message routing is delegated to the network layer by using the IP multicast protocol.

IP multicast allows applications to join one or more IP multicast groups; each group uses an IP network address that will redistribute any messages it receives to all members in its group. In this way, applications can send messages to an IP multicast address and expect the network layer to redistribute the messages appropriately (see Figure 1-3). Unlike a centralized architecture, a distributed architecture doesn't require a server for the purposes of routing messages—the network handles routing automatically. However, other server-like functionality is still required to be included with each client, such as message persistence and message delivery semantics like once-and-only-once delivery.

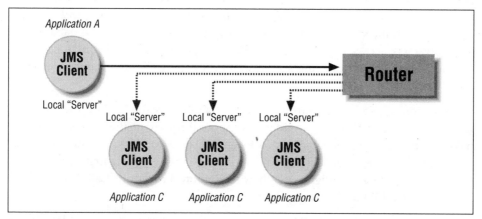

Figure 1-3. Decentralized IP multicast architecture

Hybrid Architectures

A decentralized architecture usually implies that an IP multicast protocol is being used. A centralized architecture usually implies that the TCP/IP protocol is the basis for communication between the various components. A messaging vendor's architecture may also combine the two approaches. Clients may connect to a daemon process using TCP/IP, which in turn communicate with other daemon processes using IP multicast groups.

Centralized Architecture as a Model

Both ends of the decentralized and centralized architecture spectrum have their place in enterprise messaging. The advantages and disadvantages of distributed versus centralized architectures are discussed in more detail in Chapter 7, *Deployment Considerations*. In the meantime we need a common model for discussing other aspects of enterprise messaging. In order to simplify discussions, this book uses a centralized architecture as a logical view of enterprise messaging. This is for convenience only and is not an endorsement of centralized over decentralized architectures. The term "message server" is frequently used in this book to refer to the underlying architecture that is responsible for routing and distributing messages. In centralized architectures, the message server is a middleware server or cluster of servers. In decentralized architectures, the server refers to the local server-like facilities of the client.

The Java Message Service (JMS)

The Java Message Service (JMS) is an API for enterprise messaging created by Sun Microsystems. JMS is not a messaging system itself; it's an abstraction of the interfaces and classes needed by messaging clients when communicating with messaging systems. In the same way that JDBC abstracts access to relational databases and JNDI abstracts access to naming and directory services, JMS abstracts access to MOMs. Using JMS, a messaging application's messaging clients are portable across MOM products.

The creation of JMS was an industry effort. JavaSoft took the lead on the spec and worked very closely with the messaging vendors throughout the process. The initial objective was to provide a Java API for connectivity to MOM systems. However, this changed to the wider objective of supporting messaging as a first-class Java distributed computing paradigm equally with Remote Procedure Call (RPC) based systems like CORBA and Enterprise JavaBeans:

> There were a number of MOM vendors that participated in the creation of JMS. It was an industry effort rather than a Sun effort. Sun was the spec lead and did shepherd the work but it would not have been successful without the direct involvement of the messaging vendors. Although our original objective was to provide a Java API for connectivity to MOM systems, this changed over the course of the work to a broader objective of supporting messaging as a first class Java distributed computing paradigm on equal footing with RPC.
>
> —Mark Hapner, JMS spec lead, Sun Microsystems

The result is a best-of-breed, robust specification that includes a rich set of message delivery semantics, combined with a simple yet flexible API for incorporating messaging into applications. The intent was that in addition to new vendors, existing messaging vendors would support the JMS API.

JMS Messaging Models: Publish-and-Subscribe and Point-to-Point

JMS provides for two types of messaging models, publish-and-subscribe and point-to-point queuing. The JMS specification refers to these as *messaging domains*. In JMS terminology, publish-and-subscribe and point-to-point are frequently shortened to pub/sub and p2p (or PTP), respectively. This book uses both the long and short forms throughout.

In the simplest sense, publish-and-subscribe is intended for a one-to-many broad-cast of messages, while point-to-point is intended for one-to-one delivery of mes-sages (see Figure 1-4).

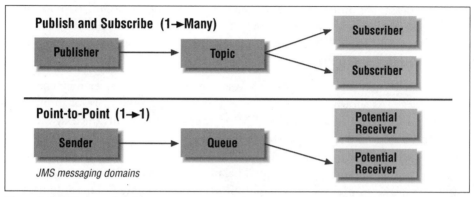

Figure 1-4. JMS messaging domains

Messaging clients in JMS are called *JMS clients*, and the messaging system—the MOM—is called the *JMS provider*. A *JMS application* is a business system composed of many JMS clients and, generally, one JMS provider.

In addition, a JMS client that produces a message is called a *producer*, while a JMS client that receives a message is called a *consumer*. A JMS client can be both a pro-ducer and a consumer. When we use the term consumer or producer, we mean a JMS client that consumes messages or produces messages, respectively. We use this terminology throughout the book.

Publish-and-subscribe

In pub/sub, one producer can send a message to many consumers through a vir-tual channel called a *topic*. Consumers, which receive messages, can choose to *subscribe* to a topic. Any messages addressed to a topic are delivered to all the topic's consumers. Every consumer receives a copy of each message. The pub/sub messaging model is by and large a push-based model, where messages are automat-ically broadcast to consumers without them having to request or poll the topic for new messages.

In the pub/sub messaging model the producer sending the message is not depen-dent on the consumers receiving the message. Optionally, JMS clients that use pub/sub can establish durable subscriptions that allow consumers to disconnect and later reconnect and collect messages that were published while they were disconnected. The pub/sub JMS messaging model is discussed in greater detail in Chapter 2, *Devel-oping a Simple Example*, and Chapter 4, *Publish-and-Subscribe Messaging*.

Point-to-point

The point-to-point messaging model allows JMS clients to send and receive messages both synchronously and asynchronously via virtual channels known as *queues*. The p2p messaging model has traditionally been a pull- or polling-based model, where messages are requested from the queue instead of being pushed to the client automatically. In JMS, however, an option exists that allows p2p clients to use a push model similar to pub/sub.

A given queue may have multiple receivers, but only one receiver may consume each message. As shown in Figure 1-4, the JMS provider takes care of doling out the work, insuring that each message is consumed once and only once by the next available receiver in the group. The JMS specification does not dictate the rules for distributing messages among multiple receivers, although some JMS vendors have chosen to implement this as a load balancing capability. P2p also offers other features, such as a queue browser that allows a client to view the contents of a queue prior to consuming its messages—this browser concept is not available in the pub/sub model. The p2p messaging model is covered in more detail in Chapter 5, *Point-to-Point Messaging*.

Application Scenarios

Until now, our discussion of enterprise messaging has been somewhat abstract. This section attempts to give some real-world scenarios to provide you with a better idea of the types of problems that enterprise messaging systems can solve.

Enterprise Application Integration

Most mature organizations have both legacy and new applications that are implemented independently and cannot interoperate. In many cases, organizations have a strong desire to integrate these applications so they can share information and cooperate in larger enterprise-wide operations. The integration of these applications is generally called Enterprise Application Integration (EAI).

A variety of vendor and home-grown solutions are used for EAI, but enterprise messaging systems are central to most of them. Enterprise messaging systems allow stovepipe applications to communicate events and to exchange data while remaining physically independent. Data and events can be exchanged in the form of messages via topics or queues, which provide an abstraction that decouples participating applications.

As an example, a messaging system might be used to integrate an Internet order processing system with an Enterprise Resource Planning (ERP) system like SAP. The Internet system uses JMS to deliver business data about new orders to a topic.

An ERP gateway application, which accesses a SAP application via its native API, can subscribe to the order topic. As new orders are broadcast to the topic, the gateway receives the orders and enters them into the SAP application.

Business-to-Business

Historically, businesses exchanged data using Electronic Data Interchange (EDI) systems. Data was exchanged using rigid, fixed formats over proprietary Value-Added Networks (VANs). Cost of entry was high and data was usually exchanged in batch processes—not as real-time business events.

The Internet, XML, and modern messaging systems have radically changed how businesses exchange data and interact in what is now called Business-to-Business (B2B). The use of messaging systems is central to modern B2B solutions because it allows organizations to cooperate without requiring them to tightly integrate their business systems. In addition, it lowers the barriers to entry since finer-grained participation is possible. Businesses can join in B2B and disengage depending on the queues and topics with which they interact.

A manufacturer, for example, can set up a topic for broadcasting requests for bids on raw materials. Suppliers can subscribe to the topic and respond by producing messages back to the manufacturer's queue. Suppliers can be added and removed at will, and new topics and queues for different types of inventory and raw materials can be used to partition the systems appropriately.

Geographic Dispersion

These days many companies are geographically dispersed. Brick-and-mortar, click-and-mortar, and dot-coms all face problems associated with geographic dispersion of enterprise systems. Inventory systems in remote warehouses need to communicate with centralized back-office ERP systems at corporate headquarters. Sensitive employee data that is administered locally at each subsidiary needs to be synchronized with the main office. JMS messaging systems can ensure the safe and secure exchange of data across a geographically distributed business.

One-to-many, push-model applications

Auction sites, stock quote services, and securities exchanges all have to push data out to huge populations of recipients in a one-to-many fashion. In many cases, the broadcast of information needs to be selectively routed and filtered on a per recipient basis. While the outgoing information needs to be delivered in a one-to-many fashion, often the response to such information needs to be sent back to the broadcaster. This is another situation in which enterprise messaging is extremely useful, since pub/sub can be used to distribute the messages and p2p can be used for responses.

Choices in reliability of delivery are key in these situations. In the case of broadcasting stock quotes, for example, absolutely guaranteeing the delivery of information may not be critical, since another broadcast of the same ticker symbol will likely happen in another short interval of time. In the case where a trader is responding to a price quote with a buy order, however, it is crucial that the response is returned in a guaranteed fashion. In this case, you mix reliability of messaging so that the pub/sub distribution is fast but unreliable while the use of p2p for buy orders from traders is very reliable. JMS and enterprise messaging provides these varying degrees of reliability for both the pub/sub and p2p models.

Building Dynamic Systems with Messaging and JMS

In JMS, pub/sub topics and p2p queues are centrally administered and are referred to as JMS *administered objects.* Your application does not need to know the network location of topics or queues to communicate with other applications; it just uses topic and queue objects as identifiers. Using topics and queues provides JMS applications with a certain level of location transparency and flexibility that makes it possible to add and remove participants in an enterprise system.

For example, a system administrator can dynamically add subscribers to specific topics on an as-needed basis. A common scenario might be if you discover a need to add an audit-trail mechanism for certain messages and not others. Figure 1-5 shows you how to plug in a specialized auditing and logging JMS client whose only job is to track specific messages, just by subscribing to the topics you are interested in.

The ability to add and remove producers and consumers allows enterprise systems to dynamically alter the routing and re-routing of messages in an already deployed environment.

As another example, we can build on the EAI scenario discussed previously. In this example, a gateway accepts incoming purchase orders, converts them to the format appropriate for a legacy ERP system, and calls into the ERP system for processing (see Figure 1-6).

In Figure 1-6, other JMS applications (A and B) also subscribe to the purchase order topic and do their own independent processing. Application A might be a legacy application in the company, while application B may be another company's business system, representing a B2B integration.

Using JMS, it's fairly easy to add and remove applications from this process. For example, if purchase orders need to be processed from two different sources, such

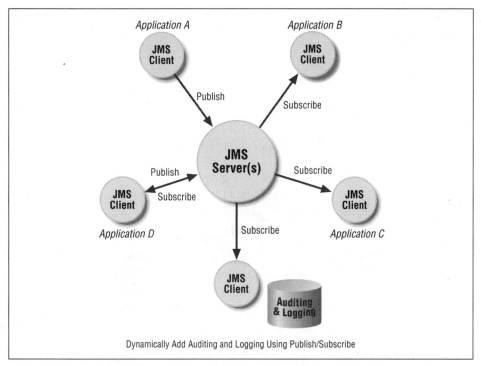

Figure 1-5. Dynamically adding auditing and logging using publish-and-subscribe

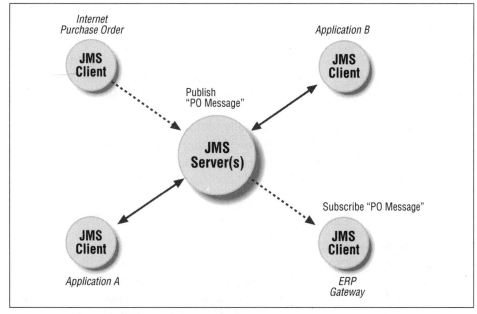

Figure 1-6. Integration of purchase order system with an ERP system

as an Internet-based system and a legacy EDI system, you can simply add the legacy purchase order system to the mix (see Figure 1-7).

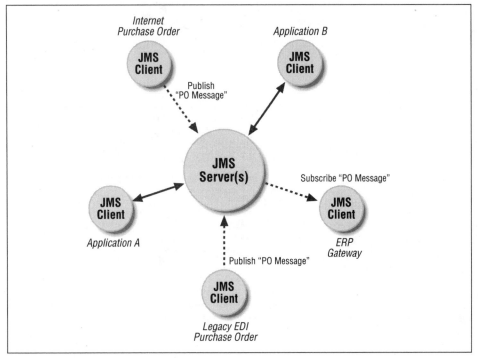

Figure 1-7. Integrating two different purchase order systems with an ERP system

What is interesting about this example is that the ERP Gateway is unaware that it is receiving purchase order messages from two completely different sources. The legacy EDI system may be an older in-house system or it could be the main system for a business partner or a recently acquired subsidiary. In addition, the legacy EDI system would have been added dynamically without requiring the shutdown and retooling of the entire system. Enterprise messaging systems make this kind of flexibility possible, and JMS allows Java clients to access many different MOMs using the same Java programming model.

RPC Versus Asynchronous Messaging

RPC (Remote Procedure Call) is a term commonly used to describe a distributed computing model that is used today by middleware technologies such as CORBA, Java RMI, and Microsoft's DCOM. Component-based architectures such as Enterprise JavaBeans are built on top of this model. RPC-based technologies have been, and will continue to be, a viable solution for many applications. However, the enterprise messaging model is superior in certain types of distributed applications. In this section we will discuss the pros and cons of each model. In Chapter 8, *J2EE, EJB, and JMS*, we will discuss a means of combining the two.

Tightly Coupled RPC

One of the most successful areas of the tightly coupled RPC model has been in building 3-tier, or *n*-tier applications. In this model, a presentation layer (1st tier), communicates using RPC with business logic on the middle tier (2nd tier), which accesses data housed on the back end (3rd tier). Sun Microsystems' J2EE platform and Microsoft's DNA are the most modern examples of this architecture.

With J2EE, JSP and Servlets represent the presentation tier while Enterprise Java-Beans is the middle tier. Microsoft's DNA is architecturally similar to J2EE, relying on ASP for presentation and COM+ for the middle tier. Regardless of the platform, the core technology used in these systems is RPC-based middleware. Whether it's the EJB or COM+, RPC is the defining communication paradigm.

RPC attempts to mimic the behavior of a system that runs in one process. When a remote procedure is invoked, the caller is blocked until the procedure completes and returns control to the caller. This synchronized model allows the developer to view the system as if it runs in one process. Work is performed sequentially, ensuring that tasks are completed in a predefined order. The synchronized nature of RPC tightly couples the client (the software making the call) to the server (the software servicing the call). The client cannot proceed—it is blocked—until the server responds.

The tightly coupled nature of RPC creates highly interdependent systems where a failure on one system has an immediate and debilitating impact on other systems. In J2EE, for example, the EJB server must be functioning properly if the servlets that use enterprise beans are expected to function.

RPC works well in many scenarios, but its synchronous, tightly coupled nature is a severe handicap in system-to-system processing where vertical applications are integrated together. In system-to-system scenarios, the lines of communication between vertical systems are many and multidirectional, as Figure 1-8 illustrates.

Consider the challenge of implementing this infrastructure using a tightly coupled RPC mechanism. There is the many-to-many problem of managing the connections between these systems. When you add another application to the mix, you have to go back and let all the other systems know about it. Also, systems can crash. Scheduled downtimes need to happen. Object interfaces need to be upgraded.

When one part of the system goes down, everything halts. When you post an order to an order entry system, it needs to make a synchronous call to each of the other

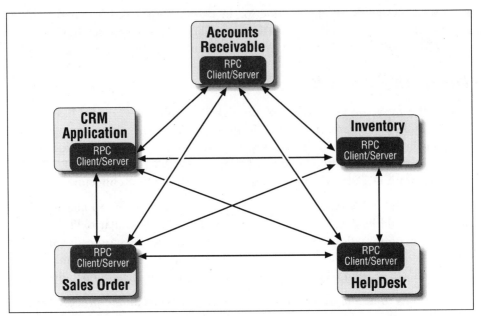

Figure 1-8. Tightly coupled with synchronous RPC

systems. This causes the order entry system to block and wait until each system is finished processing the order.*

It is the synchronized, tightly coupled, interdependent nature of RPC systems that cause entire systems to fail as a result of failures in subsystems. When the tightly coupled nature of RPC is not appropriate, as in system-to-system scenarios, messaging provides an alternative.

Enterprise Messaging

Problems with the availability of subsystems are not an issue with Message-Oriented Middleware. A fundamental concept of MOM is that communication between applications is intended to be asynchronous. Code that is written to connect the pieces together assumes there is a *one-way* message that requires no immediate response from another application. In other words, there is no blocking. Once a message is sent, the messaging client can move on to other tasks; it doesn't have to wait for a response. This is the major difference between RPC and asynchronous messaging, and is critical to understanding the advantages offered by MOM systems.

---

* Multithreading and looser RPC mechanisms like CORBA's one-way call are options, but these solutions have their own complexities and require very sophisticated development. Threads are expensive when not used wisely, and CORBA one-way calls still require application-level error handling for failure conditions.

In an asynchronous messaging system, each subsystem (Accounts Receivable, Inventory, etc.) is decoupled from the other systems (see Figure 1-9). They communicate through the messaging server, so that a failure in one does not impede the operation of the others.

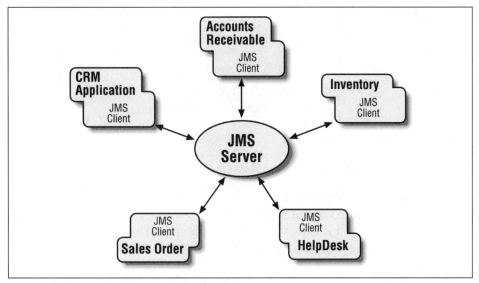

Figure 1-9. JMS provides a loosely coupled environment where partial failure of system components does not impede overall system availability

Partial failure in a networked system is a fact of life. One of the systems may have an unpredictable failure or need to be shut down at some time during its continuous operation. This can be further magnified by geographic dispersion of in-house and partner systems. In recognition of this, JMS provides *guaranteed delivery*, which ensures that intended consumers will eventually receive a message even if partial failure occurs.

Guaranteed delivery uses a *store-and-forward* mechanism, which means that the underlying message server will write the incoming messages out to a persistent store if the intended consumers are not currently available. When the receiving applications become available at a later time, the store-and-forward mechanism will deliver all of the messages that the consumers missed while unavailable (see Figure 1-10).

To summarize, JMS is not just another event service. It was designed to cover a broad range of enterprise applications, including EAI, B2B, push models, etc. Through asynchronous processing, store-and-forward, and guaranteed delivery, it provides high availability capabilities to keep business applications in continuous operation with uninterrupted service. It offers flexibility of integration by providing

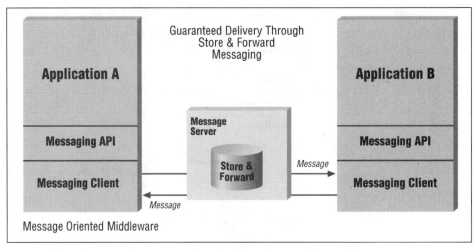

Figure 1-10. Underlying store-and-forward mechanism guarantees delivery of messages

publish-and-subscribe and point-to-point functionality. Through location transparency and administrative control, it allows for a robust, service-based architecture. And most importantly, it is extremely easy to learn and use. In the next chapter we will take a look at how simple it is by building our first JMS application.

Developing a Simple Example

Now that you understand Message-Oriented Middleware and some JMS concepts, you are ready to write your first JMS application. This chapter provides a gentle introduction to JMS using the publish-and-subscribe messaging model. You will get your feet wet with JMS and learn some of the basic classes and interfaces. Chapter 4, *Publish-and-Subscribe Messaging*, covers publish-and-subscribe in detail, and Chapter 5, *Point-to-Point Messaging*, covers the point-to-point message model.

As with all examples in this book, example code and instructions specific to several vendors is provided in the book download at O'Reilly's web site (see the Preface for details). You will need to install and configure your JMS provider according to the instructions provided by your vendor.

The Chat Application

Internet chat provides an interesting application for learning about the JMS pub/sub messaging model. Used mostly for entertainment, web-based chat applications can be found on thousands of web sites. In a chat application, people join virtual chat rooms where they can "chat" with a group of other people.

To illustrate how JMS works, we will use the JMS pub/sub API to build a simple chat application. The requirements of Internet chat map neatly onto the publish-and-subscribe messaging model. In this model, a producer can send a message to many consumers by delivering the message to a single topic. A message producer is also called a *publisher* and a message consumer is also called a *subscriber*. In reality, using JMS for a chat application would be overkill, since chat systems don't require enterprise quality service.

The following source code is a JMS-based chat client. Every participant in a chat session uses this Chat program to join a specific chat room (topic), and deliver and receive messages to and from that room:

```java
package chap2.chat;

import javax.jms.*;
import javax.naming.*;
import java.io.*;
import java.io.InputStreamReader;
import java.util.Properties;

public class Chat implements javax.jms.MessageListener{
    private TopicSession pubSession;
    private TopicSession subSession;
    private TopicPublisher publisher;
    private TopicConnection connection;
    private String username;

    /* Constructor. Establish JMS publisher and subscriber */
    public Chat(String topicName, String username, String password)
    throws Exception {
        // Obtain a JNDI connection
        Properties env = new Properties();
        // ... specify the JNDI properties specific to the vendor

        InitialContext jndi = new InitialContext(env);

        // Look up a JMS connection factory
        TopicConnectionFactory conFactory =
        (TopicConnectionFactory)jndi.lookup("TopicConnectionFactory");

        // Create a JMS connection
        TopicConnection connection =
        conFactory.createTopicConnection(username,password);

        // Create two JMS session objects
        TopicSession pubSession =
        connection.createTopicSession(false,
                                    Session.AUTO_ACKNOWLEDGE);
        TopicSession subSession =
        connection.createTopicSession(false,
                                    Session.AUTO_ACKNOWLEDGE);

        // Look up a JMS topic
        Topic chatTopic = (Topic)jndi.lookup(topicName);

        // Create a JMS publisher and subscriber
        TopicPublisher publisher =
```

```
            pubSession.createPublisher(chatTopic);
        TopicSubscriber subscriber =
            subSession.createSubscriber(chatTopic);

        // Set a JMS message listener
        subscriber.setMessageListener(this);

        // Intialize the Chat application
        set(connection, pubSession, subSession, publisher, username);

        // Start the JMS connection; allows messages to be delivered
        connection.start();

    }
    /* Initialize the instance variables */
    public void set(TopicConnection con, TopicSession pubSess,
                    TopicSession subSess, TopicPublisher pub,
                    String username) {
        this.connection = con;
        this.pubSession = pubSess;
        this.subSession = subSess;
        this.publisher = pub;
        this.username = username;
    }
    /* Receive message from topic subscriber */
    public void onMessage(Message message) {
        try {
            TextMessage textMessage = (TextMessage) message;
            String text = textMessage.getText();
            System.out.println(text);
        } catch (JMSException jmse){ jmse.printStackTrace(); }
    }
    /* Create and send message using topic publisher */
    protected void writeMessage(String text) throws JMSException {
        TextMessage message = pubSession.createTextMessage();
        message.setText(username+" : "+text);
        publisher.publish(message);
    }
    /* Close the JMS connection */
    public void close() throws JMSException {
        connection.close();
    }
    /* Run the Chat client */
    public static void main(String [] args){
        try{
            if (args.length!=3)
                System.out.println("Topic or username missing");
```

```
// args[0]=topicName; args[1]=username; args[2]=password
Chat chat = new Chat(args[0],args[1],args[2]);

// Read from command line
BufferedReader commandLine = new
  java.io.BufferedReader(new InputStreamReader(System.in));

// Loop until the word "exit" is typed
while(true){
    String s = commandLine.readLine();
    if (s.equalsIgnoreCase("exit")){
        chat.close(); // close down connection
        System.exit(0);// exit program
    } else
        chat.writeMessage(s);
    }
} catch (Exception e){ e.printStackTrace(); }
}
}
```

Getting Started with the Chat Example

To put this client to use, compile it like any other Java program. Then start your JMS server, setting up whatever topics, usernames, and passwords you want. Configuration of a JMS server is vendor-dependent, and won't be discussed here.

The Chat class includes a main() method so that it can be run as a standalone Java application. It's executed from the command line as follows:

```
java chap2.chat.Chat topic username password
```

The *topic* is the destination that we want to publish-and-subscribe to; *username* and *password* make up the authentication information for the client. Run at least two chat clients in separate command windows and try typing into one; you should see the text you type displayed by the other client.

Before examining the source code in detail, a quick explanation will be helpful. The chat client creates a JMS publisher and subscriber for a specific topic. The topic represents the chat room. The JMS server registers all the JMS clients that want to publish or subscribe to a specific topic. When text is entered at the command line of one of the chat clients, it is published to the messaging server. The messaging server identifies the topic associated with the publisher and delivers the message to all the JMS clients that have subscribed to that topic. As Figure 2-1 illustrates, messages published by any one of the JMS clients are delivered to all the JMS subscribers for that topic.

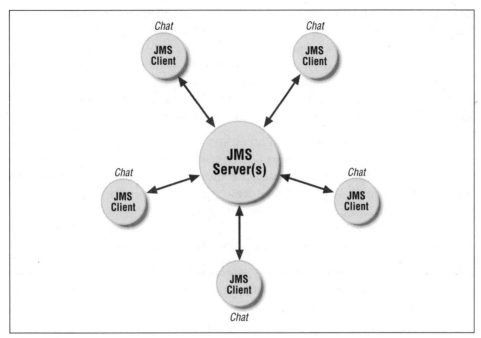

Figure 2-1. The Chat application

Examining the Source Code

Running the Chat example in a couple of command windows demonstrates *what* the Chat application does. The rest of this chapter examines the source code for the Chat application so that you can see *how* the Chat application works.

Bootstrapping the JMS client

The main() method bootstraps the chat client and provides a command-line interface. Once an instance of the Chat class is created, the main() method spends the rest of its time reading text typed at the command line and passing it to the Chat instance using the instance's writeMessage() method.

The Chat instance connects to the topic and receives and delivers messages. The Chat instance starts its life in the constructor, which does all the work to connect to the topic and set up the TopicPublisher and TopicSubscribers for delivering and receiving messages.

Obtaining a JNDI connection

The chat client starts by obtaining a JNDI connection to the JMS messaging server. JNDI is an implementation-independent API for directory and naming systems. A directory service provides JMS clients with access to ConnectionFactory and

Destinations (topics and queues) objects. ConnectionFactory and Destination objects are the only things in JMS that cannot be obtained using the JMS API—unlike connections, sessions, producers, consumers, and messages, which are manufactured using the JMS API. JNDI provides a convenient, location-transparent, configurable, and portable mechanism for obtaining Connection-Factory and Destination objects, also called JMS administered objects because they are established and configured by a system administrator.

Using JNDI, a JMS client can obtain access to a JMS provider by first looking up a ConnectionFactory. The ConnectionFactory is used to create JMS connections, which can then be used for sending and receiving messages. Destination objects, which represent virtual channels (topics and queues) in JMS, are also obtained via JNDI and are used by the JMS client. The directory service can be configured by the system administrator to provide JMS administered objects so that the JMS clients don't need to use proprietary code to access a JMS provider.

JMS servers will either work with a separate directory service (e.g., LDAP) or provide their own directory service that supports the JNDI API. For more details on JNDI, see the sidebar "Understanding JNDI."

The constructor of the Chat class starts by obtaining a connection to the JNDI naming service used by the JMS server:

```
// Obtain a JNDI connection
Properties env = new Properties();
// ... specify the JNDI properties specific to the vendor

InitialContext jndi = new InitialContext(env);
```

Creating a connection to a JNDI naming service requires that a javax.naming. InitialContext object be created. An InitialContext is the starting point for any JNDI lookup—it's similar in concept to the root of a filesystem. The InitialContext provides a network connection to the directory service that acts as a root for accessing JMS administered objects. The properties used to create an InitialContext depend on which JMS directory service you are using. The code used to create a JNDI InitialContext in BEA's Weblogic naming service, for example, would look something like this:

```
Properties env = new Properties();
env.put(Context.SECURITY_PRINCIPAL, "guest");
env.put(Context.SECURITY_CREDENTIALS, "guest");
env.put(Context.INITIAL_CONTEXT_FACTORY,
    "weblogic.jndi.WLInitialContextFactory");
env.put(Context.PROVIDER_URL, "t3://localhost:7001");

InitialContext jndi = new InitialContext(env);
```

Understanding JNDI

JNDI is a standard Java extension that provides a uniform API for accessing a variety of directory and naming services. In this respect, it is somewhat similar to JDBC. JDBC lets you write code that can access different relational databases such as Oracle, SQLServer, or Sybase; JNDI lets you write code that can access different directory and naming services, such as LDAP, Novell Netware NDS, CORBA Naming Service, and proprietary naming services provided by JMS servers.

In JMS, JNDI is used mostly as a naming service to locate administered objects. Administered objects are JMS objects that are created and configured by the system administrator. Administered objects include JMS `ConnectionFactory` and `Destination` objects like topics and queues.

Administered objects are bound to a name in a naming service. A naming service associates names with distributed objects, files, and devices so that they can be located on the network using simple names instead of cryptic network addresses. An example of a naming service is the DNS, which converts an Internet hostname like *www.oreilly.com* into a network address that browsers use to connect to web servers. There are many other naming services, such as COS-Naming in CORBA and the Java RMI registry. Naming services allow printers, distributed objects, and JMS administered objects to be bound to names and organized in a hierarchy similar to a filesystem. A directory service is a more sophisticated kind of naming service.

JNDI provides an abstraction that hides the specifics of the naming service, making client applications more portable. Using JNDI, JMS clients can browse a naming service and obtain references to administered objects without knowing the details of the naming service or how it is implemented. JMS servers are usually be used in combination with a standard JNDI driver (a.k.a. service provider) and directory service like LDAP, or provide a proprietary JNDI service provider and directory service.

JNDI is both virtual and dynamic. It is virtual because it allows one naming service to be linked to another. Using JNDI, you can drill down through directories to files, printers, JMS administered objects, and other resources following virtual links between naming services. The user doesn't know or care where the directories are actually located. As an administrator, you can create virtual directories that span a variety of different services over many different physical locations.

JNDI is dynamic because it allows the JNDI drivers for specific types of naming and directory services to be loaded dynamically at runtime. A driver maps a

—Continued—

specific kind of naming or directory service into the standard JNDI class interfaces. Drivers have been created for LDAP, Novell NetWare NDS, Sun Solaris
NIS+, CORBA COSNaming, and many other types of naming and directory
services, including proprietary ones. Dynamically loading JNDI drivers (service
providers) makes it possible for a client to navigate across arbitrary directory
services without knowing in advance what kinds of services it is likely to find.

When SonicMQ is used in combination with a third party LDAP directory service,
the connection properties would be very different. For example, the following
shows how a SonicMQ JMS client would use JNDI to access JMS administered
objects stored in a LDAP directory server:

```
Properties env = new Properties();
env.put(Context.SECURITY_PRINCIPAL, "guest");
env.put(Context.SECURITY_CREDENTIALS, "guest");
env.put(Context.INITIAL_CONTEXT_FACTORY,
    "com.sun.jndi.ldap.LdapCtxFactory");
env.put(Context.PROVIDER_URL,
    "ldap://localhost:389/o=acme.com");

InitialContext jndi = new InitialContext(env);
```

NOTE   Alternatively, the InitialContext() can be created without prop-
              erties (no-arg constructor). In this case JNDI will read the vendor-
              specific JNDI properties from a special file in the classpath named
              jndi.properties. This eliminates provider-specific code in JMS clients,
              making them more portable.

The TopicConnectionFactory

Once a JNDI InitialContext object is instantiated, it can be used to look up the
TopicConnectionFactory in the messaging server's naming service:

```
TopicConnectionFactory conFactory =
(TopicConnectionFactory)jndi.lookup("TopicConnectionFactory");
```

The javax.jms.TopicConnectionFactory is used to manufacture connections
to a message server. A TopicConnectionFactory is a type of administered object,
which means that its attributes and behavior are configured by the system administrator responsible for the messaging server. The TopicConnectionFactory is
implemented differently by each vendor, so configuration options available to system administrators vary from product to product. A connection factory might, for
example, be configured to manufacture connections that use a particular protocol, security scheme, clustering strategy, etc. A system administrator might choose

to deploy several different `TopicConnectionFactory` objects, each configured with its own JNDI lookup name.

The `TopicConnectionFactory` provides two overloaded versions of the `createTopicConnection()` method:

```
package javax.jms;

public interface TopicConnectionFactory extends ConnectionFactory {
    public TopicConnection createTopicConnection()
        throws JMSException, JMSSecurityException;
    public TopicConnection createTopicConnection(String username,
        String password) throws JMSException, JMSSecurityException;
}
```

These methods are used to create `TopicConnection` objects. The behavior of the no-arg method depends on the JMS provider. Some JMS providers will assume that the JMS client is connecting under anonymous security context, while other providers may assume that the credentials can be obtained from JNDI or the current thread.* The second method provides the client with a username-password authentication credential, which can be used to authenticate the connection. In our code, we choose to authenticate the connection explicitly with a username and password.

The TopicConnection

The `TopicConnection` is created by the `TopicConnectionFactory`:

```
// Look up a JMS connection factory
TopicConnectionFactory conFactory =
(TopicConnectionFactory)jndi.lookup("TopicConnectionFactory");

// Create a JMS connection
TopicConnection connection =
conFactory.createTopicConnection(username, password);
```

The `TopicConnection` represents a connection to the message server. Each `TopicConnection` that is created from a `TopicConnectionFactory` is a unique connection to the server.† A JMS client might choose to create multiple connections from the same connection factory, but this is rare as connections are relatively expensive (each connection requires a network socket, I/O streams, memory, etc.). Creating multiple Session objects (discussed later in this chapter)

---

* Thread-specific storage is used with the Java Authentication and Authorization Service (JAAS) to allow security credentials to transparently propagate between resources and applications.

† The actual physical network connection may or may not be unique depending on the vendor. However, the connection is considered to be logically unique so authentication and connection control can be managed separately from other connections.

from the same connection is considered more efficient, because sessions share access to the same connection. The `TopicConnection` is an interface that extends `javax.jms.Connection` interface. It defines several general-purpose methods used by clients of the `TopicConnection`. Among these methods are the `start()`, `stop()`, and `close()` methods:

```
// javax.jms.Connection the super interface
public interface Connection {
    public void start() throws JMSException;
    public void stop() throws JMSException;
    public void close() throws JMSException;
    ...
}


// javax.jms.TopicConnection extends javax.jms.Connection
public interface TopicConnection extends Connection {
    public TopicSession createTopicSession(boolean transacted,
                                     int acknowledgeMode)
    throws JMSException;
    ...
}
```

The `start()`, `stop()`, and `close()` methods allow a client to manage the connection directly. The `start()` method turns the inbound flow of messages "on," allowing messages to be received by the client. This method is used at the end of the constructor in `Chat` class:

```
    ...
    // Intialize the Chat application
    set(connection, pubSession, subSession, publisher, username);

    connection.start();


}
```

It is a good idea to start the connection *after* the subscribers have been set up, because the messages start to flow in from the topic as soon as `start()` is invoked.

The `stop()` method blocks the flow of inbound messages until the `start()` method is invoked again. The `close()` method is used to close the `TopicConnection` to the message server. This should be done when a client is finished using the `TopicConnection`; closing the connection conserves resources on the client and server. In the `Chat` class, the `main()` method calls `Chat.close()` when "exit" is typed at the command line. The `Chat.close()` method in turn calls the `TopicConnection.close()` method:

```
public void close() throws JMSException {
    connection.close();
}
```

Closing a `TopicConnection` closes all the objects associated with the connection including the `TopicSession`, `TopicPublisher`, and `TopicSubscriber`.

The TopicSession

After the `TopicConnection` is obtained, it's used to create `TopicSession` objects:

```
// Create a JMS connection
TopicConnection connection =
conFactory.createTopicConnection(username,password);

// Create two JMS session objects
TopicSession pubSession =
connection.createTopicSession(false,
                            Session.AUTO_ACKNOWLEDGE);
TopicSession subSession =
connection.createTopicSession(false,
                            Session.AUTO_ACKNOWLEDGE);
```

A `TopicSession` object is a factory for creating `Message`, `TopicPublisher`, and `TopicSubscriber` objects. A client can create multiple `TopicSession` objects to provide more granular control over publishers, subscribers, and their associated transactions. In this case we create two `TopicSession` objects, `pubSession` and `subSession`. We need two objects because of threading restrictions in JMS, which are discussed in the "Sessions and Threading" section later in the chapter.

The `boolean` parameter in the `createTopicSession()` method indicates whether the `Session` object will be transacted. A transacted `Session` automatically manages outgoing and incoming messages within a transaction. Transactions are important but not critical to our discussion at this time, so the parameter is set to `false`, which means the `TopicSession` will not be transacted. Transactions are discussed in more detail in Chapter 6, *Guaranteed Messaging, Transactions, Acknowledgments, and Failures.*

The second parameter indicates the acknowledgment mode used by the JMS client. An acknowledgment is a notification to the message server that the client has received the message. In this case we chose `AUTO_ACKNOWLEDGE`, which means that the message is automatically acknowledged after it is received by the client.

The `TopicSession` objects are used to create the `TopicPublisher` and `TopicSubscriber`. The `TopicPublisher` and `TopicSubscriber` objects are created with a `Topic` identifier and are dedicated to the `TopicSession` that created them; they operate under the control of a specific `TopicSession`:

```
TopicPublisher publisher =
    pubSession.createPublisher(chatTopic);
TopicSubscriber subscriber =
    subSession.createSubscriber(chatTopic);
```

The `TopicSession` is also used to create the `Message` objects that are delivered to the topic. The `pubSession` is used to create `Message` objects in the `writeMessage()` method. When you type text at the command line, the `main()` method reads the text and passes it to the `Chat` instance by invoking `writeMessage()`. The `writeMessage()` method (shown in the following example) uses the `pubSession` object to generate a `TextMessage` object that can be used to deliver the text to the topic:

```
protected void writeMessage(String text) throws JMSException{
    TextMessage message = pubSession.createTextMessage();
    message.setText(username+" : "+text);
    publisher.publish(message);
}
```

Several `Message` types can be created by a `TopicSession`. The most commonly used type is the `TextMessage`.

The Topic

JNDI is used to locate a `Topic` object, which is an administered object like the `TopicConnectionFactory`:

```
InitialContext jndi = new InitialContext(env);
.
.
.
// Look up a JMS topic
Topic chatTopic = (Topic)jndi.lookup(topicName);
```

A `Topic` object is a handle or identifier for an actual topic, called a *physical topic*, on the messaging server. A physical topic is an electronic channel to which many clients can subscribe and publish. A topic is analogous to a news group or list server: when a message is sent to a news group or list server, it is delivered to all the subscribers. Similarly, when a JMS client delivers a `Message` object to a topic, all the clients subscribed to that topic receive the `Message`.

The `Topic` object encapsulates a vendor-specific name for identifying a physical topic in the messaging server. The `Topic` object has one method, `getName()`, which returns the name identifier for the physical topic it represents. The name encapsulated by a `Topic` object is vendor-specific and varies from product to product. For example, one vendor might use dot (".") separated topic names, like "`oreilly.jms.chat`", while another vendor might use a completely different naming system, similar to LDAP naming, "`o=oreilly,cn=chat`". Using topic names directly will result in client applications that are not portable across brands of JMS servers. The `Topic` object hides the topic name from the client, making the client more portable.

As a convention, we'll refer to a physical topic as a *topic* and only use the term "physical topic" when it's important to stress its difference from a `Topic` object.

The TopicPublisher

A `TopicPublisher` was created using the `pubSession` and the `chatTopic`:

```
// Look up a JMS topic
Topic chatTopic = (Topic)jndi.lookup(topicName);

// Create a JMS publisher and subscriber
TopicPublisher publisher =
    pubSession.createPublisher(chatTopic);
```

A `TopicPublisher` is used to deliver messages to a specific topic on a message server. The `Topic` object used in the `createPublisher()` method identifies the topic that will receive messages from the `TopicPublisher`. In the `Chat` example, any text typed on the command line is passed to the `Chat` class's `writeMessage()` method. This method uses the `TopicPublisher` to deliver a message to the topic:

```
protected void writeMessage(String text) throws JMSException{
    TextMessage message = pubSession.createTextMessage();
    message.setText(username+" : "+text);
    publisher.publish(message);
}
```

The `TopicPublisher` objects deliver messages to the topic asynchronously. Asynchronous delivery and consumption of messages is a key characteristic of Message-Oriented Middleware; the `TopicPublisher` doesn't block or wait until all the subscribers receive the message. Instead, it returns from the `publish()` method as soon as the message server receives the message. It's up to the message server to deliver the message to all the subscribers for that topic.

The TopicSubscriber

The `TopicSubscriber` is created using the `subSession` and the `chatTopic`:

```
// Look up a JMS topic
Topic chatTopic = (Topic)jndi.lookup(topicName);

// Create a JMS publisher and subscriber
TopicPublisher publisher =
    pubSession.createPublisher(chatTopic);
TopicSubscriber subscriber =
    subSession.createSubscriber(chatTopic);
```

A `TopicSubscriber` receives messages from a specific topic. The `Topic` object argument used in the `createSubscriber()` method identifies the topic from which the `TopicSubscriber` will receive messages.

The `TopicSubscriber` receives messages from the message server one at a time (serially). These messages are pushed from the message server to the

`TopicSubscriber` asynchronously, which means that the `TopicSubscriber` does not have to poll the message server for messages. In our example, each chat client will receive any message published by any of the other chat clients. When a user enters text at the command line, the text message is delivered to all other chat clients that subscribe to the same topic.

The pub/sub messaging model in JMS includes an in-process Java event model for handling incoming messages. This is similar to the event-driven model used by Java beans.* An object simply implements the listener interface, in this case the `MessageListener`, and then is registered with the `TopicSubscriber`. A `TopicSubscriber` may have only one `MessageListener` object. Here is the definition of the `MessageListener` interface used in JMS:

```
package javax.jms;

public interface MessageListener {
    public void onMessage(Message message);
}
```

When the `TopicSubscriber` receives a message from its topic, it invokes the `onMessage()` method of its `MessageListener` objects. The `Chat` class itself implements the `MessageListener` interface and implements the `onMessage()` method:

```
public class Chat implements javax.jms.MessageListener{
    ...
    public void onMessage(Message message){
        try{
            TextMessage textMessage = (TextMessage)message;
            String text = textMessage.getText();
            System.out.println(text);
        } catch (JMSException jmse){jmse.printStackTrace();}
    }
    ...
}
```

The `Chat` class is a `MessageListener` type, and therefore registers itself with the `TopicSubscriber` in its constructor:

```
TopicSubscriber subscriber = subSession.createSubscriber(chatTopic);

subscriber.setMessageListener(this);
```

When the message server pushes a message to the `TopicSubscriber`, the `TopicSubscriber` invokes the `Chat` object's `onMessage()` method.

---

* Although the in-process event model used by `TopicSubscriber` is similar to the one used in Java beans, JMS itself is an API and the interfaces it defines are not Java beans.

NOTE   It's fairly easy to confuse the Java Message Service with its use of a
              Java event model. JMS is an API for asynchronous distributed enter-
              prise messaging that spans processes and machines across a net-
              work. The Java event model is used to synchronously deliver events
              by invoking methods on one or more objects in the same process
              that have registered as listeners. The JMS pub/sub model uses the
              Java event model so that a `TopicSubscriber` can notify its
              `MessageListener` object in the same process that a message has
              arrived from the message server.

The Message

In the `chat` example, the `TextMessage` class is used to encapsulate the messages
we send and receive. A `TextMessage` contains a `java.lang.String` as its body
and is the most commonly used message type. The `onMessage()` method receives
`TextMessage` objects from the `TopicSubscriber`. Likewise, the `writeMessage()`
method creates and publishes `TextMessage` objects using the `TopicPublisher`:

```
public void onMessage(Message message){
    try{
        TextMessage textMessage = (TextMessage)message;
        String text = textMessage.getText();
        System.out.println(text);
    } catch (JMSException jmse){jmse.printStackTrace();}
}
protected void writeMessage(String text) throws JMSException{
    TextMessage message = pubSession.createTextMessage();
    message.setText(username+" : "+text);
    publisher.publish(message);
}
```

A message basically has two parts: a *header* and *payload*. The header is comprised of
special fields that are used to identify the message, declare attributes of the message, and provide information for routing. The difference between message types
is determined largely by their payload, i.e., the type of application data the message contains. The `Message` class, which is the superclass of all message objects,
has no payload. It is a lightweight message that delivers no payload but can serve as
a simple event notification. The other message types have special payloads that
determine their type and use:

`Message`
  This type has no payload. It is useful for simple event notification.

`TextMessage`
  This type carries a `java.lang.String` as its payload. It is useful for exchang-
  ing simple text messages and also for more complex character data, such as
  XML documents.

`ObjectMessage`

This type carries a serializable Java object as its payload. It's useful for exchanging Java objects.

`BytesMessage`

This type carries an array of primitive bytes as its payload. It's useful for exchanging data in an application's native format, which may not be compatible with other existing `Message` types. It is also useful where JMS is used purely as a transport between two systems, and the message payload is opaque to the JMS client.

`StreamMessage`

This type carries a stream of primitive Java types (int, double, char, etc.) as its payload. It provides a set of convenience methods for mapping a formatted stream of bytes to Java primitives. It's an easy programming model when exchanging primitive application data in a fixed order.

`MapMessage`

This type carries a set of name-value pairs as its payload. The payload is similar to a `java.util.Properties` object, except the values must be Java primitives or their wrappers. The `MapMessage` is useful for delivering keyed data.

Sessions and Threading

The `Chat` application uses a separate session for the publisher and subscriber, `pubSession` and `subSession`, respectively. This is due to a threading restriction imposed by JMS. According to the JMS specification, a session may not be operated on by more than one thread at a time. In our example, two threads of control are active: the default main thread of the `Chat` application and the thread that invokes the `onMessage()` handler. The thread that invokes the `onMessage()` handler is owned by the JMS provider. Since the invocation of the `onMessage()` handler is asynchronous, it could be called while the main thread is publishing a message in the `writeMessage()` method. If both the publisher and subscriber had been created by the same session, the two threads could operate on these methods at the same time; in effect, they could operate on the same `TopicSession` concurrently—a condition that is prohibited.

A goal of the JMS specification was to avoid imposing an internal architecture on the JMS provider. Requiring a JMS provider's implementation of a `Session` object to be capable of safely handling multiple threads was specifically avoided. This is mostly due to one of the intended uses of JMS—that the JMS API be a wrapper around an existing messaging system, which may not have multithreaded delivery capabilities on the client.

The requirement imposed on the JMS provider is that the sending of messages and the asynchronous receiving of messages be processed serially. It is possible to publish-and-subscribe using the same session, but only if the application is publishing from within the onMessage() handler. An example of this will be covered in Chapter 4.

3

In this chapter:
• *Headers*
• *Properties*
• *Message Selectors*
• *Message Types*

Anatomy of a JMS Message

This chapter focuses on the anatomy of a message: the individual parts that make up a message (headers, properties, and the different kinds of message payloads). Appendixes B, C, and D cover additional information that will prove invaluable as a reference when developing JMS applications. Appendix B, *Message Headers*, provides in-depth information on the purpose and application of JMS headers; Appendix C, *Message Properties*, covers the rules governing the use of JMS properties; and Appendix D, *Message Selectors*, covers the syntax of message selectors. Although you do not need to read these appendixes to understand subsequent chapters in this book, you will need them as a reference when implementing real JMS applications. After you finish reading this chapter, take a look at Appendixes B, C, and D so you're familiar with their content.

The `Message` is the most important part of the entire JMS specification. All data and events in a JMS application are communicated with messages, while the rest of JMS exists to facilitate the transfer of messages. They are the lifeblood of the system.

A JMS message both carries application data and provides event notification. Its role is unique to distributed computing. In RPC-based systems (CORBA, Java RMI, DCOM), a message is a command to execute a method or procedure, which blocks the sender until a reply has been received. A JMS message is not a command; it transfers data and tells the receiver that something has happened. A message doesn't dictate what the recipient should do and the sender doesn't wait for a response. This decouples the sender from the receiver, making messaging systems and their messages far more dynamic and flexible than request-reply paradigms.

A `Message` object has two parts: the message data itself, called the payload or message body, and the message headers and properties (see Figure 3-1).

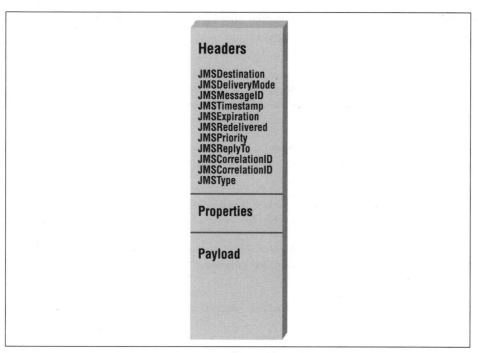

Figure 3-1. Anatomy of a message

Messages come in various types that are defined by the payload they carry. The payload itself might be very structured, as with StreamMessage and MapMessage objects, or fairly unstructured, as with TextMessage, ObjectMessage, and BytesMessage types. Messages can carry important data or simply serve as notifications of events in the system. In most cases, messages are both notifications and vehicles for carrying data.

The message headers provide metadata about the message describing who or what created the message, when it was created, how long the data is valid, etc. The headers also contain routing information that describes the destination of the message (topic or queue), how a message should be acknowledged, and a lot more. In addition to headers, messages can carry properties that can be defined and set by the JMS client. JMS consumers can choose to receive messages based on the values of certain headers and properties, using a special filtering mechanism called *message selectors.*

Headers

Every JMS message has a set of standard headers. Each header is identified by a set of accessor and mutator methods that follow the idiom setJMS<HEADER>(), getJMS<HEADER>(). Here is a partial definition of the Message interface that shows all the JMS header methods:

```
public interface Message {

    public Destination getJMSDestination() throws JMSException;
    public void setJMSDestination(Destination destination)
    throws JMSException;

    public int getJMSDeliveryMode() throws JMSException;
    public void setJMSDeliveryMode(int deliveryMode)
    throws JMSException;

    public String getJMSMessageID() throws JMSException;
    public void setJMSMessageID(String id) throws JMSException;

    public long getJMSTimestamp() throws JMSException;
    public void setJMSTimestamp(long timestamp) throws JMSException;

    public long getJMSExpiration() throws JMSException;
    public void setJMSExpiration(long expiration) throws JMSException;

    public boolean getJMSRedelivered() throws JMSException;
    public void setJMSRedelivered(boolean redelivered)
    throws JMSException;

    public int getJMSPriority() throws JMSException;
    public void setJMSPriority(int priority) throws JMSException;

    public Destination getJMSReplyTo() throws JMSException;
    public void setJMSReplyTo(Destination replyTo) throws JMSException;

    public String getJMSCorrelationID() throws JMSException;
    public void setJMSCorrelationID(String correlationID)
    throws JMSException;
    public byte[] getJMSCorrelationIDAsBytes() throws JMSException;
    public void setJMSCorrelationIDAsBytes(byte[] correlationID)
    throws JMSException;

    public String getJMSType() throws JMSException;
    public void setJMSType(String type) throws JMSException;

}
```

JMS headers are divided into two large groups: automatically assigned headers and developer-assigned headers. The next two sections discuss these two types.

Automatically Assigned Headers

Most JMS headers are automatically assigned; their value is set by the JMS provider when the message is delivered, so that values assigned by the developer using the setJMS<HEADER>() methods are ignored. In other words, for headers that are automatically assigned, using the mutator methods explicitly is fruitless.* This doesn't mean, however, that the developer has no control over the value of these headers. Some automatically assigned headers depend on declarations made by the developer when creating the Session and MessageProducer (i.e., TopicPublisher). These cases are clearly illustrated in the header definitions that follow.

JMSDestination

The JMSDestination header identifies the destination with either a Topic or Queue object, both of which are Destination types. Identifying the message's destination is valuable to JMS clients that consume messages from more than one topic or queue:

```
Topic destination = (Topic) message.getJMSDestination();
```

JMSDeliveryMode

There are two types of delivery modes in JMS: persistent and nonpersistent. A persistent message should be delivered *once-and-only-once*, which means that if the JMS provider fails, the message is not lost; it will be delivered after the server recovers. A nonpersistent message is delivered *at-most-once*, which means that it can be lost permanently if the JMS provider fails. In both persistent and nonpersistent delivery modes the message server should not send a message to the same consumer more then once, but it is possible (see the section on JMSRedelivered for more details):

```
int deliverymode = message.getJMSDeliveryMode();
if (deliverymode == javax.jms.DeliveryMode.PERSISTENT) {
    ...
} else { // equals DeliveryMode.NON_PERSISTENT
    ...
}
```

The delivery mode can be set using the setJMSDeliveryMode() method on the producer (i.e., TopicPublisher). Once the delivery mode is set on the

---

* According to the specification authors, the setJMS<HEADER>() methods were left in the Message interface for "general orthogonality," or to keep it semantically symmetrical to balance the getJMS<HEADER>() methods—a fairly strange but established justification.

MessageProducer, it is applied to all messages delivered using that producer. The default setting is PERSISTENT:

```
// Set the JMS delivery mode on the message producer
TopicPublisher topicPublisher = topicSession.createPublisher(topic);
topicPublisher.setDeliveryMode(DeliveryMode.NON_PERSISTENT);
```

JMSMessageID

The JMSMessageID is a String value that uniquely identifies a message. How unique the identifier is depends on the vendor. The JMSMessageID can be useful for historical repositories in JMS consumer applications where messages need to be uniquely indexed. Used in conjunction with the JMSCorrelationID, the JMSMessageID is also useful for correlating messages:

```
String messageid = message.getJMSMessageID();
```

JMSTimestamp

The JMSTimestamp is set automatically by the message producer when the send() operation is invoked. The timestamp is a long value that measures time in milliseconds:

```
long timestamp = message.getJMSTimestamp();
```

JMSExpiration

A Message object's expiration date prevents the message from being delivered to consumers after it has expired. This is useful for messages whose data is only valid for a period of time:

```
long timeToLive = message.getJMSExpiration();
```

The expiration time for messages is set in milliseconds on the producer (i.e., TopicPublisher) using the setTimeToLive() method:

```
TopicPublisher topicPublisher = topicSession.createPublisher(topic);
// Set time to live as 1 hour (1000 millis x 60 sec x 60 min)
topicPublisher.setTimeToLive(3600000);
```

By default the timeToLive is zero (0), which indicates that the message doesn't expire. Calling setTimeToLive() with a zero argument ensures that a message is created without an expiration date.

JMSRedelivered

The JMSRedelivered header indicates that the message was redelivered to the consumer. The JMSRedelivered header is true if the message is redelivered, and false if it's not. A message may be marked redelivered if a consumer failed to acknowledge previous delivery of the message, or when the JMS provider is not certain whether the consumer has already received the message:

```
boolean isRedelivered = message.getJMSRedelivered()
```

Message redelivery is covered in more detail in Chapter 6, *Guaranteed Messaging, Transactions, Acknowledgments, and Failures.*

JMSPriority

The message producer may assign a priority to a message when it is delivered. There are two categories of message priorities: levels 0–4 are gradations of *normal* priority; levels 5–9 are gradations of *expedited* priority. The message servers may use a message's priority to prioritize delivery of messages to consumers—messages with an expedited priority are delivered ahead of normal priority messages:

```
int priority = message.getJMSPriority();
```

The priority of messages can be declared by the JMS client using the setPriority() method on the producer:

```
TopicPublisher topicPublisher = TopicSession.createPublisher(someTopic);
topicPublisher.setPriority(9);
```

Developer-Assigned Headers

While many of the JMS headers are set automatically when the message is delivered, several others must be set explicitly on the Message object before it is delivered by the producer.

JMSReplyTo

In some cases, a JMS message producer may want the consumers to reply to a message. The JMSReplyTo header, which contains a javax.jms.Destination, indicates which address a JMS consumer should reply to. A JMS consumer is not required to send a reply:

```
message.setJMSReplyTo(topic);
...
Topic topic = (Topic) message.getJMSReplyTo();
```

JMSCorrelationID

The JMSCorrelationID provides a header for associating the current message with some previous message or application-specific ID. In most cases the JMSCorrelationID will be used to tag a message as a reply to a previous message identified by a `JMSMessageID`, but the `JMSCorrelationID` can be any value, not just a `JMSMessageID`:

```
message.setJMSCorrelationID(identifier);
...
String correlationid = message.getJMSCorrelationID();
```

JMSType

`JMSType` is an optional header that is set by the JMS client. Its main purpose is to identify the message structure and type of payload; it is currently supported by only a few vendors. Some MOM systems (IBM's MQSeries, for example) treat the message body as uninterpreted bytes. These systems often provide a message type as a simple way for applications to label the message body. So a message type can be useful when exchanging messages with non-JMS clients that require this type of information to process the payload.

Other MOM systems (e.g., Sun's JMQ) and EAI systems (e.g., SagaVista and MQIntegrator) directly tie each message to some form of external message schema, with the message type as the link. These MOM systems require a message type because they provide metadata services bound to it.

Properties

Properties act like additional headers that can be assigned to a message. They provide the developer with more information about the message. The `Message` interface provides several accessor and mutator methods for reading and writing properties. The value of a property can be a `String`, `boolean`, `byte`, `double`, `int`, `long`, or `float`.

There are three basic categories of message properties: application-specific properties, JMS-defined properties, and provider-specific properties. Application properties are defined and applied to `Message` objects by the application developer; the JMS extension and provider-specific properties are additional headers that are, for the most part, automatically added by the JMS provider.

Application-Specific Properties

Any property defined by the application developer can be an application-specific property. Application properties are set before the message is delivered. There are no predefined application properties; developers are free to define any properties that fit their needs. For example, in the chat example developed in Chapter 2,

Developing a Simple Example, a special property could be added that identifies the user sending the message:

```
TextMessage message = pubSession.createTextMessage();
message.setText(text);
message.setStringProperty("username",username);
publisher.publish(message);
```

As an application specific-property, username is not meaningful outside the Chat application; it is used exclusively by the application to filter messages based on the identity of the publisher.

Property values can be any boolean, byte, short, int, long, float, double, or String. The javax.jms.Message interface provides accessor and mutator methods for each of these property value types. Here is a subset of the Message interface definition that shows these methods:

```
package javax.jms;

public interface Message {

    public String getStringProperty(String name)
        throws JMSException, MessageFormatException;
    public void setStringProperty(String name, String value)
        throws JMSException, MessageNotWriteableException;
    public int getIntProperty(String name)
        throws JMSException, MessageFormatException;
    public void setIntProperty(String name, int value)
        throws JMSException, MessageNotWriteableException;
    public boolean getBooleanProperty(String name)
        throws JMSException, MessageFormatException;
    public void setBooleanProperty(String name, boolean value)
        throws JMSException, MessageNotWriteableException;
    public double getDoubleProperty(String name)
        throws JMSException, MessageFormatException;
    public void setDoubleProperty(String name, double value)
        throws JMSException, MessageNotWriteableException;
    public float getFloatProperty(String name)
        throws JMSException, MessageFormatException;
    public void setFloatProperty(String name, float value)
        throws JMSException, MessageNotWriteableException;
    public byte getByteProperty(String name)
        throws JMSException, MessageFormatException;
    public void setByteProperty(String name, byte value)
        throws JMSException, MessageNotWriteableException;
    public long getLongProperty(String name)
        throws JMSException, MessageFormatException;
    public void setLongProperty(String name, long value)
        throws JMSException, MessageNotWriteableException;
```

```
    public short getShortProperty(String name)
        throws JMSException, MessageFormatException;
    public void setShortProperty(String name, short value)
        throws JMSException, MessageNotWriteableException;
    public Object getObjectProperty(String name)
        throws JMSException, MessageFormatException;
    public void setObjectProperty(String name, Object value)
        throws JMSException, MessageNotWriteableException;

    public void clearProperties()
        throws JMSException;
    public Enumeration getPropertyNames()
        throws JMSException;
    public boolean propertyExists(String name)
        throws JMSException;
    ...
}
```

The object property methods (which are setObjectProperty() and getObjectProperty()) can be used with object wrappers that correspond to the allowed primitive types (java.lang.Integer, java.lang.Double, etc.) and the String type.

Once a message is produced (sent), its properties become read-only; the properties cannot be changed. If the consumer attempts to set a property, the method throws a javax.jms.MessageNotWriteableException. The properties can, however, be changed on that message by calling the clearProperties() method, which removes all the properties from the message so that new ones can be added.

The getPropertyNames() method in the Message interface can be used to obtain an Enumeration of all the property names contained in the message. These names can then be used to obtain property values using the property accessor methods; for example:

```
public void onMessage(Message message) {
    Enumeration propertyNames = message.getPropertyNames();
    while(propertyNames.hasMoreElements()){
        String name = (String)propertyNames.nextElement();
        Object value = getObjectProperty(name);
        System.out.println("\n"+name+" = "+value);
    }
}
```

JMS-Defined Properties

JMS-defined properties have the same characteristics as application properties, except that most of them are set by the JMS provider when the message is sent.

JMS-defined properties act as optional JMS headers; vendors can choose to support none, some, or all of them. The following is a list of the nine JMS-defined properties, which are described in more detail in Appendix C:

- `JMSXUserID`
- `JMSXAppID`
- `JMSXProducerTXID`
- `JMSXConsumerTXID`
- `JMSXRcvTimestamp`
- `JMSXDeliveryCount`
- `JMSXState`
- `JMSXGroupID`
- `JMSXGroupSeq`

Provider-Specific Properties

Every JMS provider can define a set of proprietary properties that can be set by the client or the provider automatically. Provider-specific properties must start with the prefix "JMS_" followed by the property name (`JMS_<vendor-property-name>`). The purpose of the provider-specific properties is to support proprietary vendor features.

Message Selectors

A message selector allows a JMS consumer to be more selective about the messages it receives from a particular destination (topic or queue). Message selectors use message properties and headers as criteria in conditional expressions. These conditional expressions use boolean logic to declare which messages should be delivered to a JMS consumer.

For example, in the chat client developed in Chapter 2, message selectors could be used to filter out messages from specific people. To accomplish this we would first declare a new property in the message that identifies the username of the JMS client publishing the message:

```
protected void writeMessage(String text) throws JMSException{
    TextMessage message = session.createTextMessage();
    message.setText(text);
    message.setStringProperty("username",username);
    publisher.publish(message);
}
```

JMS clients can now use that property to filter messages. Message selectors are declared when the message consumer is created:

```
TopicSubscriber subscriber =
session.createSubscriber(chatTopic, " username != 'William' ",false);
```

In this code, the message selector (shown in bold) tells the message server to deliver to the consumer only those messages that do *not* have a username property equal to 'William'.

NOTE   When a JMS consumer declares a message selector for a particular
           destination, the selector is applied only to messages delivered to that
           consumer. Every JMS client can have a different selector specified
           for each of its consumers.

The message selectors are based on a subset of the SQL-92 conditional expression syntax, which is used in the WHERE clauses of SQL statements. If you are familiar with SQL 92, the conditional expressions used in message selectors will be familiar to you. The syntax used for conditional expressions is covered in detail in Appendix D.

What happens to messages that are not selected for delivery to the consumer by its message selector? This depends on the message model used. In the pub/sub model, the message is simply not delivered to that consumer, but it is delivered to other consumers. This is true of both nondurable and durable subscriptions. In the p2p model, the messages remain in the queue, so other consumers of the queue can see them, but they are not visible to the consumer that used the message selector.

Message Selector Examples

Here are three complex selectors used in hypothetical environments. Although you will have to use your imagination a little, the purpose of these examples is to convey the power of the message selectors. When a selector is declared, the identifier always refers to a property name or JMS header name in the message. For example, the selector "'username != 'William'" assumes that there is a property in the message named username, which can be compared to the value 'William'.

Managing claims in an HMO

Due to some fraudulent claims, an automatic process is implemented that will audit all claims submitted by patients who are employees of the ACME manufacturing company with visits to chiropractors, psychologists, and dermatologists:

```
String selector =
  "PhysicianType IN ('Chiropracter', 'Psychologist', 'Dermatologist') "
```

```
+ "AND PatientGroupID LIKE 'ACME%'";

TopicSubscriber subscriber =
session.createSubscriber(topic, selector,false);
```

Notification of certain bids on inventory

A supplier wants notification of requests for bids on specific inventory items at specific quantities:

```
String selector =
  "InventoryID = 'S93740283-02' AND Quantity BETWEEN 1000 AND 13000";

TopicSubscriber subscriber =
session.createSubscriber(topic, selector,false);
```

Selecting recipients for a catalog mailing

An online retailer wants to deliver a special catalog to any customer that orders more then \$500.00 worth of merchandise where the average price per item ordered is greater than \$75.00 and the customer resides in one of several states. The retailer creates a special application that subscribes to the order processing topic and processes catalog deliveries for only those customers that meet the defined criteria:

```
String selector =
  "TotalCharge > 500.00 AND ((TotalCharge / ItemCount) >= 75.00) "
  + "AND State IN ('MN', 'WI', 'MI', 'OH')";

TopicSubscriber subscriber =
session.createSubscriber(topic, selector,false);
```

Message Types

The Java Message Service defines six `Message` interface types that must be supported by JMS providers. Although JMS defines the `Message` interfaces, it doesn't define their implementation. This allows vendors to implement and transport messages in their own way, while maintaining a consistent and standard interface for the JMS application developer. The six message interfaces are `Message` and its five sub-interfaces: `TextMessage`, `StreamMessage`, `MapMessage`, `ObjectMessage`, and `BytesMessage`.

The `Message` interfaces are defined according to the kind of payload they are designed to carry. In some cases, `Message` types were included in JMS to support legacy payloads that are common and useful, which is the case with the `text`, `bytes`, and `stream` message types. In other cases, the `Message` types were defined to facilitate emerging needs; for example, `ObjectMessage` can transport serializable Java objects. Some vendors may provide other proprietary message types. Progress' SonicMQ and SoftWired's iBus, for example, provide an `XMLMessage` type that extends the `TextMessage`, allowing developers to deal with the message directly through DOM or SAX interfaces. The `XMLMessage` type may become a standard message type in a future version of the specification. At the time of this writing, Sun Microsystems was starting discussions about adding an `XMLMessage` type.

Message

The simplest type of message is the `javax.jms.Message`, which serves as the base interface to the other message types. As shown below, the `Message` type can be created and used as a JMS message with no payload:

```
// Create and deliver a Message
Message message = session.createMessage();
publisher.publish(message);
...
// Receive a message on the consumer
public void onMessage(Message message){
    // No payload, process event notifiction
}
```

This type of message contains only JMS headers and properties, and is used in event notification. An event notification is a broadcast, warning, or notice of some occurrence. If the business scenario requires a simple notification without a payload, then the lightweight `Message` type is the most efficient way to implement it.

TextMessage

This type carries a `java.lang.String` as its payload. It's useful for exchanging simple text messages and more complex character data like XML documents:

```
package javax.jms;

public interface TextMessage extends Message {
    public String getText()
      throws JMSException;
    public void setText(String payload)
      throws JMSException, MessageNotWriteableException;
}
```

Text messages can be created with one of two factory methods defined in the `Session` interface. One factory method takes no arguments, resulting in a `TextMessage` object with an empty payload—the payload is added using the `setText()` method defined in the `TextMessage` interface. The other factory method takes a `String` type payload as an argument, producing a ready-to-deliver `TextMessage` object:

```
TextMessage textMessage = session.createTextMessage();
textMessage.setText("Hello!");
```

```
topicPublisher.publish(textMessage);
...
TextMessage textMessage = session.createTextMessage("Hello!");
queueSender.send(textMessage);
```

When a consumer receives a `TextMessage` object it can extract the `String` payload using the `getText()` method. If the `TextMessage` was delivered without a payload, the `getText()` method returns a `null` value or an empty `String` (`""`) depending on the JMS provider.

ObjectMessage

This type carries a serializable Java object as its payload. It's useful for exchanging Java objects:

```
package javax.jms;

public interface ObjectMessage extends Message {
    public java.io.Serializable getObject()
        throws JMSException;
    public void setObject(java.io.Serializable payload)
        throws JMSException, MessageNotWriteableException;
}
```

Object messages can be created with one of two factory methods defined in the `Session` interface. One factory method takes no arguments, so the serializable object must be added using the `setObject()`. The other factory method takes the `Serializable` payload as an argument, producing a ready-to-deliver `ObjectMessage`:

```
// Order is a serializable object
Order order = new Order();
...
ObjectMessage objectMessage  = session.createObjectMessage();
objectMessage.setObject(order);
queueSender.send(objectMessage);
...
ObjectMessage objectMessage = session.createObjectMessage(order);
topicPublisher.publish(objectMessage);
```

When a consumer receives an `ObjectMessage` it can extract the payload using the `getObject()` method. If the `ObjectMessage` was delivered without a payload, the `getObject()` method returns a `null` value:

```
public void onMessage(Message message) {
  try {
    ObjectMessage objectMessage = (ObjectMessage)message;
    Order order = (Order)objectMessage.getObject();
    ...
```

```
catch (JMSException jmse){
    ...
}
```

The `ObjectMessage` is the most modern of message types. In order for this message type to be useful, however, the consumers and producers of the message must be Java programs. In other words, `ObjectMessage` is only useful between Java clients and probably will not work with non-JMS clients.*

The class definition of the object payload has to be available to both the JMS producer and JMS consumer. If the `Order` class used in the previous example is not available to the JMS consumer's JVM, an attempt to access the `Order` object from the message's payload would result in a `java.lang.ClassNotFoundException`. Some JMS providers may provide dynamic class loading capabilities, but that would be a vendor-specific quality of service. Most of the time the class must be placed on the JMS consumer's class path manually by the developer.

BytesMessage

This type carries an array of primitive bytes as its payload. It's useful for exchanging data in an application's native format, which may not be compatible with other existing `Message` types. It is also useful where JMS is used purely as a transport between two systems, and the message payload is opaque to the JMS client:

```
package javax.jms;

public interface BytesMessage extends Message {

    public byte readByte() throws JMSException;
    public void writeByte(byte value) throws JMSException;
    public int readUnsignedByte() throws JMSException;

    public int readBytes(byte[] value) throws JMSException;
    public void writeBytes(byte[] value) throws JMSException;
    public int readBytes(byte[] value, int length)
        throws JMSException;
    public void writeBytes(byte[] value, int offset, int length)
        throws JMSException;

    public boolean readBoolean() throws JMSException;
    public void writeBoolean(boolean value) throws JMSException;

    public char readChar() throws JMSException;
    public void writeChar(char value) throws JMSException;
```

---

* It's possible that a JMS provider could use CORBA 2.3 IIOP protocol, which can handle
  `ObjectMessage` types consumed by non-Java, non-JMS clients.

```
    public short readShort() throws JMSException;
    public void writeShort(short value) throws JMSException;
    public int readUnsignedShort() throws JMSException;

    public void writeInt(int value) throws JMSException;
    public int readInt() throws JMSException;

    public void writeLong(long value) throws JMSException;
    public long readLong() throws JMSException;

    public float readFloat() throws JMSException;
    public void writeFloat(float value) throws JMSException;

    public double readDouble() throws JMSException;
    public void writeDouble(double value) throws JMSException;

    public String readUTF() throws JMSException;
    public void writeUTF(String value) throws JMSException;

    public void writeObject(Object value) throws JMSException;

    public void reset() throws JMSException;
}
```

If you've worked with the `java.io.DataInputStream` and `java.io.Data-OutputStream` classes, then the methods of the `BytesMessage` interface, which are loosely based on these I/O classes, will look familiar to you. Most of the methods defined in `BytesMessage` interface allow the application developer to read and write data to a byte stream using Java's primitive data types. When a Java primitive is written to the `BytesMessage`, using one of the `set<TYPE>()` methods, the primitive value is converted to its byte representation and appended to the stream. Here's how a `BytesMessage` is created and how values are written to its byte stream:

```
BytesMessage bytesMessage = session.createBytesMessage();

bytesMessage.writeChar('R');
bytesMessage.writeInt(10);
bytesMessage.writeUTF("OReilly");

queueSender.send(bytesMessage);
```

When a `BytesMessage` is received by a JMS consumer, the payload is a raw byte stream, so it is possible to read the stream using arbitrary types, but this will probably result in erroneous data. It's best to read the `BytesMessage`'s payload in the same order, and with the same types, with which it was written:

```
public void onMessage(Message message) {
    try {
```

```
      BytesMessage bytesMessage = (BytesMessage)message;
      char   c = bytesMessage.readChar();
      int    i = bytesMessage.readInt();
      String s = bytesMessage.readUTF();
      } catch (JMSException jmse){
  ...
}
```

In order to read and write `String` values, the `BytesMessage` uses methods based on the UTF-8 format, which is a standard format for transferring and storing Unicode text data efficiently.

UTF-8

UTF-8 encodes Unicode characters as one to four bytes. The encoding is designed for processing efficiency, ease of implementation in most existing software, and compatibility with ASCII. That is, the encoding of any character in the ASCII character set has the same encoding in UTF-8. So the letter "A" (0x41 in ASCII) is also a one-byte character with the same value, 0x41, in UTF-8. The characters in ISO 8859-1 that are above the ASCII range (i.e., above 127), when converted to Unicode and encoded in UTF-8, are two-byte characters.

Every character in the Unicode character set can be expressed in UTF-8, and there is an algorithmic conversion between the 16-bit (2-byte) form of Unicode and UTF-8 that ensures lossless transformations.

One of the key benefits of using the UTF-8 encoding is that null bytes are only used as string terminators. Some mail systems and network protocols cannot tolerate null bytes in the input stream, so the 16-bit encoding of Unicode, which might have a null value in either byte, is unacceptable for these purposes.

The methods for accessing the `short` and `byte` primitives include *unsigned* methods (`readUnsignedShort()`, `readUnsignedByte()`). These methods are something of a surprise, since the `short` and `byte` data types in Java are almost always signed. The values that can be taken by unsigned `byte` and `short` data are what you'd expect: 0 to 255 for a `byte`, and 0 to 65535 for a `short`. Because these values can't be represented by the (signed) `byte` and `short` data types, `readUnsignedByte()` and `readUnsignedShort()` both return an `int`.

In addition to the methods for accessing primitive data types, the `BytesMessage` includes a single `writeObject()` method. This is used for `String` objects and the primitive wrappers: `Byte`, `Boolean`, `Character`, `Short`, `Integer`, `Long`, `Float`, `Double`. When written to the `BytesMessage`, these values are converted to the byte form of their primitive counterparts. The writeObject() method is provided as a convenience when the types to be written aren't known until runtime.

If an exception is thrown while reading the BytesMessage, the pointer in the stream must be reset to the position it had just prior to the read operation that caused the exception. This allows the JMS client to recover from read errors without losing its place in the stream.

The reset() method returns the stream pointer to the beginning of the stream and puts the BytesMessage in read-only mode so that the contents of its byte stream cannot be further modified. This method can be called explicitly by the JMS client if needed, but it's always called implicitly when the BytesMessage is delivered.

In most cases, one of the other message types is a better option then the BytesMessage. BytesMessage should only be used if the data needs to be delivered in the consumer's native format. In some cases, a JMS client may be a kind of router, consuming messages from one source and delivering them to a destination. Routing applications may not need to know the contents of the data they transport and so may choose to transfer payloads as binary data, using a BytesMessage, from one location to another.

StreamMessage

The StreamMessage carries a stream of primitive Java types (int, double, char, etc.) as its payload. It provides a set of convenience methods for mapping a formatted stream of bytes to Java primitives. Primitive types are read from the Message in the same order they were written. Here's the definition of the StreamMessage interface:

```
public interface StreamMessage extends Message {

    public boolean readBoolean() throws JMSException;
    public void writeBoolean(boolean value) throws JMSException;

    public byte readByte() throws JMSException;
    public int readBytes(byte[] value) throws JMSException;
    public void  writeByte(byte value) throws JMSException;
    public void writeBytes(byte[] value) throws JMSException;
    public void writeBytes(byte[] value, int offset, int length)
        throws JMSException;

    public short readShort() throws JMSException;
    public void writeShort(short value) throws JMSException;

    public char readChar() throws JMSException;
    public void writeChar(char value) throws JMSException;
```

```
    public int readInt() throws JMSException;
    public void writeInt(int value) throws JMSException;

    public long readLong() throws JMSException;
    public void writeLong(long value) throws JMSException;

    public float readFloat() throws JMSException;
    public void writeFloat(float value) throws JMSException;

    public double readDouble() throws JMSException;
    public void  writeDouble(double value) throws JMSException;

    public String readString() throws JMSException;
    public void writeString(String value) throws JMSException;

    public Object readObject() throws JMSException;
    public void writeObject(Object value) throws JMSException;

    public void reset() throws JMSException;
}
```

On the surface, the StreamMessage strongly resembles the BytesMessage, but
they are not the same. The StreamMessage keeps track of the order and types of
primitives written to the stream, so formal conversion rules apply. For example, an
exception would be thrown if you tried to read a long value as a short:

```
StreamMessage streamMessage = session.createStreamMessage();
streamMessage.writeLong(2938302);

// The next line throws a JMSException
short value = streamMessage.readShort();
```

While this would work fine with a BytesMessage, it won't work with a
StreamMessage. A BytesMessage would write the long as 64 bits (8 bytes) of raw
data, so that you could later read some of the data as a short, which is only 16 bits
(the first 2 bytes of the long). The StreamMessage, on the other hand, writes the
type information as well as the value of the long primitive, and enforces a strict set
of conversion rules that prevent reading the long as a short.

Table 3-1 shows the conversion rules for each type. The left column shows the type
written, and the right column shows how that type may be read. A JMSException
is thrown by the accessor methods to indicate that the original type could not be
converted to the type requested. This is the exception that would be thrown if you
attempted to read long as a short.

Table 3-1. Type Conversion Rules

write<TYPE>()	read<TYPE>()
boolean	boolean, String
byte	byte, short, int, long, String
short	short, int, long, String
char	char, String
Long	long, String
Int	int, long, String
float	float, double, String
double	double, String
String	String, boolean, byte, short, int, long, float, double
byte []	byte []

String values can be converted to any primitive data type if they are formatted correctly. If the String value cannot be converted to the primitive type requested, a java.lang.NumberFormatException is thrown. However, most primitive values can be accessed as a String using the readString() method. The only exceptions to this rule are char values and byte arrays, which cannot be read as String values.

The writeObject() method follows the rules outlined for the similar method in the BytesMessage class. Primitive wrappers are converted to their primitive counterparts. The readObject() method returns the appropriate object wrapper for primitive values, or a String or a byte array, depending on the type that was written to the stream. For example, if a value was written as a primitive int, it can be read as a java.lang.Integer object.

The StreamMessage also allows null values to be written to the stream. If a JMS client attempts to read a null value using the readObject() method, null is returned. The rest of the primitive accessor methods attempt to convert the null value to the requested type using the valueOf() operations. The readBoolean() method returns false for null values, while the other primitive property methods throw the java.lang.NumberFormatException. The readString() method returns null or possibly an empty String ("") depending on the implementation. The readChar() method throws a NullPointerException.

If an exception is thrown while reading the StreamMessage, the pointer in the stream is reset to the position it had just prior to the read operation that caused the exception. This allows the JMS client to recover gracefully from exceptions without losing the pointer's position in the stream.

The `reset()` method returns the stream pointer to the beginning of the stream
and puts the message in a read-only mode. It is called automatically when the message is delivered to the client. However, it may need to be called directly by the
consuming client when a message is redelivered:

```
if ( strmMsg.getJMSRedelivered() )
    strmMsg.reset();
```

MapMessage

This type carries a set of *name-value* pairs as its payload. The payload is similar to a
`java.util.Properties` object, except the values can be Java primitives (or their
wrappers) in addition to `Strings`. The `MapMessage` class is useful for delivering
keyed data that may change from one message to the next:

```
public interface MapMessage extends Message {

    public boolean getBoolean(String name) throws JMSException;
    public void setBoolean(String name, boolean value)
        throws JMSException;

    public byte getByte(String name) throws JMSException;
    public void setByte(String name, byte value) throws JMSException;
    public byte[] getBytes(String name) throws JMSException;
    public void setBytes(String name, byte[] value)
        throws JMSException;
    public void setBytes(String name, byte[] value, int offset, int length)
        throws JMSException;

    public short getShort(String name) throws JMSException;
    public void setShort(String name, short value) throws JMSException;

    public char getChar(String name) throws JMSException;
    public void setChar(String name, char value) throws JMSException;

    public int getInt(String name) throws JMSException;
    public void setInt(String name, int value) throws JMSException;

    public long getLong(String name) throws JMSException;
    public void setLong(String name, long value) throws JMSException;

    public float getFloat(String name) throws JMSException;
    public void setFloat(String name, float value)
        throws JMSException;

    public double getDouble(String name) throws JMSException;
    public void setDouble(String name, double value)
        throws JMSException;
```

```
    public String getString(String name) throws JMSException;
    public void setString(String name, String value)
        throws JMSException;

    public Object getObject(String name) throws JMSException;
    public void setObject(String name, Object value)
        throws JMSException;

    public Enumeration getMapNames() throws JMSException;
    public boolean itemExists(String name) throws JMSException;
}
```

Essentially, `MapMessage` works similarly to JMS properties: any name-value pair can be written to the payload. The name must be a `String` object, and the value may be a `String` or a primitive type. The values written to the `MapMessage` can then be read by a JMS consumer using the name as a key:

```
MapMessage mapMessage = session.createMapMessage();
mapMessage.setInt("Age", 88);
mapMessage.setFloat("Weight", 234);
mapMessage.setString("Name", "Smith");
mapMessage.setObject("Height", new Double(150.32));
....
int age = mapMessage.getInt("Age");
float weight = mapMessage.getFloat("Weight");
String name = mapMessage.getString("Name");
Double height = (Double)mapMessage.getObject("Height");
```

The `setObject()` method writes a Java primitive wrapper type, `String` object, or byte array. The primitive wrappers are converted to their corresponding primitive types when set. The `getObject()` method reads `Strings`, byte arrays, or any primitive type as its corresponding primitive wrapper.

The conversion rules defined for the `StreamMessage` apply to the `MapMessage`. See Table 3-1 in the `StreamMessage` section.

A `JMSException` is thrown by the accessor methods to indicate that the original type could not be converted to the type requested. In addition, `String` values can be converted to any primitive value type if they are formatted correctly; the accessor will throw a `java.lang.NumberFormatException` if they aren't.

If a JMS client attempts to read a name-value pair that doesn't exist, the value is treated as if it was `null`. Although the `getObject()` method returns `null` for nonexistent mappings, the other types behave differently. While most primitive accessors throw the `java.lang.NumberFormatException` if a `null` value or non-existent mapping is read, other accessors behave as follows: the `getBoolean()` method returns `false` for `null` values; the `getString()` returns a `null` value or possibly an empty `String` (`""`), depending on the implementation; and the `getChar()` method throws a `NullPointerException`.

To avoid reading nonexistent name-value pairs, the `MapMessage` provides an `itemExists()` test method. In addition, the `getMapNames()` method lets a JMS client enumerate the names and use them to obtain all the values in the message. For example:

```
public void onMessage(Message message) {
    MapMessage mapMessage = (MapMessage)message;
    Enumeration names = mapMessage.getMapNames();
    while(names.hasMoreElements()){
        String name = (String)names.nextElement();
        Object value = mapMessage.getObject(name);
        System.out.println("Name = "+name+", Value = "+value);
    }
}
```

Read-Only Messages

When messages are delivered, the body of the message is made read-only. Any attempt to alter a message body after it has been delivered results in a `javax.jms.MessageNotWriteableException`. The only way to change the body of a message after it has been delivered is to invoke the `clearBody()` method, which is defined in the `Message` interface. The `clearBody()` method empties the message's payload so that a new payload can be added.

Properties are also read-only after a message is delivered. Why are both the body and properties made read-only after delivery? It allows the JMS provider more flexibility in implementing the `Message` object. For example, a JMS provider may choose to stream a `BytesMessage` or `StreamMessage` as it is read, rather than all at once. Another vendor may choose to keep properties or body data in an internal buffer so that it can be read directly without the need to make a copy, which is especially useful with multiple consumers on the same client.

Client-Acknowledged Messages

The `acknowledge()` method, defined in the `Message` interface, is used when the consumer has chosen `CLIENT_ACKNOWLEDGE` as its acknowledgment mode. There are three acknowledgment modes that may be set by the JMS consumer when its session is created: `AUTO_ACKNOWLEDGE`, `DUPS_OK_ACKNOWLEDGE`, and `CLIENT_ACKNOWLEDGE`. Here is how a pub/sub consumer sets one of the three acknowledgment modes:

```
TopicSession topic =
    topicConnection.createTopicSession(false, Session.CLIENT_ACKNOWLEDGE);
```

In `CLIENT_ACKNOWLEDGE` mode, the JMS client explicitly acknowledges each message as it is received. The `acknowledge()` method on the `Message` interface is used for this purpose. For example:

```
public void onMessage(Message message){
    message.acknowledge();

    ...
}
```

The other acknowledgment modes do not require the use of this method and are covered in more detail in Chapter 6 and Appendix B.

NOTE   Any acknowledgment mode specified for a transacted session is ignored. When a session is transacted, the acknowledgment is part of the transaction and is executed automatically prior to the commit of the transaction. If the transaction is rolled back, no acknowledgment is given. Transactions are covered in more detail in Chapter 6.

Interoperability and Portability of Messages

A message delivered by a JMS client may be converted to a JMS provider's native format and delivered to non-JMS clients, but it must still be consumable as its original `Message` type by JMS clients. Messages delivered from non-JMS clients to a JMS provider may be consumable by JMS clients—the JMS provider should attempt to map the message to its closest JMS type, or if that's not possible, to the `BytesMessage`.

JMS providers are not required to be interoperable. A message published to one JMS provider's server is not consumable by another JMS provider's consumer. In addition, a JMS provider usually can't publish or read messages from destinations (topic and queues) implemented by another JMS provider. Most JMS providers have, or will have in the future, bridges or connectors to address this issue.

Although interoperability is not required, limited message portability is required. A message consumed or created using JMS provider A can be delivered using JMS provider B. JMS provider B will simply use the accessor methods of the message to read its headers, properties, and payload and convert them to its own native format: not a fast process, but portable. This portability is limited to interactions of the JMS client, which takes a message from one provider and passes it to another.

4

In this chapter:
- *Getting Started with the B2B Application*
- *Temporary Topics*
- *Durable Subscriptions*
- *Publishing the Message Persistently*
- *JMSCorrelationID*
- *Request and Reply*
- *Unsubscribing*

Publish-and-Subscribe Messaging

This chapter focuses on the publish-and-subscribe (pub/sub) messaging model that was introduced in Chapter 2, *Developing a Simple Example*. The pub/sub messaging model allows a message producer (also called a publisher) to broadcast a message to one or more consumers (called subscribers). There are three important aspects of the pub/sub model:

- Messages are pushed to consumers, which means that consumers are delivered messages without having to request them. Messages are exchanged through a virtual channel called a *topic*. A topic is a destination where producers can publish, and subscribers can consume, messages. Messages delivered to a topic are automatically pushed to all qualified consumers.

- As in enterprise messaging in general, there is no coupling of the producers to the consumers. Subscribers and publishers can be added dynamically at runtime, which allows the system to grow or shrink in complexity over time.

- Every client that subscribes to a topic receives its own copy of messages published to that topic. A single message produced by one publisher may be copied and distributed to hundreds, or even thousands of subscribers.

In Chapter 2 you learned the basics of the pub/sub model by developing a simple chat client. In this chapter we will build on those lessons and examine more advanced features of this model, including guaranteed messaging, topic-based addressing, durable subscriptions, request-reply, and temporary topics.

Getting Started with the B2B Application

In this chapter we abandon the simple chat example for a more complex and real-world Business-to-Business (B2B) scenario. In our new example, a wholesaler wants to distribute price information to retailers, and the retailers want to respond by generating orders. We'll implement this scenario using the publish-and-sub-scribe model: the wholesaler will publish messages containing new prices and hot deals, and the retailers will respond by creating their own messages to order stock.

This scenario is typical of many Business-to-Business operations. We call the cli-ents retailers and wholesalers, but these names are really only for convenience. There's little difference between our wholesaler/retailer scenario and a stock bro-ker broadcasting stock prices to investors, or a manufacturer broadcasting bid requests to multiple suppliers. The fact that we use a retailer and a wholesaler to illustrate our example is much less important than the way we apply JMS.

Our simple trading system is implemented by two classes, both of which are JMS cli-ents: `Wholesaler` and `Retailer`. In the interest of keeping the code simple, we won't implement a fancy user interface; our application has a rudimentary command-line user interface.

Running the B2B Application

Before looking at the code, let's look at how the application works. As with the `Chat` application, the `Wholesaler` class includes a `main()` method so it can be run as a standalone Java application. It's executed from the command line as follows:

```
java chap4.B2B.Wholesaler localhost username password
```

username and *password* are the authentication information for the client. The `Retailer` class can be executed in the same manner:

```
java chap4.B2B.Retailer localhost username password
```

Start your JMS server, then run one instance of a `Wholesaler` client and a `Retailer` client in separate command windows. In the `Wholesaler` client you are prompted to enter an item description, an old price, and a new price. Enter the following as shown:

```
Bowling Shoes, 100.00, 55.00
```

Upon hitting the Enter key, you should see the `Retailer` application display information on the screen indicating that it has received a price change notice. You should then see the `Wholesaler` indicating that it has received a "buy" order from the `Retailer`. Here's the complete interaction with the `Wholesaler` and the `Retailer`:*

```
java chap4.B2B.Wholesaler localhost WHOLESALER passwd1
```

---

* WHOLESALER and RETAILER are usernames you have set up when configuring your JMS server. passwd1 and passwd2 are the passwords you've assigned to those usernames. If you are using an eval-uation version of a JMS provider, it may not be necessary to set up usernames and passwords; check your vendor's documentation for more information.

```
Enter: Item, Old Price, New Price
e.g., Bowling Shoes, 100.00, 55.00
Bowling Shoes, 100.00, 55.00
Order received - 1000 Bowling Shoes from DurableRetailer
----------------------
java chap4.B2B.Retailer localhost RETAILER passwd2
Retailer application started.
Received Hot Buy: Bowling Shoes, 100.00, 55.00
Buying 1000 Bowling Shoes
```

Here's what happened. The Wholesaler publishes a price quotation on a topic, "Hot Deals," which is intended for one or more Retailers. The Retailers subscribe to the "Hot Deals" topic in order to receive price quotes. The Retailer application has no interaction with a live user. Instead, it has an autoBuy() method that examines the old price and the new price. If the new price represents a reduction of greater than ten percent, the Retailer sends a message back to the Wholesaler on the "Buy Order" topic, telling it to purchase 1,000 items. In JMS terms, the Wholesaler is a *producer* of the "Hot Deals" topic and a *consumer* of the "Buy Order" topic. Conversely, the Retailer is a consumer of the "Hot Deals" topic and a producer of the "Buy Order" topic, as illustrated in Figure 4-1.

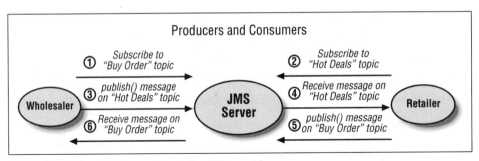

Figure 4-1. Producers and consumers in the B2B example

The B2B Source Code

The rest of this chapter examines the source code for the Wholesaler and Retailer classes, and covers several advanced subjects related to the pub/sub messaging model.

The Wholesaler class

After the listing, we will take a brief tour of the methods in this class, and discuss their responsibilities. We will go into detail about the implementation later in this chapter. Now, here is the complete definition of the Wholesaler class, which is responsible for publishing items to the "Hot Deals" topic and receiving "Buy Orders" on those deals from retailers:

```java
public class Wholesaler implements javax.jms.MessageListener{

    private javax.jms.TopicConnection connect = null;
    private javax.jms.TopicSession pubSession = null;
    private javax.jms.TopicSession subSession = null;
    private javax.jms.TopicPublisher publisher = null;
    private javax.jms.TopicSubscriber subscriber = null;
    private javax.jms.Topic hotDealsTopic = null;
    private javax.jms.TemporaryTopic buyOrdersTopic = null;

    public Wholesaler(String broker, String username, String password){
        try {
            Properties env = new Properties();
            // ... specify the JNDI properties specific to the vendor

            InitialContext jndi = new InitialContext(env);

            TopicConnectionFactory factory =
              (TopicConnectionFactory)jndi.lookup(broker);
            connect = factory.createTopicConnection (username, password);

            pubSession =
              connect.createTopicSession(false,Session.AUTO_ACKNOWLEDGE);
            subSession =
              connect.createTopicSession(false,Session.AUTO_ACKNOWLEDGE);

            hotDealsTopic = (Topic)jndi.lookup("Hot Deals");
            publisher = pubSession.createPublisher(hotDealsTopic);

            buyOrdersTopic = subSession.createTemporaryTopic();

            subscriber = subSession.createSubscriber(buyOrdersTopic);
            subscriber.setMessageListener(this);

            connect.start();

        } catch (javax.jms.JMSException jmse){
            jmse.printStackTrace(); System.exit(1);
        } catch (javax.naming.NamingException jne){
            jne.printStackTrace(); System.exit(1);
        }
    }
    private void publishPriceQuotes(String dealDesc, String username,
                                    String itemDesc,  float oldPrice,
                                    float newPrice){
        try {
```

```java
            javax.jms.StreamMessage message =
                pubSession.createStreamMessage();
            message.writeString(dealDesc);
            message.writeString(itemDesc);
            message.writeFloat(oldPrice);
            message.writeFloat(newPrice);

            message.setStringProperty("Username", username);
            message.setStringProperty("Itemdesc", itemDesc);

            message.setJMSReplyTo(buyOrdersTopic);

            publisher.publish(
                message,
                javax.jms.DeliveryMode.PERSISTENT,
                javax.jms.Message.DEFAULT_PRIORITY,
                1800000);

        } catch ( javax.jms.JMSException jmse ){
            jmse.printStackTrace();
        }
    }
    public void onMessage( javax.jms.Message message){
        try {
            TextMessage textMessage = (TextMessage) message;
            String text = textMessage.getText();
            System.out.println("\nOrder received - "+text+
                            " from " + message.getJMSCorrelationID());
        } catch (java.lang.Exception rte){
            rte.printStackTrace();
        }
    }
    public void exit(){
        try {
            connect.close();
        } catch (javax.jms.JMSException jmse){
            jmse.printStackTrace();
        }
        System.exit(0);
    }
    public static void main(String argv[]) {
        String broker, username, password;
        if  (argv.length == 3){
            broker = argv[0];
            username = argv[1];
            password = argv[2];
        } else  {
            System.out.println("Invalid arguments. Should be: ");
            System.out.println("java Wholesaler broker username password");
```

```
            return;
        }

        Wholesaler wholesaler = new Wholesaler(broker,username,password);

        try {
            // Read all standard input and send it as a message.
            java.io.BufferedReader stdin = new java.io.BufferedReader
                (new java.io.InputStreamReader( System.in ) );
            System.out.println ("Enter: Item, Old Price, New Price");
            System.out.println("\ne.g., Bowling Shoes, 100.00, 55.00");

            while ( true ){
                String dealDesc = stdin.readLine();
                if  (dealDesc != null && dealDesc.length() > 0){
                    // Parse the deal description
                    StringTokenizer tokenizer =
                    new StringTokenizer(dealDesc,",") ;
                        String itemDesc = tokenizer.nextToken();
                        String temp = tokenizer.nextToken();
                        float oldPrice =
                          Float.valueOf(temp.trim()).floatValue();
                        temp = tokenizer.nextToken();
                        float newPrice =
                          Float.valueOf(temp.trim()).floatValue();

                    wholesaler.publishPriceQuotes(dealDesc,username,
                                        itemDesc,oldPrice,newPrice);
                } else  {
                    wholesaler.exit();
                }
            }
        } catch ( java.io.IOException ioe ){
            ioe.printStackTrace();
        }
    }
}
```

The main() method creates an instance of the Wholesaler class, passing it the information it needs to set up its publishers and subscribers.

In the Wholesaler class's constructor, JNDI is used to obtain the "Hot Deals" topic identifier, which is then used to create a publisher. Most of this should look familiar to you; it's similar in many ways to the Chat application, except for the creation of a temporary topic, which is discussed in more detail later in this section.

Once the Wholesaler is instantiated, the main() method continues to monitor the command line for new "Hot Deals." When a "Hot Deal" is entered at the command prompt, the `main()` method parses the information and passes it to the `Wholesaler` instance via the `publishPriceQuotes()` method.

The `publishPriceQuotes()` method is responsible for publishing messages containing information about price quotes to the "Hot Deals" topic.

The `onMessage()` method receives messages from clients responding to deals published on the "Hot Deals" topic. The contents of these messages are simply printed to the command line.

The Retailer class

Here is the complete definition of the `Retailer` class, which subscribes to the "Hot Deals" topic and responds with "Buy Orders" on attractive deals:

```
public class Retailer implements javax.jms.MessageListener{

    private javax.jms.TopicConnection connect = null;
    private javax.jms.TopicSession session = null;
    private javax.jms.TopicPublisher publisher = null;
    private javax.jms.Topic hotDealsTopic = null;

    public Retailer( String broker, String username, String password){
        try {
            Properties env = new Properties();
            // ... specify the JNDI properties specific to the vendor

            InitialContext jndi = new InitialContext(env);

            TopicConnectionFactory factory =
            (TopicConnectionFactory)jndi.lookup(broker);

            connect = factory.createTopicConnection(username, password);
            connect.setClientID("DurableRetailer");

            session =
            connect.createTopicSession(false,Session.AUTO_ACKNOWLEDGE);

            hotDealsTopic = (Topic)jndi.lookup("Hot Deals");

            javax.jms.TopicSubscriber subscriber =
                session.createDurableSubscriber(hotDealsTopic,
                    "Hot Deals Subscription");
            subscriber.setMessageListener(this);
            connect.start();

        } catch (javax.jms.JMSException jmse){
            jmse.printStackTrace();
            System.exit(1);
```

```
        } catch (javax.naming.NamingException jne){
         jne.printStackTrace(); System.exit(1);
        }
    }
    public void onMessage(javax.jms.Message aMessage){
        try {
            autoBuy(aMessage);
        } catch (java.lang.RuntimeException rte){
            rte.printStackTrace();
        }
    }

    private void autoBuy (javax.jms.Message message){
        int count = 1000;
        try {
            StreamMessage strmMsg = (StreamMessage)message;
            String dealDesc = strmMsg.readString();
            String itemDesc = strmMsg.readString();
            float oldPrice = strmMsg.readFloat();
            float newPrice = strmMsg.readFloat();
            System.out.println("Received Hot Buy :"+dealDesc);

            // If price reduction is greater than 10 percent, buy
            if (newPrice == 0 || oldPrice / newPrice > 1.1){
                System.out.println("\nBuying " + count +" "+ itemDesc);

                TextMessage textMsg = session.createTextMessage();
                textMsg.setText(count + " " + itemDesc );

                javax.jms.Topic buytopic =
                    (javax.jms.Topic)message.getJMSReplyTo();

                publisher = session.createPublisher(buytopic);

                textMsg.setJMSCorrelationID("DurableRetailer");

                publisher.publish(
                    textMsg,
                    javax.jms.DeliveryMode.PERSISTENT,
                    javax.jms.Message.DEFAULT_PRIORITY,
                    1800000);
            } else  {
                System.out.println ("\nBad Deal- Not buying.");
            }
        } catch (javax.jms.JMSException jmse){
            jmse.printStackTrace();
        }
    }
    private void exit(String s){
```

```
        try {
            if ( s != null &&
                s.equalsIgnoreCase("unsubscribe"))
            {
                subscriber.close();
                session.unsubscribe("Hot Deals Subscription");
            }
            connect.close();
        } catch (javax.jms.JMSException jmse){
            jmse.printStackTrace();
        }
        System.exit(0);
    }
    public static void main(String argv[]) {
        String broker, username, password;
        if  (argv.length == 3){
            broker = argv[0];
            username = argv[1];
            password = argv[2];
        } else  {
            System.out.println("Invalid arguments. Should be: ");
            System.out.println
            ("java Retailer broker username password");
            return;
        }

        Retailer retailer  = new Retailer(broker, username, password);

        try {
            System.out.println("\nRetailer application started.\n");
            // Read all standard input and send it as a message.
            java.io.BufferedReader stdin =
                new java.io.BufferedReader
                ( new java.io.InputStreamReader( System.in ) );
            while ( true ){
                String s = stdin.readLine();
                if ( s == null )retailer.exit(null);
                else if ( s.equalsIgnoreCase("unsubscribe") )
                    retailer.exit ( s );
            }
        } catch ( java.io.IOException ioe ){
            ioe.printStackTrace();
        }
    }
}
```

The `main()` method of `Retailer` is much like the `main()` method of `Wholesaler`. It creates an instance of the `Retailer` class and passes it the information it needs to set up its publishers and subscribers.

The constructor of the `Retailer` class is also similar to that of the `Wholesaler` class, except that it creates a *durable* subscription using the "Hot Deals" topic. Durable subscriptions will be discussed in more detail later in this section.

Once the `Retailer` is instantiated, the `main()` method uses the `readLine()` method as a way of blocking program execution in order to monitor for message input.

The `publishPriceQuotes()` method of the `Wholesaler` class is responsible for publishing messages containing information about price quotes to the "Hot Deals" topic.

The `onMessage()` method of the `Retailer` class receives messages from the `Wholesaler` client, then delegates its work to the `autoBuy()` method. The `autoBuy()` method examines the message, determines whether the price change is significant, and arbitrarily orders 1000 items. It orders the items by publishing a persistent message back to the `Wholesaler` client's temporary topic, using the `JMSCorrelationID` as a way of identifying itself. We will examine persistent publishing and temporary topics in the next section.

Temporary Topics

In the chat example we explored in Chapter 2, we assumed that JMS clients would communicate with each other using established topics on which messages are asynchronously produced and consumed. In the next sections, we'll explore ways to augment this basic mechanism. We'll start by looking at temporary topics, which is a mechanism for JMS clients to create topics dynamically.

The constructor of the `Wholesaler` class creates a temporary topic. This topic is used as a `JMSReplyTo` destination for messages published to the "Hot Deals" topic in the `publishPriceQuotes()` method:

```
public Wholesaler(String broker, String username, String password){
    try {
        ...
        session =
        connect.createTopicSession(false,Session.AUTO_ACKNOWLEDGE);
        ...
        buyOrdersTopic = session.createTemporaryTopic();
        ...
    }
    ...
    private void publishPriceQuotes(String dealDesc, String username,
                                    String itemDesc,  float oldPrice,
                                    float newPrice){
        try {
            javax.jms.StreamMessage message = session.createStreamMessage();
            ...
```

```
message.setJMSReplyTo(buyOrdersTopic);

publisher.publish(
    message,
    javax.jms.DeliveryMode.PERSISTENT,
    javax.jms.Message.DEFAULT_PRIORITY,
    600000);
    ...
}
```

When the `Retailer` client decides to respond to a "Hot Deals" message with a buy order, it uses the `JMSReplyTo` destination, which is the temporary topic created by `Wholesaler` application:

```
private void autoBuy (javax.jms.Message message){
    int count = 1000;
    try {
        StreamMessage strmMsg = (StreamMessage)message;
        ...
        // If price reduction is greater than 10 percent, buy
        if (newPrice == 0 || oldPrice / newPrice > 1.1){
            ...
            javax.jms.Topic buytopic =
                (javax.jms.Topic)message.getJMSReplyTo();

            publisher = session.createPublisher(buytopic);
        ...
}
```

A temporary topic is a topic that is dynamically created by the JMS provider, using the `createTemporaryTopic()` method of the `TopicSession` object. A temporary topic is associated with the connection that belongs to the `TopicSession` that created it. It is only active for the duration of the connection, and it is guaranteed to be unique across all connections. Since it is temporary, it can't be durable: it lasts only as long as its associated client connection is active. In all other respects it is just like a "regular" topic.

Since a temporary topic is unique across all client connections—it is obtained dynamically through a method call on a client's session object—it is unavailable to other JMS clients unless the topic identity is transferred using the `JMSReplyTo` header. While any client may publish messages on another client's temporary topic, only the sessions that are associated with the JMS client connection that created the temporary topic may subscribe to it. JMS clients can also, of course, publish messages to their own temporary topics.

In the interest of exploring concepts like temporary topics we have designed our B2B example so that the consumer responds directly to the producer. In larger real-world applications, however, there may be many publishers and subscribers exchanging messages across many topics. A message may represent a workflow, which may take multiple hops through various stages of a business process. In that type of scenario the consumer of a message may never respond directly to the producer that originated the message. It is more likely that the response to the message will be forwarded to some other process. Thus, the JMSReplyTo header can be used as a place to specify a forwarding address, rather than the destination address of the original sender.

JMS provides a set of design patterns and helper classes for performing a direct request-reply conversation, which we will get into later in the "Request and Reply" section of this chapter.

Durable Subscriptions

A durable subscription is one that outlasts a client's connection with a message server. While a durable subscriber is disconnected from the JMS server, it is the responsibility of the server to store messages the subscriber misses. When the durable subscriber reconnects, the message server sends it all the unexpired messages that accumulated. This behavior is commonly referred to as *store-and-forward messaging*. Store-and-forward messaging is a key component of the guaranteed messaging solution. Durable subscriptions make a JMS consumer tolerant of disconnections, whether they are intentional or the result of a partial failure

We can demonstrate durable subscriptions with the B2B example. If you still have the Retailer application up and running, try simulating an abnormal shutdown by typing Ctrl-C in the command window. Leave the Wholesaler running. In the command window for the wholesaler application, type:

```
Surfboards, 500.00, 299.99
Hockey Sticks, 20.00, 9.99
```

Once the deals have been entered, restart the Retailer application:

```
java chap4.B2B.Retailer localhost username password
```

The first time you ran the Retailer application, a topic was registered as durable. When you abnormally terminated the application, the subscription information was retained by the JMS provider. When the Retailer application comes back up, the surfboards and hockey sticks messages are received, processed, and responded to. Because the Retailer had a durable subscription to the "Hot Deals" topic, the JMS server saved the messages that arrived while the Retailer was down. The messages were then delivered when the Retailer resubscribed to the topic.

Here's how we set up the durable subscription. A durable subscription is created by a `TopicSession` object, the same as with a nondurable subscription. The `Retailer` class obtains a durable subscription in its constructor:

```
public Retailer( String broker, String username, String password){
    try {
        ...
        hotDealsTopic = (Topic)jndi.lookup("Hot Deals");

        javax.jms.TopicSubscriber subscriber =
            session.createDurableSubscriber(hotDealsTopic,
            "Hot Deals Subscription");
        subscriber.setMessageListener(this);
        connect.start();
        ....
    }
}
```

The `createDurableSubscriber()` method takes two parameters: a topic name, and a subscription name. In our example we are using the `String` "Hot Deals Subscription" to identify the subscription name. While topic names are specified as being supported as JMS administered objects, subscription names are not. While not required by JMS, it is good practice for a JMS provider to provide an administration tool that monitors active subscription names, as illustrated in Figure 4-2.

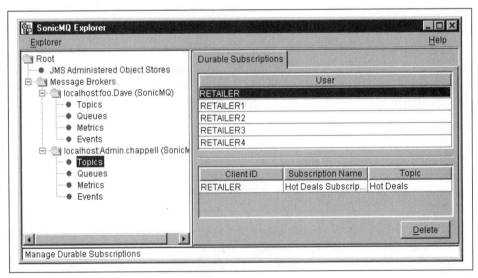

Figure 4-2. Managing active durable subscriptions

A durable subscription's uniqueness is defined by the client ID and the subscription name. In the event that the client disconnects without unsubscribing, a JMS provider will store these messages until they can be delivered later. Upon reconnecting and resubscribing, the JMS provider will match up the messages based on these two identifiers, and deliver them to the subscriber.

You might think that the client ID and the topic would be enough for the provider to uniquely identify a durable subscription. However, a client may have multiple subscriptions on the same topic; for example, a client may want to use different message selectors to sort the incoming messages. (Message selectors are discussed in detail in Appendix D, *Message Selectors.*) Therefore, durable subscriptions must be identified by their own name; simply using the topic name and the client ID will not suffice.

The JMS specification is intentionally vague about how the JMS provider determines the uniqueness of a client ID. Various provider implementations are allowed to have their own internal rules for what constitutes a unique client. The `setClientID()` method on the connection object is provided in the API as a hint. The client ID is set in the constructor of our `Retailer` example:

```
public Retailer( String broker, String username, String password){
    try {
        ....
        connect = factory.createTopicConnection (username, password);
        connect.setClientID(username);
        ....
    }
    ....
}
```

Publishing the Message Persistently

Both the `Wholesaler` and `Retailer` classes publish messages using the persistent delivery mode:

```
publisher.publish(
    message,
    javax.jms.DeliveryMode.PERSISTENT,
    javax.jms.Message.DEFAULT_PRIORITY,
    1800000);
```

Note the use of the overloaded `publish()` method, with parameters that specify delivery mode, priority, and message expiration. This method provides an alternative to using the `Message.setJMSDeliveryMode()` and `TopicPublisher.setTimeToLive()` operations, as discussed in Chapter 3, *Anatomy of a JMS Message.* In JMS, the delivery mode (persistent, nonpersistent) is a Quality of Service (QoS) setting on the message itself. Marking the message as persistent ensures that the message will be saved to a reliable persistent store by the JMS provider before the `publish()` method returns, and allows client execution to continue. More on how and why this works reliably can be found in Chapter 6, *Guaranteed Messaging, Transactions, Acknowledgments, and Failures.*

Persistent Messages and Temporary Topics

When you are using a temporary topic as a way of posting a reply to a message, you should realize that the total round trip (the initial message and the reply) isn't guaranteed to survive a certain failure condition, even if you use persistent messages. The problem is that temporary topics cannot be used for durable subscriptions. Consider the following scenario:

1. A JMS client (producer) creates a temporary topic, puts it in the JMSReplyTo header of a message, marks the message as persistent, and publishes it.

2. The subscriber gets the message and publishes a response on the temporary topic using a persistent message.

3. The original producer expects a reply on the temporary topic, but disconnects or crashes before it is received.

4. The original producer restarts, and is no longer able to subscribe to the original temporary topic that it had established in its previous life. It can't resubscribe because the temporary topic was only valid for the duration of the previous connection. Calling createTemporaryTopic() in the new session returns a new temporary topic, not the previous one.

This is a subtle point, since any client with a nondurable subscription will not get messages during a failure. In other scenarios it may be acceptable to lose messages for a time, yet still be able to start receiving newly published "responses" when the original producer of the message starts up again. In the B2B example, a failure of the Wholesaler means that the reply messages sent to the temporary topic will be lost. An alternative and superior design would use the JMSReplyTo header, with an established topic instead of a temporary one. Chapter 6 provides more detail on message delivery semantics, Quality of Service, and failure conditions.

JMSCorrelationID

In the B2B example, we are using the JMSCorrelationID as a way for the Retailer to associate its identity with its reply message, as illustrated by the following code in Retailer.autoBuy():

```
private void autoBuy (javax.jms.Message message){
    ...
    publisher = session.createPublisher(buytopic);

    textMsg.setJMSCorrelationID("DurableRetailer");
```

```
        publisher.publish(
            textMsg,
            javax.jms.DeliveryMode.PERSISTENT,
            javax.jms.Message.DEFAULT_PRIORITY,
            1800000);
        ...
    }
```

In Wholesaler, the JMSCorrelationID is extracted in the onMessage() handler, and simply printed on the command line:

```
    public void onMessage( javax.jms.Message message){
        ...
        System.out.println("Order received - "+text+
                        " from " + message.getJMSCorrelationID());
        ...
    }
```

Another way to associate the Retailer's identity with the reply message would be to store something unique in a message property, or in the message body itself.

A more common use of the JMSCorrelationID is not for the sake of establishing identity; it is for correlating the asynchronous reception of a message with a message that had been previously sent. A message consumer wishing to create a message to be used as a response may place the JMSMessageID of the original message in the JMSCorrelationID of the response message.

Request and Reply

JMS provides design patterns and helper classes to make it easier to write applications that need a direct request-reply between two end points. We have already shown two JMS features that can be used as part of a request-reply solution: temporary topics and the JMSReplyTo header. These features can be used independently or in combination to create an asynchronous request-reply conversation. On occasion you may want to create a synchronous request-reply conversation. There are two ways of doing this. You may call the TopicSubscriber.receive() method directly, or you may make use of the TopicRequestor class.

TopicSubscriber.receive()

The receive() method is defined in the MessageConsumer class, which is the superclass of TopicSubscriber. The receive() method is a way of proactively asking for the message rather than passively receiving it through the onMessage() callback. In fact, the use of the receive() method negates the use of the onMessage() callback. The default behavior of the receive() method is to block program execution until a message is retrieved from the message server. The `receive()` method effectively changes the pub/sub model from a "push" to a "pull" model. From the client's perspective, you can think of this as a polling mechanism; although that's not necessarily how it is implemented by the JMS provider.

There are three flavors of the `receive()` method:

```
package javax.jms;
public interface MessageConsumer{
    ...
    Message receive();
    Message receive(long timeout);
    Message receiveNoWait();
    ...
}
```

The `receive()` method with no parameters blocks indefinitely, until a message is received. The `receive(long timeout)` method blocks until a message is received, or until the timeout period expires, whichever comes first. The `receive()` method will return `null` if the session is closed while the method is blocking. The `receiveNoWait()` method does not block at all. It either returns a message if one is available, or it returns `null`, if there is nothing currently pending to be delivered. Here is a slightly modified version of `Wholesaler.publishPriceQuotes()` that makes use of the `receive()` method:

```
private void publishPriceQuotes(String dealDesc, String username,
                                String itemDesc,  float oldPrice,
                                float newPrice){
    ...
    System.out.println("\nInitiating Synchronous Request");

    // Publish the message persistently
    publisher.publish(
        msg,                              //message
        javax.jms.DeliveryMode.PERSISTENT, //publish persistently
        javax.jms.Message.DEFAULT_PRIORITY,//priority
        MESSAGE_LIFESPAN);                 //Time to Live

    javax.jms.Message aMessage = subscriber.receive();

    System.out.println("\nRequest Sent, Reply Received!");
    if (aMessage != null)
    {
        onMessage(aMessage);
    }
    ...
}
```

In this example the subscriber, which subscribes to the "Buy Order" temporary topic, has its `receive()` method called. The `receive()` method blocks until a message is published by the `Retailer` to the "Buy Order" topic. The `Wholesaler` client becomes a synchronous client waiting for the `Retailer` to respond. When the `receive()` method returns with a message, the `Wholesaler` simply calls `onMessage()` directly to process the message.

Due to threading restrictions imposed on a JMS session object, it is impractical to have both synchronous and asynchronous operations on a session. Hence the `Wholesaler`'s constructor does not make a call to `setMessageListener(this)`. The `onMessage()` handler will never get called automatically.

The recipient side of the conversation still looks the same as in our previous example. The `Retailer.autoBuy()` method receives the message, gets the return address from the `JMSReplyTo` header, and publishes a response using that topic.

It is erroneous for a session to be operated by more than one thread of control at any given time. In our example, there appears to be only one thread of control: the main thread of the application. However, when the `onMessage()` handler is invoked, it is being called by another thread that is owned by the JMS provider. Due to the asynchronous nature of the `onMessage()` callback, it could possibly be invoked while the main thread is blocking on a synchronous `receive()`.

TopicRequestor

The `TopicRequestor` class is distributed in source code form as a part of the JMS 1.0.2 distribution package. The class is very simple. Its constructor takes two parameters: a session and a topic. The constructor creates a temporary topic to be used for the duration of the session. Its most important method is `request()`, which looks like this:

```
public Message request(Message message) throws JMSException {
    message.setJMSReplyTo(tempTopic);
    publisher.publish(message);
    return(subscriber.receive());
}
```

The use of the `TopicRequestor` is similar to our `receive()` example, except that the calls to `publish()` and `receive()` are replaced with one call to `request()`. Here is a modified excerpt from `Wholesaler.publishPriceQuotes()` illustrating how to use a `TopicRequestor`:

```
private void publishPriceQuotes(String dealDesc, String username,
                                String itemesc,  float oldPrice,
                                float newPrice){

    ...
    System.out.println("\nInitiating Synchronous Request");

    javax.jms.TopicRequestor requestor =
```

```
    new javax.jms.TopicRequestor(session, pricetopic);

    javax.jms.Message aMessage = requestor.request(msg);

    System.out.println("\nRequest Sent, Reply Received!");
    if (aMessage != null)
    {
        onMessage(aMessage);
    }
    ...
}
```

As in our previous `receive()` example, the recipient side of the conversation remains unchanged. `Retailer.autoBuy()` receives the message, gets the return address from the `JMSReplyTo` header, and publishes a response using that topic.

As you can see, the `TopicRequestor` object is a higher-level abstraction built on top of the `TopicSubscriber.receive()` mechanism. It is very handy if you are willing to live with its limitations. Here are some reasons why you may want to call `receive()` yourself instead of using the `TopicRequestor`:

- You may want to set time-to-live or persistent properties on the message.

- You may not want to use a temporary topic. `TopicRequestor` creates its own temporary topic as its way of getting a response back.

- You want to use the alternate `receive(long timeout)` or `receiveNoWait()` options.

- You may want to publish on a topic, and receive responses on a p2p queue.

- You may want to receive more than one message in response to a request.

- `TopicRequestor.close()` will arbitrarily close the session. It may not be the behavior you are looking for.

- You may want to receive the responses using a transaction. (More on JMS transactions can be found in Chapter 6.)

Unsubscribing

Upon closing the session, the JMS provider should automatically take care of unsubscribing any nondurable subscriptions that were created by the session. But there may be cases where you want to explicitly unsubscribe a durable subscriber in a client application. Here is how that is accomplished in `Retailer.exit()`:

```
private void exit(String s){
      try {
         if ( s != null &&
            s.equalsIgnoreCase("unsubscribe"))
         {
```

```
            subscriber.close();
            session.unsubscribe("Hot Deals Subscription");
        }
        connect.close();
    } catch (javax.jms.JMSException jmse){
        jmse.printStackTrace();
    }
    System.exit(0);
}
```

For nondurable subscriptions, calling the `close()` method on the `Topic-Subscriber` class is sufficient. For durable subscriptions, there is a `unsubscribe(String name)` method on the `TopicSession` object, which takes the subscription name as its parameter. This informs the JMS provider that it should no longer store messages on behalf of this client. It is an error to call the `unsubscribe()` method without first closing the subscription. Hence both methods need to be called for durable subscriptions.

5

Point-to-Point Messaging

This chapter focuses on the point-to-point (p2p) messaging domain. Many of the concepts of p2p messaging are similar to those we learned in Chapter 4, *Publish-and-Subscribe Messaging*. To avoid redundancy, this chapter highlights the areas where the two models are the same, and focuses on the areas where the two models differ.

In the p2p model, the producer is called a *sender* and the consumer is called a *receiver*. The most important characteristics of the point-to-point model are:

- Messages are exchanged through a virtual channel called a queue. A queue is a destination to which producers send messages, and a source from which receivers consume messages.

- Each message is delivered only to one receiver. Multiple receivers may connect to a queue, but each message in the queue may only be consumed by one of the queue's receivers.

- Messages are ordered. A queue delivers messages to consumers in the order they were placed in the queue by the message server. As messages are consumed they are removed from the head of the queue.

- There is no coupling of the producers to the consumers. Receivers and senders can be added dynamically at runtime, allowing the system to grow or shrink in complexity over time. (This is a characteristic of messaging systems in general.)

In this chapter, we introduce new versions of our Wholesaler and Retailer classes, called QWholesaler and QRetailer. QWholesaler still uses pub/sub to broadcast price quotes, while QRetailer uses a p2p queue to respond with "buy" orders instead of publishing to a temporary topic.

The rest of the chapter focuses on the unique capabilities offered by p2p: examining a queue using the `QueueBrowser` interface, and load balancing among multiple recipients of a queue.

Point-to-Point and Publish-and-Subscribe

Like publish/subscribe messaging, point-to-point messaging is based on the concept of sending a message to a named destination. The actual network location of the destination is transparent to the sender, because the p2p client works with a `Queue` identifier obtained from a JNDI namespace, the same way that a pub/sub client uses a `Topic` identifier.

The pub/sub model is based on a push model, which means that consumers are delivered messages without having to request them. Messages are exchanged through a virtual channel called a topic. From the viewpoint of the receiver, a p2p queue can either push or pull messages, depending on whether it uses the asynchronous `onMessage()` callback, or a synchronous `receive()` method. Both of these methods are explained in more detail later.

In the p2p model, as in the pub/sub model, there is no direct coupling of the producers to the consumers. The destination queue provides a virtual channel that decouples consumers from producers. In the pub/sub model, multiple consumers that subscribe to the same topic each receive their own copy of every message addressed to that topic. In the p2p model, multiple consumers can use the same queue, but each message delivered to the queue can only be received by one of the queue's consumers. How messages delivered to a queue are distributed to the queue's consumers depends on the policies of the JMS provider. Some JMS providers use load-balancing techniques to distribute messages evenly among consumers, while others will use more arbitrary policies.

Messages intended for a p2p queue can be either persistent or nonpersistent. Persistent messages survive JMS provider failures, while nonpersistent messages do not. Messages may have a priority and an expiration time. One important difference between point-to-point and publish/subscribe messaging is that p2p messages are always delivered, regardless of the current connection status of the receiver. Once a message is delivered to a queue, it stays there even if there is no consumer currently connected. More details on failure scenarios can be found in Chapter 6, *Guaranteed Messaging, Transactions, Acknowledgments, and Failures*.

The interfaces for connecting, creating, sending and receiving are similar to the interfaces for topics, as shown in Table 5-1.

Table 5-1. Interfaces for Topics and Queues

Topic	Queue
TopicConnectionFactory	QueueConnectionFactory
TopicSession	QueueSession
TopicPublisher	QueueSender
TopicSubscriber	QueueReceiver
createTopicConnection()	createQueueConnection()
createTopicSession()	createQueueSession()
createTemporaryTopic()	createTemporaryQueue()
...	...

When to Use Point-to-Point Messaging

First, let's talk about why two distinct models exist. The rationale behind the two models lies in the origin of the JMS specification. JMS started out as a way of providing a common API for accessing existing messaging systems. At the time of its conception, some messaging vendors had a p2p model, and some had a pub/sub model. Hence JMS needed to provide an API for both models to gain wide industry support. The JMS 1.0.2 specification does not require a JMS provider to support both models, although most JMS vendors do.

Almost anything that can be done with the pub/sub model can be done with point-to-point, and vice versa. An analogy can be drawn to developers' programming language preferences. In theory, any application that can be written with Pascal can also be written with C. Anything that can be written in C++ can also be written in Java. In some cases it comes down to a matter of preference, or which model you are already familiar with.

In most cases, the decision about which model to use depends on the distinct merits of each model. With pub/sub, any number of subscribers can be listening on a topic, all receiving copies of the same message. The publisher may not care if everybody is listening, or even if nobody is listening. For example, consider a publisher that broadcasts stock quotes. If any particular subscriber is not currently connected and misses out on a great quote, the publisher is not concerned. Likewise, our Wholesaler class didn't care whether there were any subscribers when it sent price quotes: if a Retailer missed a great price, that wasn't the Wholesaler's problem. In contrast, a point-to-point session is likely to be intended for a one-on-one conversation with a specific application at the other end. In this scenario, every message really matters.

The range and variety of the data that the messages represent can be a factor as well. Using pub/sub, messages are dispatched to the consumers based on filtering that is provided through the use of specific topics. Even when messaging is being used to establish a one-on-one conversation with another known application, it can be advantageous to use pub/sub with multiple topics to segregate different kinds of messages. Each kind of message can be dealt with separately through its own unique consumer and onMessage() handler.

Point-to-point is more convenient when you want one receiver to process any given message once-and-only-once. This is perhaps the most critical difference between the two models: point-to-point guarantees that only one consumer processes a given message. This is extremely important when messages need to be processed separately but in tandem, balancing the load of message processing across many JMS clients. Another advantage is that the point-to-point model provides a QueueBrowser that allows the JMS client to peek ahead on the queue to see messages waiting to be consumed. Pub/sub does not include a browsing feature. We'll talk more about the QueueBrowser later in this chapter.

The QWholesaler and QRetailer

Let's rethink our wholesaler/retailer scenario in terms of the distinction between the two message models. The pub/sub model is well suited for sending price quotes, since that is naturally a one-to-many broadcast. However, when the retailer responds with a "buy" order, it is more appropriate to use a point-to-point queue. In the real world, retailers naturally deal with many wholesalers, and you would only send a purchase order to the wholesaler that offered the quote.

From the user's perspective, the QWholesaler and QRetailer examples that we'll develop now are functionally equivalent to the Wholesaler and Retailer examples introduced in Chapter 4. The difference lies in the use of the point-to-point queue for responses to price quotes. If you wish to see these classes in action, start your JMS provider and execute the following commands, each in a separate command window:

```
java chap5.B2B.QWholesaler localhost username password
java chap5.B2B.QRetailer localhost username password
```

The QRetailer Class

Here is the listing for the QRetailer class in its entirety. Later, we will examine this class in detail:

```
import java.util.StringTokenizer;
import java.util.Properties;
import javax.naming.InitialContext;
import javax.jms.TopicConnectionFactory;
import javax.jms.QueueConnectionFactory;
import javax.jms.Topic;
import javax.jms.Queue;
```

```java
import javax.jms.Session;
import javax.jms.StreamMessage;
import javax.jms.TextMessage;

public class QRetailer implements javax.jms.MessageListener {

    private javax.jms.QueueConnection qConnect = null;
    private javax.jms.QueueSession qSession = null;
    private javax.jms.QueueSender qSender = null;

    private javax.jms.TopicConnection tConnect = null;
    private javax.jms.TopicSession tSession = null;

    private javax.jms.Topic hotDealsTopic = null;
    private javax.jms.TopicSubscriber tsubscriber = null;
    private static boolean useJNDI = false;
    private static String uname = null;

    public QRetailer( String broker, String username, String password){
        try  {
            TopicConnectionFactory tFactory = null;
            QueueConnectionFactory qFactory = null;
            InitialContext jndi = null;
            uname = username;

            Properties env = new Properties();
            // ... specify the JNDI properties specific to the vendor
            jndi = new InitialContext(env);
            tFactory =
                (TopicConnectionFactory)jndi.lookup(broker);
            qFactory =
                (QueueConnectionFactory)jndi.lookup(broker);
            tConnect =
                tFactory.createTopicConnection (username, password);
            qConnect =
                qFactory.createQueueConnection (username, password);
            tConnect.setClientID(username);
            qConnect.setClientID(username);

            tSession =
                tConnect.createTopicSession(false,
                    Session.AUTO_ACKNOWLEDGE);
            qSession =
                qConnect.createQueueSession(false,
                    javax.jms.Session.AUTO_ACKNOWLEDGE);

            hotDealsTopic = (Topic)jndi.lookup("Hot Deals");

            tsubscriber =
```

```
                    tSession.createDurableSubscriber(hotDealsTopic,
                                         "Hot Deals Subscription");
            tsubscriber.setMessageListener(this);
            tConnect.start();

        } catch  (javax.jms.JMSException jmse){
            jmse.printStackTrace();
            System.exit(1);
        } catch (javax.naming.NamingException jne){
         jne.printStackTrace(); System.exit(1);
        }
    }
    public void onMessage(javax.jms.Message aMessage){
        try  {
            autoBuy(aMessage);
        } catch  (java.lang.RuntimeException rte){
            rte.printStackTrace();
        }
    }
    private void autoBuy (javax.jms.Message message){
        try  {
            StreamMessage strmMsg = (StreamMessage)message;
            String dealDesc = strmMsg.readString();
            String itemDesc = strmMsg.readString();
            float oldPrice = strmMsg.readFloat();
            float newPrice = strmMsg.readFloat();
            System.out.println("Received Hot Buy: "+dealDesc);

            // If price reduction is greater than 10 percent, buy
            if (newPrice == 0 || oldPrice / newPrice > 1.1) {
                int count = (int)(java.lang.Math.random()*(double)1000);
                System.out.println("\nBuying " + count +" "+ itemDesc);

                TextMessage textMsg = tSession.createTextMessage();
                textMsg.setText(count + " " + itemDesc );
                textMsg.setIntProperty("QTY", count);

                textMsg.setJMSCorrelationID(uname);

                Queue buyQueue = (Queue)message.getJMSReplyTo();

                qSender = qSession.createSender(buyQueue);
                qSender.send( textMsg,
                            javax.jms.DeliveryMode.PERSISTENT,
                            javax.jms.Message.DEFAULT_PRIORITY,
                            1800000);
            } else {
                System.out.println ("\nBad Deal.  Not buying");
            }
        } catch  (javax.jms.JMSException jmse){
```

```
                        jmse.printStackTrace();
                }
        }
        private void exit(String s){
            try {
                if ( s != null &&
                    s.equalsIgnoreCase("unsubscribe"))
                {
                    tsubscriber.close();
                    tSession.unsubscribe("Hot Deals Subscription");
                }
                tConnect.close();
                qConnect.close();
            } catch (javax.jms.JMSException jmse){
                jmse.printStackTrace();
            }
            System.exit(0);
        }
        public static void main(String argv[]) {
            String broker, username, password;
            if (argv.length == 3){
                broker = argv[0];
                username = argv[1];
                password = argv[2];
            } else {
                System.out.println("Invalid arguments. Should be: ");
                System.out.println
                ("java QRetailer broker username password");
                return;
            }

            QRetailer retailer  = new QRetailer(broker, username, password);

            try {
                System.out.println("\nRetailer application started.\n");
                // Read all standard input and send it as a message
                java.io.BufferedReader stdin =
                    new java.io.BufferedReader
                    ( new java.io.InputStreamReader( System.in ) );
                while ( true ){
                    String s = stdin.readLine();
                    if ( s == null )retailer.exit(null);
                    else if ( s.equalsIgnoreCase("unsubscribe") )
                        retailer.exit ( s );
                }
            } catch ( java.io.IOException ioe ){
                ioe.printStackTrace();
            }
        }
    }
```

Now let's look at the code in detail. A session can either be a QueueSession (point-to-point) or a TopicSession (publish/subscribe). It cannot be both at the same time. Similarly, a connection can be either a QueueConnection or a Topic-Connection. Therefore we create a connection and a session for each model in the QRetailer's constructor:

```
public QRetailer( String broker, String username, String password){
    ...
        tFactory =
            (TopicConnectionFactory)jndi.lookup(broker);
        qFactory =
            (QueueConnectionFactory)jndi.lookup(broker);
        tConnect =
            tfactory.createTopicConnection (username, password);
        qConnect =
            qfactory.createQueueConnection (username, password);

        tConnect.setClientID(username);
        qConnect.setClientID(username);

        tSession =
            tConnect.createTopicSession(false,
                Session.AUTO_ACKNOWLEDGE);
        qSession =
            qConnect.createQueueSession(false,
                javax.jms.Session.AUTO_ACKNOWLEDGE);


    ...
```

The autoBuy() method is responsible for sending the "Buy Order" messages. This method is invoked by the onMessage() handler for the "Hot Deals" topic:

```
private void autoBuy (javax.jms.Message message){
    ...
    textMsg.setJMSCorrelationID("DurableRetailer");

    Queue buyQueue = (Queue)message.getJMSReplyTo();

    qSender = qSession.createSender(buyQueue);
            qSender.send( textMsg,
    javax.jms.DeliveryMode.PERSISTENT,
    javax.jms.Message.DEFAULT_PRIORITY,
    1800000);
    ...
}
```

The Message object itself is independent of the domain being used to transport it. All of the same headers and properties apply to each. Therefore, we can set a correlation ID, extract an object to reply to (this time, it's a Queue), and use the

Queue to create a sender. The QueueSender.send() method is identical in form to the TopicPublisher.publish() method. Here is the interface definition for the QueueSender object:

```
public interface QueueSender
        Extends MessageProducer
{
        Queue getQueue() throws JMSException;
        void send(Message message) throws JMSException,
            MessageFormatException, InvalidDestinationException;

        void send(Message message, int deliveryMode,
        int priority, long timeToLive) throws JMSException,
            MessageFormatException, InvalidDestinationException;

        void send(Queue queue, Message message) throws JMSException,
            MessageFormatException, InvalidDestinationException;

        void send(Queue queue, Message message, int deliveryMode,
        int priority, long timeToLive) throws JMSException,
            MessageFormatException, InvalidDestinationException;
}
```

The QueueSender object is created as part of the onMessage() handler, using the call to the createSender() method. As an alternative, we could have created the QueueSender once in the QRetailer's constructor using null as a parameter, then specified buyQueue as a parameter to the send() operation each time the onMessage() method is invoked. For most applications, this would be more efficient; the example recreates the QueueSender for clarity.

The QWholesaler Class

Here is the complete listing for the QWholesaler class:

```
import java.util.StringTokenizer;
import java.util.Properties;
import javax.naming.InitialContext;
import javax.jms.TopicConnectionFactory;
import javax.jms.QueueConnectionFactory;
import javax.jms.Topic;
import javax.jms.Queue;
import javax.jms.QueueReceiver;
import javax.jms.Session;
import javax.jms.TextMessage;

public class QWholesaler implements javax.jms.MessageListener{

    private javax.jms.TopicConnection tConnect = null;
    private javax.jms.TopicSession tSession = null;
```

```java
    private javax.jms.TopicPublisher tPublisher = null;

    private javax.jms.QueueConnection qConnect = null;
    private javax.jms.QueueSession qSession = null;
    private javax.jms.Queue receiveQueue = null;

    private javax.jms.Topic hotDealsTopic = null;
    private javax.jms.TemporaryTopic buyOrdersTopic = null;

public QWholesaler(String broker, String username, String password){
    try  {
        TopicConnectionFactory tFactory = null;
        QueueConnectionFactory qFactory = null;
        InitialContext jndi = null;

        Properties env = new Properties();
        // ... specify the JNDI properties specific to the vendor
        jndi = new InitialContext(env);

        tFactory =
            (TopicConnectionFactory)jndi.lookup(broker);
        qFactory =
            (QueueConnectionFactory)jndi.lookup(broker);
        tConnect = tFactory.createTopicConnection (username, password);
        qConnect = qFactory.createQueueConnection (username, password);
        tSession =
            tConnect.createTopicSession(false,Session.AUTO_ACKNOWLEDGE);
        qSession =
            qConnect.createQueueSession(false,Session.AUTO_ACKNOWLEDGE);

        hotDealsTopic = (Topic)jndi.lookup("Hot Deals");
        receiveQueue = (Queue)jndi.lookup("SampleQ1");

        tPublisher = tSession.createPublisher(hotDealsTopic);

        QueueReceiver qReceiver = qSession.createReceiver(receiveQueue);
        qReceiver.setMessageListener(this);

        // Now that setup is complete, start the Connection
        qConnect.start();
        tConnect.start();
    } catch  (javax.jms.JMSException jmse){
        jmse.printStackTrace(); System.exit(1);
    } catch (javax.naming.NamingException jne){
        jne.printStackTrace(); System.exit(1);
    }
}
private void publishPriceQuotes(String dealDesc, String username,
                               String itemDesc,  float oldPrice,
                               float newPrice){
```

```
        try  {
          javax.jms.StreamMessage message =
                tSession.createStreamMessage();
          message.writeString(dealDesc);
          message.writeString(itemDesc);
          message.writeFloat(oldPrice);
          message.writeFloat(newPrice);

          message.setStringProperty("Username", username);
          message.setStringProperty("itemDesc", itemDesc);

          message.setJMSReplyTo(receiveQueue);

          tPublisher.publish(
             message,
             javax.jms.DeliveryMode.PERSISTENT,
             javax.jms.Message.DEFAULT_PRIORITY,
             1800000);
        } catch  ( javax.jms.JMSException jmse ){
           jmse.printStackTrace();
        }
    }
    public void onMessage( javax.jms.Message message){
        try  {
           TextMessage textMessage = (TextMessage) message;
           String text = textMessage.getText();
           System.out.println("Order received - "+text+
                            " from " + message.getJMSCorrelationID());
        } catch  (java.lang.Exception rte){
           rte.printStackTrace();
        }
    }
    public void exit(){
        try  {
          tConnect.close();
          qConnect.close();
        } catch  (javax.jms.JMSException jmse){
          jmse.printStackTrace();
        }
        System.exit(0);
    }
    public static void main(String argv[]) {
        String broker, username, password;
        if (argv.length == 3){
           broker = argv[0];
           username = argv[1];
           password = argv[2];
        } else {
```

```
           System.out.println("Invalid arguments. Should be: ");
           System.out.println
                 ("java QWholesaler broker username password");
           return;
       }

       QWholesaler wholesaler = new QWholesaler(broker, username, password);

       try {
           // Read all standard input and send it as a message
           java.io.BufferedReader stdin = new java.io.BufferedReader
               (new java.io.InputStreamReader( System.in ) );
           System.out.println ("Enter: Item, Old Price, New Price");
           System.out.println("\ne.g. Bowling Shoes, 100.00, 55.00");

           while ( true ){
               String dealDesc = stdin.readLine();
               if (dealDesc != null && dealDesc.length() > 0){
                   // Parse the deal description
                   StringTokenizer tokenizer =
                   new StringTokenizer(dealDesc,",") ;
                       String itemDesc = tokenizer.nextToken();
                       String temp = tokenizer.nextToken();
                       float oldPrice =
                         Float.valueOf(temp.trim()).floatValue();
                       temp = tokenizer.nextToken();
                       float newPrice =
                         Float.valueOf(temp.trim()).floatValue();

                   wholesaler.publishPriceQuotes(dealDesc,username,
                                             itemDesc, oldPrice,newPrice);
               } else {
                   wholesaler.exit();
               }
           }
       } catch ( java.io.IOException ioe ){
           ioe.printStackTrace();
       }
   }
}
```

The job of QWholesaler is to establish a publisher for broadcasting the price quotes, and to establish a QueueReceiver for consuming the "Buy Order" messages. These objects are created in the constructor:

```
public QWholesaler(String broker, String username, String password){
   ...
       tSession =
           tConnect.createTopicSession(false,Session.AUTO_ACKNOWLEDGE);
```

```
    qSession =
        qConnect.createQueueSession(false,Session.AUTO_ACKNOWLEDGE);

    hotDealsTopic = (Topic)jndi.lookup("Hot Deals");
    receiveQueue = (Queue)jndi.lookup("SampleQ1"); // Buy Order

    tPublisher = tSession.createPublisher(hotDealsTopic);

    QueueReceiver qReceiver = qSession.createReceiver(receiveQueue);
    qReceiver.setMessageListener(this);
    qConnect.start();
    ...
}
```

Here we are creating a QueueSession using the createQueueSession() method
on the QueueConnection object. We are creating a receiver using the
createReceiver() method on the QueueSession object. These methods are
identical to their counterparts in the pub/sub domain.

There is very little left to explain. The publishPricesQuotes() method works
exactly as it did in Chapter 4, with the exception that it now places a Queue in the
JMSReplyTo header:

```
private void publishPriceQuotes(String dealDesc, String username,
                                String itemDesc,  float oldPrice,
                                float newPrice){

    ...

    message.setJMSReplyTo(receiveQueue);

    tPublisher.publish(
        message,
        javax.jms.DeliveryMode.PERSISTENT,
        javax.jms.Message.DEFAULT_PRIORITY,
        1800000);
    ...
}
```

The onMessage() method also works exactly as it did before. The programming
model is the same whether we use a Queue or a Topic. Likewise we could have
used the alternate QueueReceiver.receive() method to do a synchronous
receive. This method is the same as the TopicSubscriber.recieve() method
discussed in Chapter 4.

The similarity between this code and the code in Chapter 4 is the beauty of JMS.
Even though there are two separate messaging domains, the interfaces follow the
same idiom, making it easier to remember and easy to change from one domain to
the other.

Creating a Queue Dynamically

The setup and configuration of queues tends to be vendor-specific. A queue may be used exclusively by one consumer, or shared by multiple consumers. It may have a size limit (limiting the number of unconsumed messages held in the queue) with options for in-memory storage versus overflow to disk. In addition, a queue may be configured with a vendor-specific addressing syntax, or special routing capabilities.

JMS doesn't attempt to define a set of APIs for all the possible options on a queue. It should be possible to set these options administratively, using the vendor-specific administration capabilities. Figure 5-1 shows what a graphical administration tool for queues would look like. Most vendors supply a command-line administration tool, a graphical administration tool, or an API for administering queues at runtime. Some vendors supply all three.

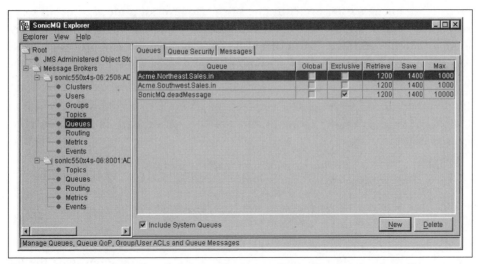

Figure 5-1. Queues are created and administered using vendor-specific administration tools

Using vendor-specific administration APIs to create and configure a queue may be convenient at times. However, it is not very portable, and may require that the application have administrator privileges.

JMS provides a QueueSession.createQueue(String queueName) method, but this is not intended to define a new queue in the messaging system. It is intended to return a Queue object that represents an existing queue. There is also a JMS-defined method for creating a temporary queue that can only be consumed by the JMS client that created it: QueueSession.createTemporaryQueue(). A temporary queue is similar to a temporary topic, and could have been used in our example just like the TemporaryTopic was used in Chapter 4.

Load Balancing Using Multiple QueueSessions

A queue may have multiple receivers attached to it for the purpose of distributing the workload of message processing. The JMS specification states that this capability must be implemented by a JMS provider, although it does not define the rules for how the messages are distributed among consumers. A sender could use this feature to distribute messages to multiple instances of an application, each of which would provide its own receiver.

When multiple receivers are attached to a queue, each message in the queue is delivered to one receiver. The absolute order of messages cannot be guaranteed, since one receiver may process messages faster than another. From the receiver's perspective, the messages it consumes should be in relative order; messages delivered to the queue earlier are consumed first. However, if a message needs to be redelivered due to an acknowledgment failure, it is possible that it could be delivered to another receiver. The other receiver may have already processed more recently delivered messages, which would place the redelivered message out of the original order.

If you would like to see multiple recipients in action, try starting two instances of QWholesaler and three or more instances of QRetailer, each in a separate command window:

```
java chap5.B2B.QWholesaler localhost WHOLESALER1 password
java chap5.B2B.QWholesaler localhost WHOLESALER2 password

java chap5.B2B.QRetailer localhost RETAILER1 password
java chap5.B2B.QRetailer localhost RETAILER2 password
java chap5.B2B.QRetailer localhost RETAILER3 password
```

In the command window for one of the QWholesaler applications, type the following command:

```
Surfboards, 999.99, 499.99
```

Upon hitting the enter key, each instance of QRetailer will get the price quote, and respond with a "Buy" order. If you have three QRetailers up and running, you should see two of the messages going to one of the QWholesalers, and one going to the other.

NOTE   If you don't see this behavior, load balancing may not be broken. It
            may mean that vendor-specific queue settings are preventing load
            balancing; you may need to send more than three messages simulta-
            neously to populate the queue enough to cause the messages to be
            delivered to more than one consumer. For example, in SonicMQ
            there is a configurable pre-fetch count that determines how many
            messages may be batched together as they are delivered to a con-
            sumer. The default is three messages, so the messages get delivered
            to each consumer three at a time. The SonicMQ version of these
            samples has some code that sets the value to one, which makes load
            balancing work properly with only three clients:

```
...
qReceiver.setPrefetchThreshold(0);
qReceiver.setPrefetchCount(1);
...
```

            It is likely that other vendors have the same kind of optimization, so
            you should check that possibility if you are using a vendor other than
            SonicMQ and don't see the proper behavior.

Examining a Queue

A QueueBrowser is a specialized object that allows you to peek ahead at pending
messages on a Queue without actually consuming them. This feature is unique to
point-to-point messaging. Queue browsing can be useful for monitoring the contents of a queue from an administration tool, or for browsing through multiple
messages to locate a message that is more important than the one that is at the
head of the queue. The latter scenario is what we chose to explore in our new version the wholesaler application, the QWBrowser.

QWBrowser sends out price quotes to multiple instances of QRetailer, which
respond with "Buy" orders. To make this more interesting, we'll modify the
retailer so that each order requests a random number of items. The QWBrowser
may not be able to fulfill all of the orders from its on-hand inventory.

In order to sell as many items from inventory as possible without going into back-
order, QWBrowser examines all of the responses that are pending in the queue,
then finds the one order with a quantity that most closely fits the amount it has in
inventory. It then synchronously consumes all of the messages using Queue-
Receiver.receive(long timeout), fulfills the desired order, and places the rest
of them in a back-order status.

If you would like to see this in action, shut down all the other wholesalers and retailers you may have running. Start one instance of QWBrowser and four or more instances of QRetailer, each in a separate command window:

```
java chap5.B2B.QWBrowser localhost WHOLESALER1 password
```

```
java chap5.B2B.QRetailer localhost RETAILER1 password
java chap5.B2B.QRetailer localhost RETAILER2 password
java chap5.B2B.QRetailer localhost RETAILER3 password
java chap5.B2B.QRetailer localhost RETAILER3 password
```

In the command window for the QWBrowser, type the following command:

```
Surfboards, 999.99, 499.99
```

When you press Enter, each instance of QRetailer will get the price quote, and respond with a "Buy Order." Each order will request a different quantity. You should see output in the QWBrowser window indicating that it is browsing the queue, placing the order for one of the messages, and placing the rest on back-order status.

The QWBrowser Source Code

The QueueBrowser object is simple to use. We will examine this listing from QWBrowser.examineQueue() in detail:

```java
private int examineQueue(int inStockQty)
{
    int cnt = 0;
    int bestQty = 0;
    try {
        System.out.println("In Stock QTY: " + inStockQty);
        System.out.print ( "Creating QueueBrowser..." );
        javax.jms.QueueBrowser browser
            = qSession.createBrowser(receiveQueue);
        System.out.println ("[done]");

        java.util.Enumeration e = browser.getEnumeration();
        while(e.hasMoreElements()){
            System.out.print(" --> getting message "
            + String.valueOf(++cnt) + "...");
            javax.jms.TextMessage message =
                (javax.jms.TextMessage) e.nextElement();
            System.out.println("[" + message.getText() + "]");
            if (message != null){
                int orderQty = message.getIntProperty("QTY");
                if ( orderQty > bestQty && orderQty <= inStockQty)
                    bestQty = orderQty;
            }
        }
    }
```

```
                // Free any resources in the browser
                browser.close();
            } catch ( javax.jms.JMSException jmse ){
                jmse.printStackTrace();
            }
            System.out.println("\nBestQty: " + bestQty);
            return bestQty;
        }
```

First, note the call to create the QueueBrowser:

```
        System.out.print ( "Creating QueueBrowser..." );
        javax.jms.QueueBrowser browser
            = qSession.createBrowser(receiveQueue);
        System.out.println ("[done]");
```

The method createQueueBrowser() is a session method. It takes a Queue object as a parameter and returns a QueueBrowser object. The createQueueBrowser() method, in additon, allows you to set a message selector using an overloaded method signature.

The QueueBrowser object contains a java.util.Enumeration that holds the messages in the queue. Here's how to use it:

```
        ...
        java.util.Enumeration e = browser.getEnumeration();
        while(e.hasMoreElements()){
            javax.jms.TextMessage message =
                (javax.jms.TextMessage) e.nextElement();
            System.out.println("[" + message.getText() + "]");
        ...
```

When the browser has served its purpose, it must be closed. This informs the JMS provider that it is no longer needed, thus allowing the provider to clean up any resources it may have allocated on the browser's behalf:

```
        // Free any resources in the browser
        browser.close();
```

Now let's look at the main input loop, which publishes the prices quotes, browses the queue, then uses a synchronous QueueReceiver to consume the messages after it has browsed them:

```
    public void processInput(){
        try {
            ...
            System.out.println ("Enter: Item, Old Price, New Price");
            System.out.println("\ne.g. Bowling Shoes, 100.00, 55.00");
            String dealDesc = stdin.readLine();
            ...
            publishPriceQuotes(dealDesc,uname,
```

```
                        itemDesc, oldPrice,newPrice);

          int inStockQty =
             (int)(java.lang.Math.random() * (double)1000);
          int bestQty = examineQueue(inStockQty);
          qConnect.start(); // Start the connection
          javax.jms.TextMessage textMessage = null;
          while( true ){
             textMessage =
                (javax.jms.TextMessage)qReceiver.receive(1000);
             if ( textMessage == null ){
                qConnect.stop();
                break;  // No more messages to get
             }
             String text = textMessage.getText();
             int qty = textMessage.getIntProperty("QTY");
             System.out.println("\nOrder received - "+text+
                " from " + textMessage.getJMSCorrelationID());

             if (qty == bestQty){
                System.out.println("Fulfilling order");
                // Do some processing to fulfill order
             } else {
                System.out.println("Placing in BACK-ORDER status");
                // Do some processing to create BACK-ORDER status
             }
          }
       ...
    }
```

Messages obtained from a QueueBrowser are copies of messages contained in the queue and are not considered to be consumed—they are merely for browsing.

It is important to note that the QueueBrowser is not guaranteed to have a definitive list of messages in the queue. The JMS specification allows the QueueBrowser to contain a snapshot, or a copy of, the queue as it appears at the time the QueueBrowser is created. The behavior may vary depending on vendor implementation, since the contents of the queue may change between the time the browser is created and the time you examine its contents. No matter how small that window of time is, new messages may arrive and other messages may be consumed by other JMS clients. Some JMS providers will update QueueBrowsers as the status of the queue changes while others will not.

6

Guaranteed Messaging, Transactions, Acknowledgments, and Failures

We have been introducing the notion of *guaranteed messaging* in bits and pieces throughout the book. Until now, we have assumed that you would take our word that guaranteed messaging ensures that messages are faithfully delivered once-and-only-once to their intended consumers.

This chapter examines *why* guaranteed messaging works, and provides a thorough discussion of the subject. We will examine the message acknowledgment protocols that are part of guaranteed messaging, and how to use client acknowledgments in applications. We will explore the design patterns of JMS that enable you to build guaranteed messaging into applications, and discuss failure scenarios, the rules that apply to recovery, and how to deal with recovery semantics in a JMS application.

Guaranteed Messaging

Guaranteed messaging is more than just a mechanism for handling disconnected consumers. It is a crucial part of the messaging paradigm, and is the key to under-. standing the design of a distributed messaging system. There are three main parts to guaranteed messaging: message autonomy, store-and-forward, and the underlying message acknowledgment semantics.

Before we discuss the parts of guaranteed messaging, we need to review and define some new terms. A JMS client application uses the JMS API. Each JMS vendor provides an implementation of the JMS API on the client, which we call the *client runtime*. In addition to the client runtime, the JMS vendor also provides some kind of message "server" that implements the routing and delivery of messages. The client runtime and the message server are collectively referred to as the *JMS provider*. Regardless of the architecture used by a JMS provider, the logical parts of a JMS system are the same. The number of processes and their location on the network is unimportant for this discussion. (In Chapter 7, *Deployment Considerations,* we'll see that some providers use a multicast architecture in which there is no central server.) The upcoming sections make use of diagrams that describe the logical pieces, and do not necessarily reflect the process architecture of any particular JMS provider.

A *provider failure* refers to any failure condition that is outside of the domain of the application code. It could mean a hardware failure that occurs while the provider is entrusted with the processing of a message, or an unexpected exception, or the abnormal end of a process due to a software defect, or network failures.

Message Autonomy

Messages are self-contained autonomous entities. This fact needs to be foremost in your mind when designing a distributed messaging application. A message may be sent and resent many times across multiple processes throughout its lifetime. Each JMS client along the way will consume the message, examine it, execute business logic, modify it, or create new messages in order to accomplish the task at hand.

In a sense, a JMS client has a contract with the rest of the system: when it receives a message, it does its part of the processing, and may deliver the message (or new message) to another topic or queue. When a JMS client sends a message, it has done its job. The messaging server guarantees that any other interested parties will receive the messages. This contract between the sender and the message server is much like the contract between a JDBC client and a database. Once the data is delivered, it is considered "safe" and out of the hands of the client.

Store-and-Forward Messaging

When messages are marked *persistent,* it is the responsibility of the JMS provider to utilize a store-and-forward mechanism to fulfill its contract with the sender. The storage mechanism is used for persisting messages to disk (or some other reliable medium) in order to ensure that the message can be recovered in the event of a provider failure or a failure of the consuming client. The implementation of the storage mechanism is up to the JMS provider. The messages may be stored centrally (as is the case with centralized architectures), or locally, with each sending or receiving client (the solution used by decentralized architectures). Some vendors use a flat-file storage mechanism, while others use a database. Some use an intelligent combination of both. The forwarding mechanism is responsible for retrieving messages from storage, and subsequently routing and delivering them.

Message Acknowledgments and Failure Conditions

JMS specifies a number of acknowledgment modes. These acknowledgments are a
key part of guaranteed messaging. A message acknowledgment is part of the protocol that is established between the client runtime portion of the JMS provider and
the server. Servers acknowledge the receipt of messages from JMS producers and
JMS consumers acknowledge the receipt of messages from servers. The acknowledgment protocol allows the JMS provider to monitor the progress of a message so
that it knows whether the message was successfully produced and consumed. With
this information, the JMS provider can manage the distribution of messages and
guarantee their delivery.

Message Acknowledgments

The message acknowledgment protocol is the key to guaranteed messaging, and
support for acknowledgment is required by the semantics of the JMS API. This section provides an in-depth explanation of how the acknowledgment protocol works
and its role in guaranteed messaging.

We will begin by examining the AUTO_ACKNOWLEDGE mode. We will revisit this discussion later as it pertains to CLIENT_ACKNOWLEDGE, DUPS_OK_ACKNOWLEDGE, and
JMS transacted messages. An understanding of the basic concepts of AUTO_
ACKNOWLEDGE will make it easy to grasp the fundamental concepts of the other
modes.

The acknowledgment mode is set on a JMS provider when a Session is created:

```
tSession =
    tConnect.createTopicSession(false, Session.CLIENT_ACKNOWLEDGE);

qSession =
    qConnect.createQueueSession(false, Session.DUPS_OK_ACKNOWLEDGE);
```

AUTO_ACKNOWLEDGE

We'll look at the AUTO_ACKNOWLEDGE mode from the perspective of a message
producer, the message server, and the message consumer.

The producer's perspective

Under the covers, the TopicPublisher.publish() or QueueSender.send()
methods are synchronous. These methods are responsible for sending the message
and blocking until an acknowledgment is received from the message server. Once
an acknowledgment has been received, the thread of execution resumes and the
method returns; processing continues as normal. The underlying acknowledgment

is not visible to the client programming model. If a failure condition occurs during this operation, an exception is thrown and the message is considered undelivered.

The server's perspective

The acknowledgment sent to the producer (sender) from the server means that the server has received the message and has accepted responsibility for delivering it. From the JMS server's perspective, the acknowledgment sent to the producer is not tied directly to the delivery of the message. They are logically two separate steps.* For persistent messages, the server writes the message out to disk (the *store* part of store-and-forward), then acknowledges to the producer that the message was received (see Figure 6-1). For nonpersistent messages, this means the server may acknowledge the sender as soon as it has received the message and has the message in memory. If there are no subscribers for the message's topic, the message may be discarded depending on the vendor.

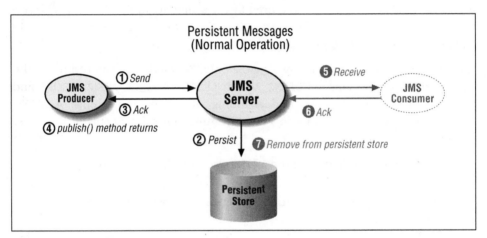

Figure 6-1. Send and receive are separate operations

In a publish-and-subscribe model, the message server delivers a copy of a message to each of the subscribers. For durable subscribers, the message server does not consider a message fully delivered until it receives an acknowledgment from all of the message's intended recipients. It knows on a per-consumer basis which clients have received each message and which have not.

Once the message server has delivered the message to all of its known subscribers and has received acknowledgments from each of them, the message is removed from its persistent store (see Figure 6-2).

---

* In reality, these two operations may likely happen in parallel, but that depends on the vendor.

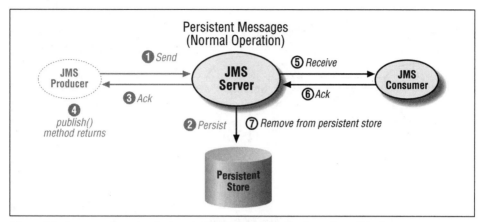

Figure 6-2. A message is removed when the last known subscriber has acknowledged

If the subscriptions are durable and the subscribers are not currently connected, then the message will be held by the message server until either the subscriber becomes available, or the message expires. This is true even for nonpersistent messages. If a nonpersistent message is intended for a disconnected durable subscriber, the message server saves the message to disk as though it were a persistent message. In this case, the difference between persistent and nonpersistent messages is subtle, but very important. For nonpersistent messages, there may be a window of time after the message server has acknowledged the message to the sender and before it has had a chance to write the message out to disk on behalf of the disconnected durable subscribers. If the JMS provider fails during this window of time the message may be lost (see Figure 6-3).*

With persistent messages, a provider may fail and recover gracefully, as illustrated in Figure 6-4 and Figure 6-5. Since the messages are held in persistent storage, they are not lost, and will be delivered to consumers when the provider starts up again. If the messages are sent using a p2p queue, they are guaranteed to be delivered. If the messages were sent via publish-and-subscribe, they are only guaranteed to be delivered if the consumers' subscriptions are durable. The delivery behavior for nondurable subscribers may vary from vendor to vendor.

The consumer's perspective

There are also rules governing acknowledgments and failure conditions from the consumer's perspective. If the session is in AUTO_ACKNOWLEDGE mode, the JMS provider's client runtime must automatically send an acknowledgment to the server

---

* In practice the JMS provider may not allow this condition to happen. However, the JMS specification does infer that this failure condition can occur.

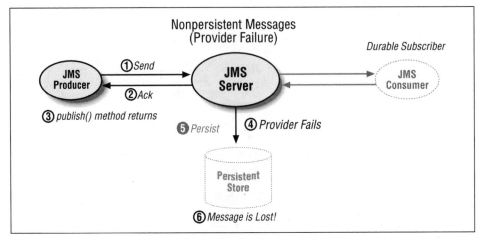

Figure 6-3. Nonpersistent messages with durable subscribers may be lost

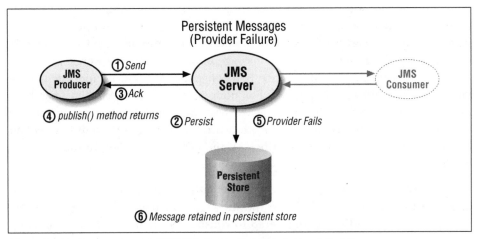

Figure 6-4. Persistent messages will NOT be lost in the event of a provider failure

as each consumer gets the message. If the server doesn't receive this acknowledgment, it considers the message undelivered and may attempt redelivery.

Message redelivery

The message may be lost if the provider fails while delivering a message to a consumer with a nondurable subscription. If a durable subscriber receives a message, and a failure occurs before the acknowledgment is returned to the provider (see Figure 6-6), then the JMS provider considers the message undelivered and will attempt to redeliver it (see Figure 6-7). In this case the once-and-only-once requirement is in doubt. The consumer may receive the message again, because when delivery is guaranteed, it's better to risk delivering a message twice than to

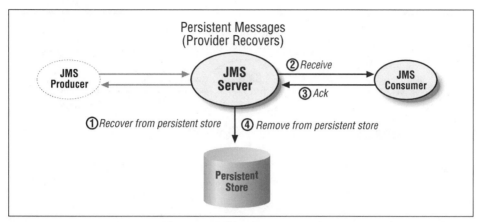

Figure 6-5. Persistent messages are delivered upon recovery of the provider

risk losing the message entirely. A redelivered message will have the JMSRedelivered flag set. A client application can check this flag by calling the getJMSRedelivered() method on the Message object. Only the most recent message received is subject to this ambiguity.

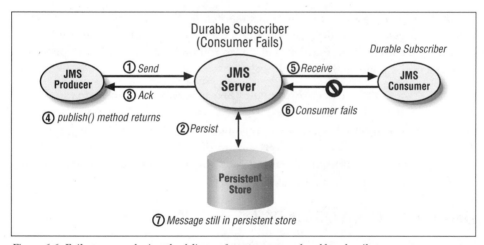

Figure 6-6. Failure occurs during the delivery of a message to a durable subscriber

To guard against duplicate messages while in AUTO_ACKNOWLEDGE mode, an application must check whether a redelivered message was already processed. One common technique for checking is to use a database table that is keyed on the JMSMessageID header. A JMSMessageID is unique for all messages and is intended for historical monitoring of messages in a repository. The JMSMessageID is therefore guaranteed to retain its uniqueness across provider

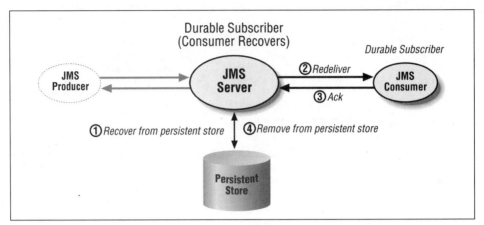

Figure 6-7. Durable subscriber recovers

failures. An alternate approach would be to use the CLIENT_ACKNOWLEDGE mode, or to use a transacted message, which we will discuss in detail shortly.

Point-to-point queues

For point-to-point queues, messages are marked by the producer as either persistent or nonpersistent. If they are persistent, they are written to disk and subject to the same acknowledgment rules, failure conditions, and recovery as persistent messages in the publish-and-subscribe model.

From the receiver's perspective the rules are somewhat simpler, since only one consumer can receive a particular instance of a message. A message stays in a queue until it is either delivered to a consumer or it expires. This is analogous to a durable subscriber in that a receiver can be disconnected while the message is being produced without losing the message. If the messages are nonpersistent they are not guaranteed to survive a provider failure.

DUPS_OK_ACKNOWLEDGE

Specifying the DUPS_OK_ACKNOWLEDGE mode on a session instructs the JMS provider that it is OK to send a message more than once to the same destination. This is different from the once-and-only-once or the at-most-once delivery semantics of AUTO_ACKNOWLEDGE. The DUPS_OK_ACKNOWLEDGE delivery mode is based on the assumption that the processing necessary to ensure once-and-only-once delivery incurs extra overhead and hinders performance and throughput of messages at the provider level. An application that is tolerant of receiving duplicate messages can use the DUPS_OK_ACKNOWLEDGE mode to avoid incurring this overhead.

In practice, the performance improvement that you gain from DUPS_OK_
ACKNOWLEDGE may be insignificant or even nonexistent, depending on the JMS
vendor. It is even conceivable that a JMS provider could perform better in AUTO_
ACKNOWLDEGE mode because it would receive its acknowledgments sooner rather
than later. This could allow it to clean up resources more quickly, or reduce the
size of persistent storage and in-memory queues. At first glance it seems reasonable that fewer acknowledgments result in less network traffic. However, the network may not be the bottleneck under heavy load conditions with large numbers
of clients. In summary, the benefits of DUPS_OK_ACKNOWLEDGE are something you
may want to measure before designing your application around it.

CLIENT_ACKNOWLEDGE

With AUTO_ACKNOWLEDGE mode, the acknowledgment is always the last thing to
happen implicitly after the onMessage() handler returns. The client receiving the
messages can get finer-grained control over the delivery of guaranteed messages by
specifying the CLIENT_ACKNOWLEDGE mode on the consuming session.

The use of CLIENT_ACKNOWLEDGE allows the application to control when the
acknowledgment is sent. For example, an application can acknowledge a message—thereby relieving the JMS provider of its duty—and perform further processing of the data represented by the message. The key to this is the acknowledge()
method on the Message object, as shown in the following example:

```
public void onMessage(javax.jms.Message message){
    int count = 1000;
    try {
    // Perform some business logic with the message
        ...
        message.acknowledge();
        // Perform more business logic with the message
        ...
    } catch (javax.jms.JMSException jmse){
        // Catch the exception thrown and undo the results
        // of partial processing
        ...
    }
}
```

The acknowledge() method informs the JMS provider that the message has been
successfully received by the consumer. This method throws an exception to the client if a provider failure occurs during the acknowledgment process. The provider
failure results in the message being retained by the JMS server for redelivery.
Therefore, the exception handling code should undo the results of any partially

processed business logic in preparation for receiving the message again, or it should log the message as processed so that the redelivered message can be ignored. The acknowlege() method should only be used with the CLIENT_ ACKNOWLEDGE mode; if used with the AUTO_ACKNOWLEDGE or DUPS_OK_ ACKNOWLEDGE mode, the call is ignored by the JMS provider.

Grouping multiple messages

The CLIENT_ACKNOWLEDGE mode also gives you the ability to batch together multiple message receipts and consume them in an all-or-nothing fashion. A consuming client may receive several messages in a sequence and treat them as a group. CLIENT_ACKNOWLEDGE does not provide the capability to consume messages selectively. A single acknowledgment for the last message in the group implicitly acknowledges all previously unacknowledged messages for the current session. This means that if the client application fails before the last message is acknowledged, it may recover when it comes back up. All of the unacknowledged messages will be resent with the JMSRedelivered flag set on each of the unacknowledged messages. A JMS client may also call the recover() method on a Session object, to force the redelivery of all previously unacknowledged messages, even if there hasn't been a failure.

JMS also provides a transaction model for grouping multiple sends and receives. We cover this in detail later in the "Transacted Messages" section of this chapter.

Message Groups and Acknowledgment

When multiple messages need to be dealt with as a group, the application needs to be able to store or cache interim messages until the entire group has been delivered. This requirement typically means that the asynchronous invocation of the onMessage() handler would result in business logic getting executed, and data would be placed temporarily in a database table in preparation for processing the group of messages as a whole. When the last message of the group arrives, the application can then go to the database to retrieve the data from the previous messages to establish any context it may need.

Handling Redelivery of Messages in an Application

JMS provides strict rules that govern when the redelivered flag is set. In AUTO_ ACKNOWLEDGE mode, only the most recently consumed message is subject to ambiguous redelivery. In other modes, multiple messages may have the redelivered flag set. It is up to the application designer to isolate the conditions under which ambiguity can occur, and to account for it in the application.

Message Groups in QRetailer

A message that has been redelivered should be reconciled against any application state to resolve ambiguities related to the reason for redelivery. To see this in action, run the QWholesaler and QRetailer applications in separate command windows using the following command-line options:

```
java chap6.B2B.QWholesaler localhost username password
java chap6.B2B.QRetailer localhost username password
```

In the QWholesaler application, enter the following two lines at the prompt (Item description, Old Price, New Price):

```
Surfboards, 999.99, 499.99
Wetsuits, 299.99, 149.99
```

The QRetailer application does not respond with a "Buy Order" until you hit the Enter key on the second line-item, because QRetailer knows that it can't buy 1000 surfboards without also buying 1000 wetsuits to go with them. Here is the code for the autoBuy() method, which contains this logic:

```
private void autoBuy (javax.jms.Message message){
        int count = 1000;
        try {
            StreamMessage strmMsg = (StreamMessage)message;
            String dealDesc = strmMsg.readString();
            String itemDesc = strmMsg.readString();
            float oldPrice = strmMsg.readFloat();
            float newPrice = strmMsg.readFloat();
            System.out.println( "Received Hot Buy: "+dealDesc );

            // "saveDesc" is our "saved" data
            if ( saveDesc == null )
            {
                if (message.getJMSRedelivered())
                    processCompensatingTransaction();
                processInterimMessages( itemDesc );
                return;
            }

            // If price reduction is greater than 10 percent, buy
            if ((newPrice == 0 || oldPrice / newPrice > 1.1)){
                TextMessage textMsg = tsession.createTextMessage();
                textMsg.setText(count + " " + saveDesc + ", "
                    + count + " " + itemDesc );

                textMsg.setJMSCorrelationID("DurableRetailer");

                Queue buyQueue = (Queue)message.getJMSReplyTo();

                System.out.println ("\nBuying " + count + " "
```

```
                            + saveDesc + " " + count + " " + itemDesc);

                    qsender = qsession.createSender(buyQueue);
                    qsender.send( textMsg,
                                    javax.jms.DeliveryMode.PERSISTENT,
                                    javax.jms.Message.DEFAULT_PRIORITY,
                                    1800000);
                    // Acknowledge the original message
                    try {
                        System.out.println("\nAcknowledging messages");
                        message.acknowledge();
                        System.out.println("\nMessage acknowledged");
                        saveDesc = null;
                    } catch (javax.jms.JMSException jmse){
                        System.out.println("\nAcknowledgment failed." +
                        "\nProcessing compensating transaction for "+
                        "interim messages");

                        processCompensatingTransaction();
                    }
                } else {
                    System.out.println ("\nBad Deal.  Not buying");
                }
            } catch (javax.jms.JMSException jmse){
                jmse.printStackTrace();
            }
        }
```

The first message (surfboards) is processed by the call to a very simple helper
method, processInterimMessages(), that exists only to simulate the processing of the initial message:

```
    private void autoBuy (javax.jms.Message message){
        int count = 1000;
        try {
            ...
            if ( saveDesc == null){
                if (message.getJMSRedelivered())
                    processCompensatingTransaction();
                processInterimMessages( itemDesc );
                return;
            }
            ...
        }
    }
    private String saveDesc = null;
    private void processInterimMessages(String itemDesc)
    {
        saveDesc = itemDesc;
    }
```

`processInterimMessages()` saves the item description, which will be used later when the second message arrives. In a real application, you can envision that the call to `processInterimMessages()` would perform some real work, executing some business logic and placing data in a database table in preparation for the next message. We will get to the redelivered case shortly.

The next important piece to examine is the placement of the call to the `acknowledge()` method. It is called once, after both messages have been received:

```
private void autoBuy (javax.jms.Message message){
    int count = 1000;
    try {
        ...
        try {
            System.out.println("\nAcknowledging messages");
            message.acknowledge();
            System.out.println("\nMessage acknowledged");
            saveDesc = null;
        } catch (javax.jms.JMSException jmse){
        ...
    }
```

Calling the `acknowledge()` method on a message acknowledges the current message and all previously unacknowledged messages. Because the `autoBuy()` logic does not respond with a buy order until it sees the second message, it also does not explicitly acknowledge the receipt of the message until it knows it can process both at the same time. This logic avoids processing the first message if the second message fails to be delivered. If the messages were to be separately acknowledged, the client could fail after the first message was acknowledged, but before the second message was fully processed. If this occurred, the first message would be considered delivered by the JMS provider, yet not fully processed by the client. It would be effectively lost. Delaying acknowledgment provides a way to write the application so that it behaves correctly when failures occur. If you still have your B2B application up and running, try typing the request for surfboards in the command window for the QWholesaler application:

```
Surfboards, 999.99, 499.99
```

Notice that some output appears in the QRetailer window to indicate that the message was received. Kill the QRetailer application by hitting Ctrl-C in its command window. Next, type in the second line item in the QWholesaler application:

```
Wetsuits, 299.99, 149.99
```

Now restart the QRetailer application. You should see output in the QRetailer window indicating that both the Surfboard message and the Wetsuits message have been received. This new instance of the QRetailer receives both messages because the earlier instance of QRetailer never sent an acknowledgment for the first message. Therefore, when we restarted the QRetailer, the JMS provider redelivered the Surfboard message, and then sent the Wetsuits message. A single acknowledgment is now sent, acknowledging both messages. The JMS provider has now fullfilled its part of the contract with the receiving application, and can remove the messages from its persistent store.

Compensating transactions

In the code that deals with the redelivered flag, we introduced a call to processCompensatingTransaction():

```
private void autoBuy (javax.jms.Message message){
    int count = 1000;
    try {
            ...
            if ( saveDesc == null )
            {
                if ( message.getJMSRedelivered() )
                    processCompensatingTransaction();
                processInterimMessages( itemDesc );
                return;
            }
            ...
    }
}
```

This code is executed when the client restarts and receives redelivered messages, as was the case in the client failure exercise we just went through. The first message of the sequence will have the redelivered flag set on the message, causing the processCompensatingTransactions() method to be invoked:

```
private void processCompensatingTransaction()
    {
        saveDesc = null;  // null out "saved" work
    }
```

In our case, this method really doesn't do anything. In a real application, you can envision that the initial call to processInterimMessages() would execute some business logic , and place data in a database table in preparation for the next message. Upon failure of the client, restart, and subsequent redelivery of the first message, processCompensatingTransaction() would clean up or reinitialize any application specific data that may have been left in an unclean state.

Another place we have used this technique is in the exception handler for the call to the acknowledge() method. This situation is harder to deal with programmatically. The exception is caught for the failed acknowledgment, but the "Buy Order" message has already been sent. Historically, some messaging solutions have dealt with this problem by requiring the initiation of a *compensating transaction* at the application level, as we have done in this example. In our case, a compensating transaction would involve sending another message back to the QWholesaler to cancel the "Buy Order" message. However, if the exception was thrown because of a critical provider failure, then sending another message to cancel an order might not be possible for the time being.

We could have acknowledged the messages first, then sent the buy order. This would avoid the problem, but then the send could fail for the buy order, or the application could fail before sending it. This would leave us back in a situation where the messages have been acknowledged by the consumer but not really dealt with by the application.

This is a good argument for message autonomy. Each message should be self-contained. When multiple messages need to depend on each other, the application should be written like a finite state machine where the results of the processing of one message are saved so that the application's state can be re-established at a later time. The next message can then independently re-establish all of the context it needs to do its work. This is a perfectly viable and valid application design and should be considered in lieu of, or in conjunction with, other approaches.

Transacted Messages

Our discussion of message acknowledgment shows that producers and consumers have different perspectives on the messages they exchange. The producer has a contract with the message server that ensures the message will be delivered as far as the server. The server has a contract with the consumer that ensures the message will be delivered to it. The two operations are separate, which is a key benefit of asynchronous messaging. It is the role of the JMS provider to ensure that messages get to where they are supposed to go. Having all producers and all consumers participate in one global transaction would defeat the purpose of using a loosely coupled asynchronous messaging environment.

JMS transactions follow the convention of separating the send operations from the receive operations. Figure 6-8 shows a transactional send, in which a group of messages are guaranteed to get to the message server, or none of them will. From the sender's perspective, the messages are cached by the JMS provider until a commit() is issued. If a failure occurs, or a rollback() is issued, the messages are discarded. Messages delivered to the message server in a transaction are not forwarded to the consumers until the producer commits the transaction.

The JMS provider will not start delivery of the messages to its consumers until the producer has issued a commit() on the session. The scope of a JMS transaction can include any number of messages.

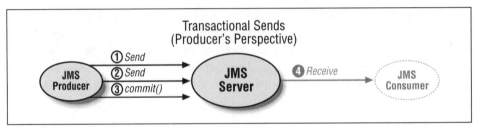

Figure 6-8. Transactional messages are sent in an all-or-nothing fashion

It should be no surprise that JMS also supports transactional receives, in which a group of transacted messages are received by the consumer on an all-or-nothing basis (see Figure 6-9). From the transacted receiver's perspective, the messages are delivered to it as expeditiously as possible, yet they are held by the JMS provider until the receiver issues a `commit()` on the session object. If a failure occurs or a `rollback()` is issued, then the provider will attempt to redeliver the messages, in which case the messages will have the redelivered flag set.

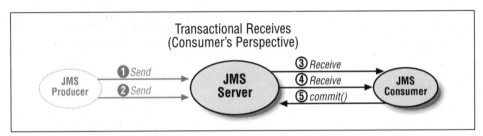

Figure 6-9. Transactional messages are received by a consumer in an all-or-nothing fashion

Transacted producers and consumers can exchange messages with non-transacted consumers and producers. The scope of the transaction is limited to the producer's or consumer's session with the message server. Transacted producers and transacted consumers can, however, be grouped together in a single transaction, provided that they are created from the same session object, as shown in Figure 6-10. This allows a JMS client to produce and consume messages as a single unit of work. If the transaction is rolled back, the messages produced within the transaction will not be delivered by the JMS provider. The messages consumed within the same transaction will not be acknowledged and will be redelivered.

Grouping together a receive followed by a send within a single transaction is useful. However, you should never group together a send followed by a receive within a single transaction. If you are intending to do this in a request-reply fashion, the result will be deadlock. The request message will never get to the replier until the transaction is commited. The requestor will wait indefinitely for a reply that will never arrive.

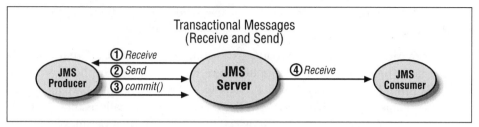

Figure 6-10. Sends and receives may be grouped together in one transactional session

Creating and Using a JMS Transaction

Now that you understand the concepts of transactional sends and receives, we can take a look at some code. The first step in creating a transactional message is the initialization of the `Session` object:

```
// pub/sub connection creates a transacted TopicSession
javax.jms.TopicSession session =
        connect.createTopicSession(true,Session.AUTO_ACKNOWLEDGE);
// p2p connection creates a transacted QueueSession
javax.jms.QueueSession =
        connect.createQueueSession(true,Session.AUTO_ACKNOWLEDGE);
        ...
}
```

The first parameter of a `createTopicSession()` or `createQueueSession()` method is a `boolean` indicating whether this is a transacted session. That is all we need to create a transactional session. There is no explicit `begin()` method. When a session is transacted, all messages sent or received using that session are automatically grouped in a transaction. The transaction remains open until either a `session.rollback()` or a `session.commit()` happens, at which point a new transaction is started.[*] An additional `Session` method, `isTransacted()`, returns `true` or `false` indicating whether or not the current session is transactional.

The Transacted Retailer Example

To demonstrate how to use transactions, we will develop a modified version of our publish-and-subscribe `Wholesaler` and `Retailer` from Chapter 4, *Publish-and-Subscribe Messaging*. The use of JMS transactions for sending or receiving just one message is only mildly interesting. You get one message, then decide whether it should be committed or rolled back. In this new example we will show:

- A new technique for grouping multiple messages together

- Multiple receives and sends grouped in one transaction

---

[*] This is called "transaction chaining," which means that the end of one transaction automatically starts another.

- Handling of message redelivery, and how to distinguish between redelivery due to failure and redelivery due to a transaction rollback

In this scenario, the wholesaler broadcasts a group of "special deals" that can only be purchased together. The separate items are each contained in their own messages, yet are related to each other. Today's special deals are surfboards and wetsuits. The retailer has logic that looks at the messages individually as they arrive. If the price is acceptable, the orders are placed for each item on a per-message basis. When the retailer sees that all of the messages in the group have an acceptable price discount, the orders are placed. If any one of the prices in the group is unacceptable, all the orders are cancelled. All this takes place without the knowledge of the wholesaler. The wholesaler never sees a thing unless the retailer decides that it is OK to place all of the orders. To accomplish this, the retailer uses a JMS transaction either to place all of the orders (commit) or to cancel them (rollback).

Before getting into the details of the example, run the version of the wholesaler and retailer applications in this chapter. Start the `Wholesaler` and `Retailer` applications in separate command windows:

```
java chap6.Wholesaler localhost username password
java chap6.Retailer localhost username password
```

First, we will study the case in which all the prices are acceptable. We start with acceptable price reductions for both items. When prompted by the `Wholesaler` application, enter:

```
Surfboards, 999.99, 499.99
Wetsuits, 299.99, 149.99
```

When you enter these new prices, the `Retailer` should indicate that it is purchasing 1000 surfboards. You shouldn't see anything in the `Wholesaler` window to indicate that it received the order, because the `Retailer` is using a transacted session to send the "Buy Order" messages. The Wholesaler won't receive the message until the `Retailer` commits the session. Now go back to the `Wholesaler` and type "end".

While the `Retailer` is using transactions in this example, the `Wholesaler` is not. When you type in the word "end" on the command line, `Wholesaler` sends a message to `Retailer` indicating that it is finished with its group of messages, as shown in this excerpt from `Wholesaler`'s command-line processing loop:

```
...
while ( true ){
    String dealDesc = stdin.readLine();
    if ( dealDesc != null && dealDesc.length() > 0 ){
        if ( dealDesc.substring(0,3).equalsIgnoreCase("END") ){
            wholesaler.sendSequenceMarker( "END_SEQUENCE" );
        } else {
...
```

`Wholesaler.sendSequenceMarker()` simply creates a message, sets a property on it, and publishes it:

```
private void sendSequenceMarker(String sequenceMarker){
    try {
        javax.jms.StreamMessage message = session.createStreamMessage();
        message.setStringProperty("SEQUENCE_MARKER",sequenceMarker);

        publisher.publish(
            message,
            javax.jms.DeliveryMode.PERSISTENT,
            javax.jms.Message.DEFAULT_PRIORITY,
            1800000);
    } catch ( javax.jms.JMSException jmse ){
        jmse.printStackTrace();
    }
}
```

This message has no body. We set the user-defined property `"SEQUENCE_MARKER"`, which the receiving application uses to know when the group of "Hot Deals" messages is completed. In this example, we are using a message as an event, instead of transporting meaningful business data.

The `Retailer` now indicates in its output window that it has received the second "Hot Buy" message and is placing an order. You will now see the messages for both the `Surfboards` and the `Wetsuits` in the `Wholesaler` window. The messages appear now because the order was placed using a transactional session. The `Retailer` published each message separately as it saw the "Hot Deals" coming in. However, since these messages were part of a transaction, the messages were held by the JMS provider, and not delivered. When `Retailer` saw the `"SEQUENCE_MARKER"` message, it performed a `commit()` on the transaction, causing the JMS provider to deliver both messages to `Wholesaler`.

The basic logic that makes this work is in the `autoBuy()` method of `Retailer`:

```
private void autoBuy (javax.jms.Message message){
    ...

    if ( strmMsg.propertyExists("SEQUENCE_MARKER") ){
        String sequence = strmMsg.getStringProperty( "SEQUENCE_MARKER" );
        if ( sequence.equalsIgnoreCase("END_SEQUENCE") ){
            ...
            session.commit();
        }
        return;
    }
    ...
```

If you peeked ahead at the full example, note that the logic is more complex than this. The rest of the logic handles the rollback and redelivered conditions.

Now let's look at the other case, in which one of the items doesn't have an acceptable price. Enter the following in the `Wholesaler` command window:

```
Surfboards, 999.99, 499.99
Wetsuits, 299.99, 299.99
end
```

This time, the new price for the wetsuits is the same as the old price—hence a "bad deal." You should see a "bad deal" message in the `Retailer` command window, with a number of indicators that messages are being redelivered. Let's review the part of `Retailer`'s `autoBuy()` that makes all this happen. It's a little complex, but we will walk through it step by step:

```
private void autoBuy (javax.jms.Message message){
int count = 1000;
try {
    boolean redelivered = message.getJMSRedelivered();
    StreamMessage strmMsg = (StreamMessage)message;
    if ( redelivered ){
        System.out.println("\nMessage redelivered, inRollback: "
            + inRollback + " rollbackOnly: " + rollbackOnly );
        strmMsg.reset();
    }

    if ( strmMsg.propertyExists("SEQUENCE_MARKER") ){
        String sequence = strmMsg.getStringProperty( "SEQUENCE_MARKER" );
        if ( sequence.equalsIgnoreCase("END_SEQUENCE") )
        {
            if ( redelivered && inRollback ){  // At the end, start fresh
                inRollback = false;
                rollbackOnly = false;
                session.commit();
            }
            else if ( rollbackOnly ){
                inRollback = true;
                session.rollback();
            }
            else
                session.commit();
        }
        return;
    }
    if ( rollbackOnly )
        return; // Ignore all other messages while in rollback mode

    ...
```

```
    // If price reduction is greater than 10 percent, buy
    if (newPrice == 0 || oldPrice / newPrice > 1.1){
        System.out.println ("\nBuying " + count + " " + itemDesc);
        ...
        publisher.publish(
            buyTopic,
            textMsg,
            javax.jms.DeliveryMode.PERSISTENT,
            javax.jms.Message.DEFAULT_PRIORITY,
            1800000);
    } else {
        System.out.println ("\nBad Deal.  Not buying");
        rollbackOnly = true;
    }
```

First we will examine what makes the rollback happen:

```
    // If price reduction is greater than 10 percent, buy
    if (newPrice == 0 || oldPrice / newPrice > 1.1){
    ...
    } else {
        System.out.println ("\nBad Deal.  Not buying");
        rollbackOnly = true;
    }
```

The `rollbackOnly` variable is a `boolean` used by the application to signal that a rollback needs to occur. If you are familiar with the EJB transaction model, this is similar to calling the `setRollbackOnly()` method on an EJB entity bean. The messages in the transaction are either all commited, or they are all rolled back. Setting the rollback-only flag indicates a deferred rollback. The processing of any message in the group can set the `rollbackOnly` flag. Since the "Buy Order" messages are all part of the same transaction, they will be retained by the JMS provider and will go no further. When the `"END_SEQUENCE"` message arrives, the `rollbackOnly` flag is examined:

```
        if ( sequence.equalsIgnoreCase("END_SEQUENCE") )
        {
            if ( redelivered && inRollback ){  // at the end, start fresh
                inRollback = false;
                rollbackOnly = false;
                session.commit();
            }
            else if ( rollbackOnly ){
                inRollback = true;
                session.rollback();
            }
            else
                session.commit();
        }
        return;
```

The logic is fairly simple: if the message is NOT redelivered AND it is NOT already in a rollback, AND the `rollbackOnly` flag is `true`, THEN roll back the transaction. Otherwise commit the transaction.

The `inRollback` flag is needed because of the behavior of the `Session.rollback()` method. It causes all of the messages to be redelivered. In our case, that includes the `"SEQUENCE_MARKER"` message, which will always be the last message that is redelivered as a result of the rollback.[*] Without this flag, it would be impossible to tell whether the messages are being redelivered as a result of the transaction rollback, or for some other reason.

Now you can see the reason for using the delayed rollback. This allows us to isolate the `commit()`, `rollback()`, and message redelivery logic in the handling of the `"SEQUENCE_MARKER"` message. Dealing with the rollback individually as each message arrives can quickly become unwieldy.

Finally, let's try this redelivery logic out by simulating a failure. In the `Wholesaler` window, type:

```
Surfboards, 999.99, 499.99
Wetsuits, 299.99, 149.99
```

Before you type `end`, simulate an abnormal shut down of the `Retailer` application by typing Ctrl-C in the `Retailer` command window. Then type "end" in the `Wholesaler` window.

Now restart the `Retailer` application. When the retailer app comes back up, it shows that it is receiving the surfboard and wetsuit messages as redelivered messages and is placing the order again. The JMS provider knew that the `Retailer` had failed in the middle of a transaction. When the `Retailer` came back up and reconnected, the JMS provider redelivered the messages to it. The `Retailer` logic knew that the message was being redelivered as a result of a failure, as shown in the following section of `autoBuy()`. The logic is fairly simple. If we are at the end marker:

```
if ( sequence.equalsIgnoreCase("END_SEQUENCE") )
{
```

AND we are both redelivered AND in a rollback (we aren't in a rollback):

```
if ( redelivered && inRollback ){  // At the end, start fresh
    inRollback = false;
    rollbackOnly = false;
    session.commit();
}
```

---

[*] This illustrates the importance of the JMS provider's role in maintaining proper delivery order, especially in the redelivery case.

Else if we are in `rollbackOnly` mode (we aren't, but we could be and it would still work):

```
else if ( rollbackOnly ){
    inRollback = true;
    session.rollback();
}
```

Else, commit (that's what just happened):

```
else
    session.commit();
    }
    return;
```

Otherwise, just continue on and process the message.

Point-to-point queues have the same transactional capabilities as publish-and-subscribe, with one caveat: when a `rollback()` occurs on a `QueueSession`, the messages are placed back on the queue. Because a queue may have multiple recipients, the messages could now go to another consuming client. This may result in messages being processed out of order, since the other client could have processed newer messages while the older messages were being rolled back. This is an area where behavior may vary, depending on how your vendor interprets the standard.

Finally, you may have noticed that we used `Wholesaler` and `Retailer` for this example instead of their "Q" counterparts. This is because a publish-and-subscribe session and point-to-point session cannot jointly particpate in a JMS transaction. JMS transactions cannot span multiple sessions without the use of a JTA-compliant transaction manager (see the next section, "Distributed Transactions"). We wanted to show the use of JMS as first-class middleware in its own right, without using a supporting application server just to provide a shared transaction between a p2p and a pub/sub session. The inability of p2p and pub/sub sessions to share a transaction is a weakness in JMS that may be addressed in a future version of the specification.

Distributed Transactions

Distributed systems sometimes use a *two-phase commit* (2PC) process that allows multiple distributed resources to participate in one transaction. This typically involves an underlying transaction manager that takes care of coordinating the prepare, commit, or rollback of each resource participating in the transaction. In most cases, the resources involved in the transaction are databases, but they can be other things, like JMS providers.

Transactions can be either local transactions or global transactions. Local transactions involve work performed on a single resource: one database or JMS provider. Global transactions involve work performed across several different resources, i.e., some combination of databases and JMS providers. JMS provides transaction facilities for both local and global transactions. The transacted sessions discussed previously are local transactions in JMS; they involve a single JMS provider.

The 2PC protocol is designed to facilitate global transactions, transactions that span multiple resources. As an example, an enterprise application may need to process (consume and produce) messages as well as make changes to a database. In some cases, the processing of messages and database updates needs to be treated as a single unit of work, so that a failure to update the database or consume a message will cause the entire unit of work to fail. This is the basic premise behind a transaction: all the tasks must complete or fail together. To create a unit of work that spans different resources, the resources must be able to cooperate with a transaction manager in a 2PC.

The 2PC protocol is used by a transaction manager to coordinate the interactions of resources in a global transaction. A resource can only participate in a global transaction if it supports the 2PC protocol, which is usually implemented using the XA interface developed by The Open Group. In the Java enterprise technologies, the XA interface is implemented by the Java Transaction API and XA interfaces (`javax.transaction` and `javax.transaction.xa`). Any resource that implements these interfaces can be enrolled in a global transaction by a transaction manager that supports these interfaces.

JMS providers that implement the JTA XA APIs can therefore participate as a resource in two-phase commit. The JMS specification provides XA versions of the following JMS objects: `XAConnectionFactory`, `XAQueueConnection`, `XAQueue-ConnectionFactory`, `XAQueueSession`, `XASession`, `XATopicConnection`, `XATopicConnectionFactory`, and `XATopicSession`.

Each of these objects works like its corresponding non-XA–compliant object. The `XATopicSession`, for example, provides the same methods as the `TopicSession`. An application server's transaction manager uses these XA interfaces directly, but a JMS client only sees the nontransactional versions. The following code shows a JMS client that uses JDBC and JMS together in one transaction managed by an external transaction manager. JNDI is used to obtain all the resources including the JTA `TransactionManager`, the JDBC `XADataSource`, and the JMS `XATopicConnectionFactory`:

```
InitialContext jndiContext = new InitialContext(env);

// Obtain the JTA TransactionManager a JNDI namespace
TransactionManager txMngr =jndiContext.lookup("../../tx/txmngr");
```

```
// Start the Global Transaction
txMngr.begin();

// Get the transaction object that represents the new global transaction
Transaction transaction = txMnger.getTransaction();

// Obtain the JDBC DataSource from a JNDI namespace
XADataSource dataSrc = jndiContext.lookup("../../jdbc/data");

// Obtain an XA-compliant Connection
XAConnection jdbcCon = dataSrc.getConnection();

// Obtain the XAResource from the connection
XAResource jdbcXA = jdbcCon.getXAResource();

/*
 * Enlist the XAResource in the transaction. This adds the JDBC
 * resource to the global transaction.
 */
transaction.enlist(jdbcXA);

//... do some JDBC work

// Obtain an XA-compliant TopicConnectionFactory from a JNDI namespace
XATopicConnectionFactory factory = jndiContext.lookup("../.../jms/factory");

// Obtain an XA-compliant TopicConnection
XATopicConnection jmsCon = factory.createXATopicConnection();

// Obtain an XA-compliant Session
XATopicSession session = jmsCon.createXATopicSession();

// Obtain the XAResource from the session
XAResource jmsXA = session.getXAResource();

/*
 * Enlist the XAResource in the transaction. This adds the JMS
 * resource to the global transaction.
 */
transaction.enlist(jmsXA);

// ... do some JMS work

/*
 * Committing the global transaction will allow both the JDBC
 * work (all updates and inserts) as well as the JMS work
 * (all the message sends and receives) to be commited as a single
 * unit of work. They all succeed or fail together.
 */
transaction.commit();
```

All XA-compliant resources (JDBC or JMS) provide an XAResource object that is an interface to the underlying resource (in JMS, the JMS provider). The XAResource object is used by the TransactionManager to coordinate the 2PC commit. In the previous example, the application associates the XAResource for the JDBC driver and the JMS provider with the current transaction so that all the work performed using those resources is bound together in one transaction. When the transaction is committed, all the work performed by the JDBC connection and JMS session is committed. If the transaction had been rolled back, all the work performed by the JDBC connection and JMS session would have been rolled back. All the work performed across these two resources either succeeds together or fails together.

An application server, such as an EJB server, may itself be a JMS client. In this case, whether the interfaces are exposed depends on how the JMS server and the application server are integrated. If the integration is hidden within the implementation, as is the case with EJB, then the container may use the XA-compliant version of these objects directly. Since the XA interfaces in JMS are not intended for application developers—they are intended to be implemented by vendors—we will not go into them in detail in this book. The important thing to understand is that JMS providers that implement the XA interfaces properly can be used in a 2PC transaction. If your application server (i.e., EJB server) supports 2PC, then these kinds of JMS providers can be used with other resources in global transactions.

Lost Connections

When the network connection between the client and server is lost, a JMS provider must make every reasonable attempt to re-establish the connection. In the event that the JMS provider cannot automatically reconnect, the provider must notify the client of this condition by throwing an exception when the client invokes a method that would cause network traffic to occur. However, it is reasonable to expect that a JMS client may only be a receiver using the Message-Listener interface, and not a producer that makes any outbound publish() or send() calls. In this case, the client is not invoking JMS methods—it is just listening for messages—so a dropped connection won't be detected.

JMS provides an ExceptionListener interface for trapping a lost connection and notifying the client of this condition. The ExceptionListener is bound to the connection—unlike MessageListeners, which are bound to sessions. The definition of the ExceptionListener is:

```
public interface ExceptionListener{
    void onException(JMSException exception);
}
```

It is the responsibility of the JMS provider to call the onException() method of all registered ExceptionListeners after making reasonable attempts to reestablish the connection automatically. The JMS client can implement the ExceptionListener so that it can be alerted to a lost connection, and possibly attempt to reestablish the connection manually.

How can the JMS provider call an ExceptionListener if the client has been disconnected? Every JMS provider has some amount of functionality that resides in the client application. We have been referring to this as the *client runtime* portion of the JMS provider. It is the responsibility of the client runtime to detect the loss of connection and call the ExceptionListener.

The Wholesaler Becomes an ExceptionListener

To make our Wholesaler into an ExceptionListener, we start by changing the formal declaration of the class to implement the javax.jms.ExceptionListener interface:

```
public class Wholesaler implements
    javax.jms.MessageListener,
    javax.jms.ExceptionListener
{
...
```

Next, we remove the connection setup information from the constructor and isolate it in its own method, establishConnection():

```
public Wholesaler(String broker, String username, String password){
        mBroker = broker;
        mUsername = username;
        mPassword = password;

        establishConnection( broker, username, password );
}
```

establishConnection() sets up the connection, the publisher, and the subscriber. The new addition is the retry logic on the TopicConnectionFactory's createTopicConnection() method, which continually retries the connection every ten seconds until it is established:

```
private void establishConnection(String broker, String username,
                                  String password)
{
    ...
    while (connect == null)
    {
            try {
```

```
            connect =
            factory.createTopicConnection (username, password);
        } catch (javax.jms.JMSException jmse)
        {
        try {
            Thread.sleep(10000);
            } catch (java.lang.InterruptedException ie) { }
            continue;
        }
    }
    System.out.println("\nConnection established");
...
}
```

The establishConnection() method then registers the ExceptionListener with the connection via the setExceptionListener() method:

```
connect.setExceptionListener( (javax.jms.ExceptionListener) this);
```

Last, but not least, is the implementation of the onException() listener method. Its task is to call the establishConnection() method again to re-establish a connection with the JMS provider:

```
public void onException ( javax.jms.JMSException jmse)
{
    // Tell the user that there is a problem
    System.err.println ("\n\nThere is a problem with the connection.");
    System.err.println ("  JMSException: " + jmse.getMessage());

    System.err.println ("Please wait while the application tries to "+
                        "reestablish the connection...");
    connect = null;
    establishConnection(mBroker, mUsername, mPassword);
}
```

When a connection is dropped and reestablished, all of the sessions, queues, publishers, and subscribers need to be reestablished in order for the application to continue normal processing. This is why we isolated all the connection logic in the establishConnection() method, so that it can be used during startup and reused if the connection is lost.

JMS does not define any reason codes for a dropped connection. However, a JMS provider may provide a finer level of granularity by defining reason codes. Depending on the host operating system's network settings, it may take a while for the provider to notice that a connection has been dropped. Some providers implement a ping capability as a configurable setting to detect a network loss.

Dead Message Queues

JMS provides mechanisms for guaranteed delivery of messages between clients, utilizing the mechanisms we have discussed in this chapter. However, there are cases where guaranteed delivery, acknowledgments, and transactional semantics are just not enough. Many conditions may cause a message to be undeliverable. Messages may expire before they reach their intended destination, or messages are viewed by the provider as undeliverable due to some other reason such as a deployment configuration problem. A message need not have an expiration associated with it, which means it would never expire. Forever is a long time. Realistically, it would be more prudent if the JMS provider could notify an application if a message cannot be delivered within a reasonable amount of time.

Although these issues are not specifically addressed by the JMS specification, some messaging vendors have the notion of a "Dead Letter Queue" or "Dead Message Queue" to deal with messages that are deemed undeliverable.

The extent of Dead Message Queue (DMQ) support varies from vendor to vendor. In the simplest case, it is the responsibility of the messaging system to put all undeliverable messages in the DMQ, and it is the responsibility of the application to monitor its contents. In addition, a JMS provider may support administrative events that notify the application when something is placed in the DMQ. The notification may go to the sender, or it may go to a centralized management tool. A specialized JMS client may be written to receive all DMQ notifications.

A DMQ can be treated just like a normal queue in most respects; it can be consumed, or it can be browsed. There is one respect in which a DMQ behaves differently from other queues: the destination of a message, as obtained via `Message.getJMSDestination()`, would be the original destination the message was intended for, not the DMQ. The message may also contain additional properties, such as a vendor-defined reason code indicating why the message was placed in the DMQ.

It's important to know whether the JMS provider you are using supports Dead Message Queues. If it does, and you don't provide the application support to monitor it and peel things from the DMQ in a timely fashion, then the DMQ may fill up over time without your knowledge.

7

*Deployment
Considerations*

An enterprise application's performance, scalability, and reliability should be among the foremost concerns in a real deployment environment. The underlying messaging middleware is critical to that environment.

Performance, Scalability, and Reliability

Every JMS vendor claims to be the fastest in the marketplace. Some claim to be fast *and* scalable to thousands of clients. It is hard to take any one vendor's word for having the fastest and most scalable product. Different application architectures have different demands. The industry has no accepted messaging benchmark. Thus, the proof of any vendor's claims lies in your own testing and measurement.

Performance and scalability are terms commonly used together, but they are not interchangeable. *Performance* refers to the speed at which the JMS provider can process a message through the system from the producer to the consumer. *Scalability* refers to the number of concurrently connected clients that a JMS provider can support. When used together, the terms refer to the effective rate at which a JMS provider can concurrently process a large volume of messages on behalf of a large number of simultaneously connected producers and consumers. The distinction between performance and scalability, as well as the implications of what it means to combine them, is very important, as you will soon see. A simple test using one or two clients will differ drastically from a test using hundreds or thousands of clients. The following section is intended to be used as a guide to help with performance and scalability testing.

Determining Message Throughput Requirements

Before you embark on your performance and scalability testing effort, consider what you are trying to accomplish. Since any particular vendor may do well with one scenario and not so well in others, the makeup of your application is important to define. Here are some key things to consider:

- The potential size of the user community for your application. While this may be hard to project, it is important to try to predict how it will grow over time.

- The average load required by the application. Given a total size of the user community for your application, how many are going to be actively using it at any given time?

- The peak load required by the application. Are there certain times of the day, or certain days in a month, when the number of concurrent users will surge?

- The number of JMS client connections used by the application. In some cases, the number of JMS clients does not correspond to the number of application users. Middleware products, such as EJB servers, share JMS connections across application clients, requiring far fewer JMS client connections than other applications. On the other hand, some applications use multiple JMS connections per client application, requiring more JMS client connections than users. Knowing the ratio of users to JMS clients helps you determine the number of messages being processed per client.

- The amount of data to be processed through the messaging system over a given period of time. This can be measured in messages per second, bytes per second, messages per month, etc.

- The typical size of the messages being processed. Performance data will vary depending on the message size.

- Any atypical message sizes being produced. If 90% of the messages being processed through the system are 100 bytes in size, and the other 10% are 10 megabytes, it would be important to know how well the system can handle either scenario.

- The messaging domain to be used, and how it will be used. Does the entire application use one p2p queue? Are there many queues? Is it pub/sub with 1,000 topics? One-to-many, many-to-one, or many-to-many?

- The message delivery modes to be used. Persistent? Nonpersistent? Durable subscribers? Transacted messages? A mixture? What is the mixture?

Testing the Real-World Scenario

Any vendor can make any software product run faster, provided the company has the right amount of time, proper staffing, commitment, and enough hardware to analyze and test a real-world deployment environment.

The simplest scenario for a vendor to optimize is the fastest performance throughput possible with one or two clients connected. This is also the easiest scenario to test, but is not the kind of testing we recommend; for one thing, it's difficult to imagine a realistic application that only has one or two clients. More complex testing scenarios that better match your system's real-world environment are preferable.

It is important to know ahead of time if the vendor you have chosen will support the requirements of your application when it is deployed. Because JMS is a standard, you may switch JMS vendors at any time. However, you may soon find yourself building vendor-specific extensions and configurations into your application. It's always possible to change vendors, if you're willing to expend some effort. However, if you wait to find out whether or not your application scales, you may no longer be able to afford the time to switch to another vendor.

This is not intended to imply that using JMS is a risky proposition. These same issues apply to any distributed infrastructure, whether third-party or home-grown, whether it is based on a MOM or based on CORBA, COM, EJB, or RMI, and whether it is based on an established vendor or an emerging one. Everything should be sized and tested prior to deployment.

Testing with one client

The most important thing to realize is this:

```
performanceWithOneClient != performanceWithManyClients;
```

Many issues come into play once a message server starts to scale up to a large number of clients. New bottlenecks appear under heavy load that would never have occurred otherwise. Examples include thread contention, overuse of object allocation, garbage collection, and overflow of shared internal buffers and queues.

A vendor may have chosen to optimize message throughput with hundreds or thousands of concurrent clients at the expense of optimizing for throughput with one client. Likewise, a vendor may have optimized for a small number of clients at the expense of scalability with larger client populations.

The best approach is to start with something small and build up the number of clients and the number of messages in increments. For example, run a test with 10 senders and 10 receivers, and 100,000 messages. Next try 100 senders and 100 receivers, and run a test with 1,000,000 messages. Try as many clients as you can, within the limitations of the hardware you have available, and watch for trends.

Send rate versus receive rate

It is extremely important to measure both the send rates and the receive rates of the messages being pumped through the messaging system. If the send rate far exceeds the receive rate, what is happening to the messages? They are being buffered at the JMS provider level. That's OK, right? That is what a messaging product does—it queues things. In some cases that may be acceptable based on the predetermined throughput requirements of your application, and the predictable size and duration of the surges and spikes in the usage of the application. If these factors are not extremely predictable, it is important to measure the long-term effects of unbalanced send and receive rates.

In reality everything has a limit. If the send rate far exceeds the receive rate, the messages are filling up in-memory queues and eventually overflowing the memory limits of the system, or perhaps the in-memory queues are overflowing to disk storage, which also has a limit. The closer the system gets to its hardware limits, the more the JVM and the operating system thrash to try to compensate, further limiting the JMS provider's ability to deliver messages to its consumers.

Determining hardware requirements

The hardware required to perform testing varies from vendor to vendor. You should have the hardware necessary to do a full-scale test, or be prepared to purchase the hardware as soon as possible. If the JMS provider's deployment architecture uses one or more server processes (as in a hub and spoke model), then a powerful server (like a quad-processor) and lightweight clients are appropriate. If the vendor's architecture requires that the persistence and routing functionality be located on the client machine, then many workstations may be required.

If you have limited hardware for testing, do the best you can to run a multi-client load test within the limitations of your hardware. You typically won't see any reasonably indicative results until you have at least 20 JMS clients. You must therefore be able to find a machine or a set of machines that can handle at least that much.

Assuming your client population will be large, truly indicative results start showing up with over 100 JMS clients. Your goal should be to use as many clients as possible within the limits of the testing hardware and to see whether the message throughput gets better or gets worse. A good guideline is to stop adding clients when the average resource utilization on each test machine (both clients and servers) approaches 80 percent CPU or memory use. At 80 percent, you realistically measure the throughput capacity of the JMS provider for a given class of machine and eliminate the possibility of having exceeded the limits of your hardware.

If the CPU or memory utilization does not approach its maximum, and the message throughput does not continue to improve as you add clients, then the bottleneck is probably disk I/O or network throughput. Disk I/O is most likely to be the bottleneck if you are using persistent messaging.

Finding or building a test bed

Building a test bed suitable for simulating a proper deployment environment itself can be a moderately sized effort. Most JMS vendors provide a performance test environment freely downloadable from their web site. In most cases, they provide a test bed sufficient for testing with one client.*

Long duration reliability

Testing your application over a long period of time is very important. After all, it is expected to perform continuously once deployed. Verifying that the middleware behaves reliably is the first step toward ensuring long-term application reliability.

Once you have a multi-client test bed in place, try running it for an extended period of time to ensure that the performance throughput is consistent. Start out by running the test bed while you can be there to monitor the behavior. Any long-term trends are likely to be detected in the first few hours. Things to watch for are drops in performance throughput, increase in memory usage, CPU usage, and disk usage. When you feel comfortable with the results you see, you may progressively start running tests overnight, over the weekend, or over a week.

Memory leaks

The term "memory leak" refers to a condition that can happen when new memory gets allocated and never freed over a period of time, usually through a repeated operation, such as repeatedly pumping messages through a messaging system. Eventually, the system runs out of available memory; as a result, it will perform badly and may eventually crash.

Although Java has built-in memory management through garbage collection, it is an oversimplification to think that garbage collection permanently solves the problem of memory links. Garbage collection works effectively only when the developer follows explicit rules for the scoping of Java objects. A Java object can be garbage collected only if it has gone out of scope and there are no other objects currently referencing it. Even the best code can contain memory leaks, if the developer has mistakenly overlooked an object reference in a collection class that never goes out of scope.

Therefore, you need to monitor for memory leaks during testing. Memory that leaks in small increments may be not be noticable at first, but eventually these leaks could seriously impact performance. To detect them quickly, it helps to use a memory leak detection tool like OptimizeIt! or Jprobe. Even if the JMS provider

---

* As of publication, SonicMQ is the only vendor providing a multiclient test bed.

and other third-party Java products you are using contain obfuscated classes, tools like these still help you prove that your memory requirements are growing (possibly the result of a memory leak), which is a good start.

To Multicast or Not to Multicast

An increasing number of vendors are releasing products based on IP multicasting. To understand the tradeoffs involved in these products, you need a basic understanding of how the TCP/IP protocol family works, and how multicasting fits into the bigger picture.* We won't discuss any particular JMS implementations, or suggest that one vendor might be better than another; our goal is to give you the tools that you need to ask intelligent questions, evaluate different products, and map out a deployment strategy.

TCP/IP

TCP/IP is the name for a family of protocols that includes TCP (Transmission Control Protocol), UDP (User Datagram Protocol), and IP (Internet Protocol). The protocols are layered: IP provides low-level services; both TCP and UDP sit "on top of" IP.

TCP is a reliable, connection-oriented protocol. A process wishing to establish communication with one or more processes across a network creates a connection to each of the other processes and sends and receives data using those connections. The network software, rather than the application, is responsible for making sure that all the data arrives, and that it arrives in the correct order. It takes care of acknowledging that data has been received, automatically discards duplicate data, and performs many other services for the application. If something happens with the connection, the process on either side of the connection will know *almost* immediately that the connection has been permanently broken.†

Most high-level network protocols (and most JMS implementations) are built on top of TCP, for obvious reasons: it's a lot easier to use a protocol that takes care of reliability for you. However, reliability comes with a cost: a lot of work is involved in setting up and tearing down connections, and additional overhead is required to acknowledge data that's sent and received. Therefore, TCP is slower than its unreliable relative, UDP.

---

* This is not the place for a comprehensive discussion of TCP/IP networking. If you want detailed treatment of these protocols, see *Internet Core Protocols*, by Eric Hall (O'Reilly). If you're interested in network programming in Java, see *Java Network Programming*, by Elliotte Rusty Harold (O'Reilly).

† If a connection is not sending or receiving any data, it could take a while before the owning process is signaled about a problem, depending on the network settings.

UDP

UDP (User Datagram Protocol) is an unreliable protocol: you send data to a destination, but there's no guarantee that the data will arrive. If it doesn't arrive, you'll never find out; furthermore, the process receiving the data will never know that you sent anything.

This sounds like a bad basis for reliable software, but it really only means that applications using UDP have to take reliability into their own hands: they need to come up with their own mechanism for verifying that data was received, and for retransmitting data that went astray. In practice, applications that need reliability guarantees can either use TCP, or can incorporate software to build reliability on top of UDP. Most applications have taken the easier route, but a few important applications (like DNS and the early versions of NFS) make extensive use of UDP.

IP Multicast

The simplicity of UDP makes possible a kind of service that's completely different from anything in the TCP world. Because it is connection-oriented, TCP is fundamentally limited to point-to-point communications. UDP offers the notion of a "multicast," in which an application can send data to a group of recipients. Multicasting is based on a special class of addresses, known as Class D addresses.* Class D addresses are not assigned to individual hosts; they're assigned to multicast groups. Hosts can join and leave groups that they have an interest in. Data sent to a multicast address will only be received by the hosts in the multicast group. At least from the network's standpoint, multicast is much more efficient when you need to send a message to many recipients.

Multicasting maps naturally into the sorts of things we want messaging systems to do. Many messaging products use multicasting for one-to-many pub/sub broadcast of messages. Most have built some level of reliability on top of UDP. If this issue is important to you, it would be in your interest to delve deeper and find out exactly what your JMS vendor has, or has not, implemented. Multicast has its drawbacks as well. UDP traffic is usually not allowed through a firewall, so you may have to negotiate with your network administrators or find some workaround if you need to get multicast traffic through your company's firewalls. Furthermore, multicast relies heavily on special routing software. Most modern routers support multicast, but lots of old routers are still in service. Even if you have up-to-date routers within your corporate network, and your network administrators know how to configure multicast routing, there's still the Internet; multicasting does not realistically

---

* A Class D network address is one defined as having the range of 224.0.0.0 through 239.255.255.255. Class D network addresses are reserved for IP multicast.

work across the Internet (see the section "Network routers and firewalls" later in this chapter). As a configuration and maintenance consideration, multicast addresses must be coordinated across the network to avoid collisions. These drawbacks are especially important if you are building an application that you want to sell to others, who in turn expect to deploy it easily.

Messaging Over IP Multicast

In the following section we will explore the tradeoffs of using messaging over an IP multicast architecture. It is important for you to understand the issues as you map out your deployment strategy.

Duplication, ordering, and reliability of messages

If a messaging vendor wishes to provide full reliability for IP multicast and UDP it must build TCP-like semantics into the JMS provider layer to compensate for duplicate datagrams, out of order datagrams, and datagrams that could never possibly get to the intended destination. Either the JMS provider has to incur the overhead of detecting and compensating for duplicate datagrams, or the application needs to be tolerant of duplicate messages. If the duplication of datagrams is not dealt with at the JMS provider level, it is only really viable for DUPS_OK_ ACKNOWLEDGE. No matter what, a messaging vendor has to implement the reliability necessary to ensure guaranteed ordering, since UDP doesn't ensure that packets are received in the same order that they are sent.

A messaging vendor should support some sort of error detection to know when a UDP datagram is lost. Ideally it should know that a client can't be reached due to a network boundary across an unsupported network router (see the section "Network routers and firewalls" later in this chapter). The JMS specification allows for a nondurable JMS subscriber to miss messages, but is intentionally vague about this since it is not a goal of the specification to impose an architecture on a JMS provider. However, for all practical purposes, nonguaranteed messaging means that messages *may* be lost, and that should mean they may only be lost once in a while. For both cases, some sort of acknowledgment semantics are required.

Centralized and decentralized architectures

A TCP-based messaging system generally uses a hub-and-spoke architecture whereby a centralized message server, or cluster of message servers, communicates with JMS clients using TCP/IP, SSL, or HTTP connections. The centralized server is responsible for knowing who is publishing and who is subscribing at any given time. Message servers may operate in a cluster spread across multiple machines, but to the clients there only appears to be a single logical server.

Message servers operating in a cluster can intelligently route messages to other servers. Clustering may provide load balancing, and may help to optimize network traffic by selectively filtering and routing only the messages that need to get to a particular node. The servers are also responsible for persistence of guaranteed messages, and for Access Control Lists (ACLs) that grant permissions to subscribers on a per-topic basis. The messages are only delivered to the subscribers that are interested in a particular topic, and only to those that have the permissions to get them. A centralized server also makes it easier to add subscribers: when a new subscriber comes online; only the message server needs to know about it.

At the same time, a centralized architecture may introduce a single point of failure: if the main server in a cluster (the server to which clients initially connect) goes down, the entire cluster may become unavailable. A JMS provider may solve this problem by distributing the connections across multiple servers in the cluster. If one server goes down, the other servers can continue to operate, thus minimizing the impact of the failure. Reconnect logic may also be built into the client, enabling it to find another server if its initial server goes down.

Multicasting implies a drastically different architecture, in which there usually is no centralized server. Because there is no central server, there is no single point of failure; each JMS client broadcasts directly to all other JMS clients. One consequence of this architecture is that every publisher and every subscriber may have local configuration information about every other JMS client on the system. This can be an extremely important consideration for deployment administration. In the absence of a higher-level administrative framework, local configurations have to be updated on every client whenever a new client or a new topic is added.

A decentralized architecture may also mean that the persistence mechanism for guaranteed messaging is pushed out to the client machines. No matter how efficient the storage algorithm, disk I/O is always going to be the biggest bottleneck. Choosing to use such an architecture would require that the client machines have disk storage that is both fast and large.

There is disagreement as to whether guaranteed messaging (storing persistent messages) benefits from a decentralized architecture. Proponents of a decentralized architecture argue that the I/O load is distributed among the clients and is therefore faster. On the other hand, client I/O is not nearly as reliable, nor is it as fast as a centralized server with a powerful disk system.

Network routers and firewalls

Although technically possible, it is unlikely that a firewall administrator will allow UDP traffic to pass through a firewall. Firewalls typically disallow all traffic, except for traffic to or from specific hosts, using specific protocols. UDP traffic is rarely allowed through a firewall for various reasons.

In recognition of the problems with IP multicast (lack of support, and firewall blocking), messaging vendors that use IP multicast provide software bridge processes to carry messaging traffic across routers and firewalls. The bridges may consist of one or more processes connected together by HTTP, SSL, or TCP/IP.

If you're considering a vendor that supports multicasting, it is worth considering what percentage of your message traffic is going through one of these bridges. If all of your messages are going through the firewall over an SSL or HTTP connection, there will be little point in using multicasting behind the firewall for performance reasons. If the routers in your deployment environment require that a number of TCP/IP-based bridges be put in place, the performance benefits of multicast are diminished, depending on how many of these you have to put in place and administer. The messaging system is only as fast as its slowest link.

If most of the message traffic is confined to your corporate LAN or a VPN and you have full control over it, IP multicasting is a very attractive option.

Some vendors support both centralized and decentralized architectures

In recognition of these issues, the vendors who support IP multicast also provide centralized servers using TCP/IP socket connections. This could mean you have two different architectures to configure and support: one configuration for the nonguaranteed one-to-many pub/sub multicast of messages within a subnet on your corporate LAN, and another for everything else. It is important to consider what it will mean to choose one of these architectures at deployment time, or how you will switch from one mode to the other after your application is deployed.

The Bottom Line

IP multicast has significant network throughput benefits in a one-to-many broadcast of information. A single multicast message to multiple recipients will always cause less network traffic than sending the message to each recipient via a TCP connection. A messaging vendor picks and chooses how much reliability to build on top of UDP based on the quality of service required for the message as defined by JMS.

However, the choice is not that simple when it is applied to a deployment environment in a messaging product. The performance advantages of IP multicasting are only viable for a certain deployment environment. These advantages can diminish depending on the types of messages in your application, the networking hardware at your site, the deployment environment (intranet, extranet, internet), and the complexity of administration.

Make sure to benchmark your application carefully before making a final decision, using the guidelines we discussed earlier in this chapter. You may be surprised at what you see. When a JMS provider is put under heavy stress with lots of clients, there are so many other factors involved that the speed at which network packets go across the wire is not usually a significant factor. You may see that one vendor's implementation of messaging over IP multicast will perform vastly differently from another's—even with the use of nonguaranteed messaging. You may even find that one vendor's TCP-based implementation performs better than another vendor's multicast implementation.

Security

In this section, we are only going to concern ourselves with those aspects of security that are commonly supported by JMS providers. You need to think about three aspects of security: authentication, authorization, and secure communication. How these aspects of security are implemented is vendor-specific, and each vendor uses its own combination of available technologies to authenticate, authorize, and secure communication between JMS clients.

We will also discuss firewalls and HTTP tunneling as a solution to restrictions placed on JMS applications by organizations.

Authentication

Simply put, authentication verifies the identity of the user to the messaging system; it may also verify the identity of the server to the JMS client. The most common kind of authentication is a login screen that requires a username and a password. This is supported explicitly in the JMS API when a `Connection` is created, as well as in the JNDI API when an `InitialContext` is created. JMS providers that use username/password authentication may support either of these solutions:

```
Properties env = new Properties();

env.put(Context.SECURITY_PRINCIPAL, "username");
env.put(Context.SECURITY_CREDENTIALS, "password");
TopicFactory topicFactory = jndiContext.lookup("...");
...
TopicConnection con =
  topicFactory.createTopicConnection("username", "password");
```

JMS providers may also use more sophisticated mechanisms for authentication, such as secret or public key authentication. Secret key authentication, most commonly used in Kerberos, requires the participation of a Kerberos server.* Public key authentication, most commonly used in SSL, is based on a chain of certifying authorities. Each of these systems has its supporters and detractors, but the end result is the same: the connecting client is given permission to access the system.

Authorization

Authentication is only the first step in the security process, but it's the basis for what follows. Once you have verified the identify of the user, you can make intelligent decisions about what that user is allowed to do. That's where authorization comes in. Authorization (a.k.a. access control) applies security policies that regulate what a user can and cannot do within a system. Authorization policies are usually set up as access control lists by the system administrators. Authorized users are given an identity in the system and assigned to user groups, which may themselves be a part of a larger group. Groups and individual users (identities) are assigned permissions dictating which topics, queues, or connection factories they are allowed to access. Permissions may be configured to grant all members of a group access except for some specified members, or deny all members of a group except some specified members. Some JMS providers may choose to check access control lists on every message delivered, while others simply control the destinations or connection factory that a JMS client can obtain from the JNDI namespace. Generally, authorization policies work better in a centralized messaging system, since it can be centrally managed.

Most JMS providers provide hierarchical topic trees that allow consumers to subscribe to different levels of topics using wildcard substitution. For example, topics could be divided into "ACME.SALES.SOUTHWEST.ANVILS" and "ACME.SALES. NORTHEAST.ANVILS". A subscriber can subscribe to "ACME.SALES.*" and see all the messages published for all the sales of ACME, though that may not be the desire of the system administrator. A companion security feature allows permissions to be set at each level in the topic tree, thus making access control much easier to manage by providing more finely grained access control.

Secure Communication

Communication channels between a client and a server are frequently the focus of security concerns. A channel of communication can be secured by physical isolation (like a dedicated network connection) or by encrypting the communication

---

* Although a system may use Kerberos to authenticate a user, the system will probably use SSL for secure communications.

between the client and the server. Physically securing communication is expensive, limiting, and pretty much impossible on the Internet, so we will focus on encryption. When communication is secured by encryption, the messages passed are encoded so that they cannot be read or manipulated while in transit. This normally involves the exchange of cryptographic keys between the client and the server. The keys allow the receiver of the message to decode and read the message.

There are two basic ways that messages are encrypted by JMS providers today: SSL and Payload Encryption. SSL (Secure Socket Layer) is an industry-standard specification for secure communication used extensively in Internet applications. With SSL, the JMS provider's protocol is encrypted, protecting every aspect of the JMS client's exchanges with the message service. Payload Encryption allows messages to be encrypted on a per-topic, per-queue basis. This unusual variance minimizes overhead by encrypting only the messages that need it, rather than everything on the whole connection.* For example, Wholesaler may not need to encrypt the broadcast of price quotes since that same information is being replicated to every Retailer with an authenticated connection. The response message with the "Buy Order" would more likely be encrypted since that is sensitive data that is unique to each Retailer. Payload Encryption can also ensure end-to-end security between a producer and a consumer. Without it, there may be nothing preventing a sender from connecting to the message server using a SSL connection and receiving an unencrypted message using a non-SSL connection.

Firewalls and HTTP Tunneling

Firewalls are systems that serve as the gateway between an organization and a broader network such as the Internet. These gateways filter all incoming and outgoing messages. Firewalls only allow packets of a predetermined type and protocol to pass between computers within the organization and those in the broader network. Firewalls help to stop malicious attacks against an organization's information systems by outside parties.

In most cases, firewalls allow HTTP traffic to flow without restriction. Since HTTP is not the native protocol of most JMS providers, JMS providers must piggy-back their protocol on top of HTTP to penetrate a firewall and exchange messages. This is commonly referred to as *HTTP tunneling*. HTTP tunneling is not really complicated. It involves nesting a JMS provider's native protocol inside HTTP requests and responses. Because the JMS provider's protocol is nested in HTTP, it's hidden from the firewall and effectively tunnels through unnoticed.

---

* At the time of this writing only SonicMQ supports Payload Encryption in addition to SSL encryption.

In any JMS application that must communicate across a variety of firewalls with large user populations, HTTP tunneling is a necessity. This is especially true when the clients are not centrally managed and may be added and removed at will, which is often the case in B2B applications.

The level of support for tunneling varies, depending on the JMS provider. In addition to tunneling through server-side firewalls, it is important to know if the JMS client can tunnel through a client-side firewall, and if HTTP proxies are supported. It is also important to know if the vendor supports HTTP 1.1 Persistent Connections, HTTP 1.0 Keep-Alive Connections, or simple HTTP 1.0 Connections.

Connecting to the Outside World

There are often entities outside your corporation that you need to interact with. You may have trading partners, financial institutions, and vertical business portals to connect to and communicate with. These outside entities usually have established protocols that they already use for electronic communication. An Electronic Data Interchange (EDI) system may have nightly batch jobs that export flat files to an FTP site. A trading partner may expect to send and receive HTTP transmissions as its way of communicating with the outside world. A supply chain portal may require that you install one of their clients on your site in order to communicate with them through whatever protocol they dictate. Sometimes email is required as a way of sending a "Thank you for your order" message.

Ideally each of these outside entities would have a close working relationship with you, and would allow you to install a JMS client at each site. That would make communication very easy—but it's not how the world works. These other communication mechanisms may have been in place for a number of years, and their users aren't about to rip them out just because you want them to. They may not be capable of changing the way their systems work just to accommodate your JMS provider. These are "legacy systems"; in the future, they may gradually disappear, but for the time being, we have to figure out how to work with them.

Someday JMS may provide on-the-wire interoperability, and be ubiquitous. Until then, we are left to building bridges, or connectors to those other protocols. As illustrated in Figure 7-1, a connector is simply a JMS client. Its sole purpose is to receive data using the foreign protocol, create a JMS message, and send it along through your JMS-based system. Likewise an outbound connector would listen for messages from your JMS-based system and transmit the message out into the world using the protocol expected by the entity at the other end.

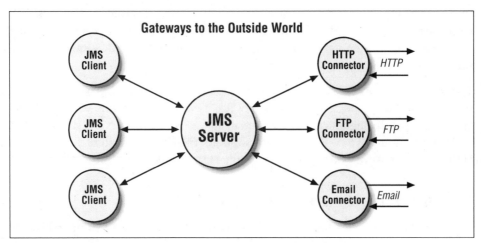

Figure 7-1. JMS clients can be dedicated as protocol connectors to the outside world

The JMS specification does not suggest this notion of connectors.* However, legacy systems are a fact of life. In recognition of this, most JMS vendors are starting to provide connectors to legacy systems as a way to provide added value. If your JMS provider does not support the connector you are looking for, it is typically easy enough to write your own. In fact, this is an ideal situation for using CLIENT_ ACKNOWLEDGE mode. As illustrated in Figure 7-2, a JMS consumer can explicitly acknowledge the receipt of the message once its data transmission has been successfully completed.

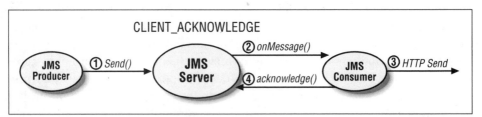

Figure 7-2. Using CLIENT_ACKNOWLEDGE, a JMS consumer can still ensure reliability when bridging to other protocols

It is important to know that end-to-end quality of service may not be guaranteed when using bridges to other protocols. In Figure 7-2, the HTTP send may succeed, yet the acknowledge() may fail.

---

* The use of the term "connector" in this discussion should not be confused with "connectors" as defined by the J2EE connector specification—a different thing altogether.

Bridging to Other Messaging Systems

JMS does not provide for interoperability between JMS providers. A JMS client from one vendor cannot talk directly to a JMS server from another vendor. Interoperability between vendors was not a goal of the specification's creators, since the architecture of messaging vendors can be so vastly different. One solution to this problem is to build a connector process that is a client of both providers. Its sole purpose is to act as a pass-through mechanism between the two providers, as shown in Figure 7-3. This is one of the reasons why the message itself is required to be interoperable between vendors, as explained in Chapter 3, *Anatomy of a JMS Message*. The message need not be recreated as it is passed along to the other JMS client.

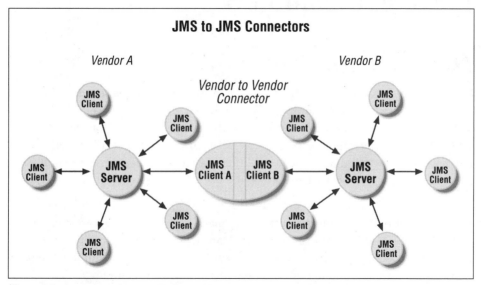

Figure 7-3. Connecting from one JMS provider to another is a simple pass-through process that is a client of both

End-to-end quality of service should be a consideration when building or using such a bridge. The robustness of JMS vendor-provided bridges may vary in this respect.

Since JMS is a standard, and it is easy enough to remove one vendor's implementation and swap in another one, you may ask "Why would anyone want to do this?" The main reason today is to bridge an IBM MQSeries legacy application with an application that is based on a more modern JMS provider.

In recognition of this need, most JMS vendors are providing bridges to MQSeries. It's in their best interest to do so, since MQSeries is a strong established player in the messaging market.

8

In this chapter:
• *J2EE Overview*
• *J2EE: A United Platform*
• *The JMS Resource in J2EE*
• *The New Message-Driven Bean in EJB 2.0*

J2EE, EJB, and JMS

J2EE Overview

Java 2, Enterprise Edition (J2EE) is a specification that unites several other Java enterprise technologies, including JMS, into one complete platform. J2EE is built on three main components: Enterprise JavaBeans, Servlets, and JavaServer Pages (JSP). Many other technologies, such as JMS, JDBC, JavaMail, JTA, CORBA, and JNDI. are also included as services in J2EE. The Java Message Service actually has two roles in J2EE: it is both a service and the basis for a new enterprise bean type.

To get a better understanding of what J2EE is, and why it is important, we need to discuss the three main components and explain how they are drawn together to form the unified J2EE platform. It is important to keep in mind that all the technologies discussed here are paper specifications licensed and implemented by vendors—a central theme in Sun Microsystems' enterprise technologies.

Enterprise JavaBeans

Enterprise JavaBeans (EJB) 2.0 defines a Java component model for component transaction monitors (CTMs). A CTM is a marriage of two technologies: distributed objects and transaction processing monitors (TPMs). Distributed object technologies such as CORBA, Java RMI-JRMP, and DCOM provide a networking and routing infrastructure that allows applications to access objects hosted on other processes or computers. A TPM, such as CICS or TUXEDO, provides a robust, secure, and scalable environment for running transactional applications. A CTM combines these technologies into transactional distributed objects that run in a robust, secure, and scalable environment. There are three main CTM technologies today: Sun's Enterprise JavaBeans, Microsoft's COM+ (a.k.a. MTS), and the Object Management Group's CORBA Component Model (CCM). J2EE is built on

EJB, which provides it with powerful transactional components that can be used to model and run an organization's business logic.

NOTE   Enterprise JavaBeans are not at all like Java Beans. Enterprise Java-Beans are nonvisual components that run on an application server. Java beans are used as visual widgets (buttons, graphs, etc.). Other than the common name "Bean" and the fact that they are both Java component technologies from Sun Microsystems, EJB and Java Beans have very little in common.

In Enterprise JavaBeans 2.0, bean components come in three main flavors: session, entity, and message-driven beans. *Session beans* model processes and act as server-side extensions of their clients (they can manage a client's session state). *Entity beans* model persistent business objects; and combine business logic and database data. *Message-driven beans*, the newest bean type, are JMS clients that can consume messages concurrently in a robust and scalable EJB environment. The EJB 2.0 bean components are shown in Figure 8-1.

Application developers create custom enterprise beans by implementing one of the main bean interfaces and developing the bean according to conventions and policies dictated by the EJB specification. Entity beans are usually used for modeling business concepts that have persistent data and may be accessed by many clients concurrently. Entity beans might be used to model customers, orders, vehicles, locations, and similar objects. Session beans model business processes that may or may not have session state. Session beans might be used to model business concepts like a securities broker, an online shopping cart, loan calculation, medical claim processor—any process or mediator-type business concept. Message-driven beans are used to model stateless JMS consumers. A message-driven bean will have a pool of instances at runtime, each of which is a `MessageListener`. The bean instances can concurrently consume hundreds of messages delivered to the message-driven bean, which makes the message-driven bean scalable. Similar to session beans, message-driven beans model business processes by coordinating the interaction of other beans and resources according to the messages received and their payloads.

In addition to the Java classes that define a bean, every bean has an XML configuration file called a *deployment descriptor*. The deployment descriptor allows the bean developer to declare many of a bean's runtime behaviors including transaction policies, access control policies, and the resources (services) available. Resources (JMS, JDBC, JavaMail, etc.) that are declared in the deployment descriptor are accessed via JNDI from the bean's environment naming context (ENC). The ENC is simply a default read-only JNDI namespace that is available to every bean at runtime. Each bean deployment has its own JNDI ENC. In addition

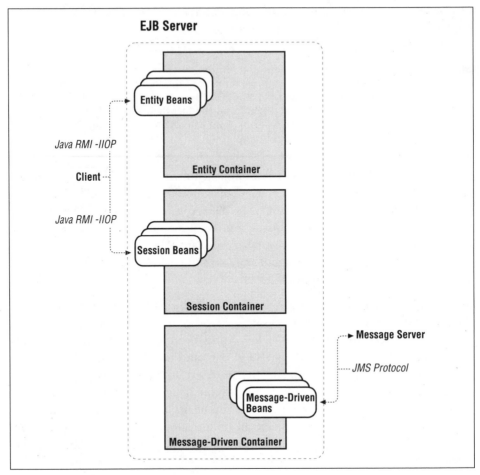

Figure 8-1. The EJB 2.0 bean components

to providing a bean with access to resources such as JDBC, JavaMail, JTA, and URL and JMS connection factories, the JNDI ENC is used to access properties and other enterprise beans. Resources accessed from the JNDI ENC are managed implicitly by the EJB server so that they are pooled and then are automatically enrolled in transactions as needed.

All enterprise beans (session, entity, and message-driven) can be developed separately, packaged in a JAR file and distributed. As components, packaged beans can be reused and combined with various other beans to solve any number of application requirements. In addition, enterprise beans are portable so that they can be combined and deployed on any application server that is EJB-compliant.

Session and entity beans are accessed as distributed objects via Java RMI-IIOP, which provides some level of location transparency; clients can access the beans on the server somewhat like local objects. Entity and session beans are based on the RPC distributed computing paradigm. Message-driven beans are JMS clients that process JMS messages; they are *not* accessed as distributed objects. Message-driven beans are based on the asynchronous enterprise messaging paradigm.

There is a lot more to Enterprise JavaBeans than is provided in this simple overview. You can learn more about EJB by reading *Enterprise JavaBeans,* by Richard Monson-Haefel (O'Reilly).

Servlets

The servlet specification defines a server-side component model that can be implemented by web server vendors. Servlets provide a simple but powerful API for generating web pages dynamically. (Although servlets can be used for many different request-reply protocols, they are predominantly used to process HTTP requests for web pages.)

Servlets are developed in the same fashion as enterprise beans; they are Java classes that extend a base component class and may have a deployment descriptor. Servlets do not implicitly support transactions and are *not* accessed as distributed objects. Servlets respond to requests recieved from an input stream, usually HTTP, and respond by writing to an output stream. Once a servlet is developed and packaged in a JAR file, it can be deployed in a web server. When a servlet is deployed, it is assigned to handle requests for a specific web page or assist other servlets in handling page requests.

The servlet specification is simple and elegant. It's a powerful server-side component model. You can learn more about servlets in *Java™ Servlet Programming,* by Jason Hunter and William Crawford (O'Reilly).

JavaServer Pages

JavaServer Pages (JSP) is an extension of the servlet component model that simplifies the process of generating HTML dynamically. JSP essentially allows you to incorporate Java directly into an HTML page as a scripting language. JSP pages (text documents) are translated and compiled into Java servlets, which are then run in a web server just like any other servlet—some servers do the compilation automatically at runtime. JSP can also be used to generate XML documents dynamically.

J2EE: A United Platform

Servlets and JSP, collectively called web components, provide a powerful technology for dynamically generating HMTL using server side components. As EJB matured it became obvious that a synergy existed between EJB and web components. EJB provides scalable, secure, transactional access to business logic and data, while web components provide a flexible model for dynamically generating HTML user interfaces. Together these technologies strike a nice balance between the need for a robust infrastructure and a lightweight, web-based, and easily distributed user interface.

To create a united platform, J2EE standardizes the use of XML deployment descriptors and the JNDI ENC across both enterprise beans and web components. In J2EE, both servlets and JSP scripts can access resources like JDBC, JavaMail, and JMS connection factories via their own JNDI ENC. The ability to consistently access a JMS connection factory from a servlet, JSP script, or enterprise bean enables any of these components to become a JMS client.

In addition to web components and enterprise bean components, J2EE introduces the *application client component*. The application client component runs on the client machine in its own container (see Figure 8-2). It is simply a Java application that has a deployment descriptor and a JNDI ENC that allows it the same ease of access to resources that other components enjoy. The application client can access JMS through its JNDI ENC, so it too can become a JMS client.

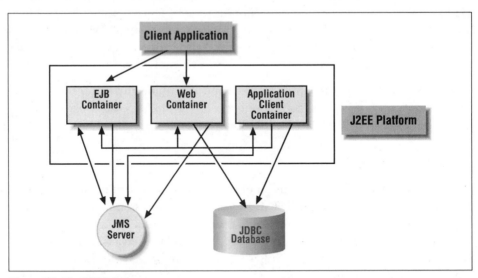

Figure 8-2. The J2EE platform

The J2EE specification ensures a certain amount of portability between vendors. A J2EE application that runs on Vendor A's platform should, with a little work, be able to run on Vendor B's J2EE platform. As long as proprietary extensions are not used, web, enterprise bean, and application client components developed to the J2EE specification will run on any J2EE platform.

The JMS Resource in J2EE

The JNDI Environment Naming Context (ENC) is central to the J2EE platform. The JNDI ENC specifies that JMS connection factories (Topic-ConnectionFactory and QueueConnectionFactory) can be bound within a JNDI namespace and made available to any J2EE component at runtime. This allows any J2EE component to become a JMS client.

For example, the Wholesaler JMS client developed in Chapter 4, *Publish-and-Subscribe Messaging*, could be modeled as a J2EE application client, which would allow it to access a JMS connection factory through the JNDI ENC:

```
public class Wholesaler implements javax.jms.MessageListener{
   public Wholesaler(String username, String password){
      try{

         InitialContext jndiEnc = new InitialContext();

         TopicConnectionFactory factory = (TopicConnectionFactory)
            jndiEnc.lookup("java:comp/env/jms/broker");
         connect = factory.createTopicConnection (username, password);

         session =
          connect.createTopicSession(false,Session.AUTO_ACKNOWLEDGE);

         hotDealsTopic=(Topic)
             jndiEnc.lookup("java:comp/env/jms/HotDeals");
         publisher = session.createPublisher(hotDealsTopic);

         ...

      } catch (javax.jms.JMSException jmse){
         jmse.printStackTrace(); System.exit(1);
      } catch (javax.naming.NamingException jne){
         jne.printStackTrace(); System.exit(1);
      }
   }
   ...
```

Notice that the InitialContext did not need a set of vendor specific properties and that the lookup() operations referenced a special namespace, "java:comp/env/jms/", to access the connection factories. The JNDI ENC allows the J2EE component to remain ignorant of the actual network location of the administered objects, and even of the vendor that implements them. This allows the J2EE components to be portable across JMS providers as well as J2EE platforms. In addition, the JNDI names used to locate objects are logical bindings, so the topics or

queues bound to these names can change independently of the actual bindings
used by the JMS provider.

In the XML deployment descriptor for the Wholesaler application client, the
component developer declares that a JMS connection factory and destination
need to be bound within the JNDI ENC:

```
<application-client>
  <display-name>Wholesaler Applicaton</display-name>
    <resource-ref>
      <description>Hot Deals Broker</description>
      <res-ref-name>jms/broker</res-ref-name>
      <res-type>javax.jms.TopicConnectionFactory</res-type>
      <res-auth>Container</res-auth>
    </resource-ref>
  ...
    <resource-env-ref>
      <description>Hot Deals Topic</description>
      <resource-env-ref-name>jms/HotDeals</resource-env-ref-name>
      <resource-env-ref-type>javax.jms.Topic</resource-env-ref-type>
    </resource-env-ref>
  ...
```

When the component is deployed, the J2EE vendor tools generate code to trans-
late the JNDI ENC resource references into JMS-administered objects. This translation is done when the bean is deployed using administration tools.

Any J2EE component can access JMS connection factories and destinations using
the JNDI ENC. As an example, the Wholesaler client can be rewritten as a stateless session bean that uses the JNDI ENC to obtain a JMS connection factory and
destination:

```
public class WholesalerBean implements javax.ejb.SessionBean{

    ...

    public void setSessionContext(SessionContext cntx){
        try {

            InitialContext jndiEnc = new InitialContext();

            TopicConnectionFactory factory = (TopicConnectionFactory)
                jndiEnc.lookup("java:comp/env/jms/broker");
            connect = factory.createTopicConnection (username, password);

            session =
             connect.createTopicSession(false,Session.AUTO_ACKNOWLEDGE);

            hotDealsTopic=(Topic)
```

```
            jndiEnc.lookup("java:comp/env/jms/HotDeals");
        publisher = session.createPublisher(hotDealsTopic);


            ...

        }
        ...

    }
    public void publishPriceQuotes(String dealDesc, String username,
                                   String itemDesc,  float oldPrice,
                                   float newPrice){
        try {
            javax.jms.StreamMessage message =
                    session.createStreamMessage();
            message.writeString(dealDesc);
            ...

            publisher.publish(
                message,
                javax.jms.DeliveryMode.PERSISTENT,
                javax.jms.Message.DEFAULT_PRIORITY,
                1800000);

        } catch ( javax.jms.JMSException jmse ){
            jmse.printStackTrace();
        }
    }
    ...

}
```

Although session, entity, and web components can all act as JMS producers, these components can only consume JMS messages *synchronously* using the `MessageConsumer.receive()` methods. Calling one of the `receive()` methods causes the JMS client to pole the queue or topic and wait for a message.* These methods are used to consume messages synchronously, while `MessageListener` objects are used to consume messages asynchronously.

Only the message-driven bean and application client components can both produce and consume asynchronous messages. The web, session, and entity components cannot act as asynchronous JMS consumers because they are driven by synchronous request-reply protocols, not asynchronous messages. Web components respond to HTTP requests while entity and session beans respond to Java RMI-IIOP requests.

---

* It's recommended that the component developer use the nonblocking method, `receiveNoWait()`, to conserve resources and avoid blocking. Unrestricted blocking is not limited to any length of time, and is therefore risky.

The fact that neither web components nor session and entity beans can asynchronously consume JMS messages was one of the things that led to development of the message-driven bean. The message-driven bean provides J2EE developers with a server-side JMS consumer that can consume asynchronous messages, something they didn't have before EJB 2.0.

The New Message-Driven Bean in EJB 2.0

While most JMS vendors provide the message-brokering facilities for routing messages from producers to consumers, the responsibility for implementing JMS clients is left to the application developer. In many cases the JMS clients that consume and process messages need a lot of infrastructure in order to be robust, secure, fault-tolerant, and scalable. JMS clients may access databases and other resources, use local and distributed transactions, require authentication and authorization security, or need to process a large load of concurrent messages. Fulfilling these needs is a tall order, requiring that a significant amount of work be done by the application developer. In the end, the kind of infrastructure needed to support powerful JMS consumers is not unlike the infrastructure needed for session and entity beans, which can produce but not consume messages asynchronously.*

In recognition of this need, EJB 2.0 now includes the `MessageDrivenBean` type, which can consume JMS messages, and process them in the same robust component-based infrastructure that session and entity beans enjoy. The `MessageDrivenBean` type (message-driven bean) is a first-class enterprise bean component that is designed to consume asynchronous JMS messages. Like stateless session beans, message-driven beans don't maintain state between requests; they may also have instance variables that are maintained throughout the bean instance's life, but that may not store conversational state. Unlike all other bean types, a message-driven bean does not have a remote or home interface, because the message-driven bean is not an RPC component. It does not have business methods that are invoked by EJB clients. A message-driven bean consumes messages delivered by other JMS clients through a message server.

In addition to providing the container infrastructure for message-driven beans, EJB 2.0 provides another important advantage: concurrent processing. In EJB 2.0, a message-driven bean is deployed as a JMS consumer. It subscribes to a topic or connects to a queue and waits to receive messages. At runtime, the EJB container actually instantiates many instances of the same message-driven bean and keeps those instances in pool. When a message is delivered to a message-driven bean, one instance of that bean is selected from a pool to handle the message. If several

---

* Entity and session beans can technically consume JMS messages synchronously by polling the destination using the `MessageConsumer.receive()` methods.

messages are delivered at the same time, the container can select a different bean instance to process each message; the messages can be processed concurrently. Because a message-driven bean can consume messages concurrently in a robust server environment, it is capable of much higher throughput and better scalability than most traditional JMS clients.

Message-driven beans are composed of a bean class and an XML deployment descriptor. The bean class must implement both the `javax.ejb.MessageDrivenBean` interface and the `javax.jms.MessageListener` interface. The `MessageDrivenBean` interface defines three methods:

```
package javax.ejb;
import javax.jms.Message;

public interface MessageDrivenBean {
  public void ejbCreate( );
  public void ejbRemove( );
  public void setMessageDrivenContext(MessageDrivenContext mdc);
}
```

The `MessageListener` interface defines the `onMessage()` method:

```
package javax.jms;

public interface MessageListener {
  public void onMessage( );
}
```

The `setMessageDrivenContext()` is called on each instance right after it is instantiated. It provides the instance with a `MessageDrivenContext`, which is based on a standard container interface, `EJBContext`. The `ejbCreate()` method is invoked on each instance after the `setMessageDrivenContext()` method, but before the bean instance is added to the pool for a particular message-driven bean. Once the message-driven bean has been added to the pool, it's ready to process messages. When a message arrives, the instance is removed from the pool and its `onMessage()` method is invoked. When the `onMessage()` method returns, the bean instance is returned to the pool and is ready to process another message. The `ejbRemove()` method is invoked on an instance when it is discarded. This might happen if the container needs to reduce the size of the pool. The lifecycle of a message-driven bean is shown in Figure 8-3.

The `Retailer` JMS client developed in Chapter 4 can easily be converted to a message-driven bean. When messages are received from the wholesalers, `RetailerMessageBean` can process them quickly and efficiently, providing a more scalable option then the JMS clients we developed in Chapter 4:

```
public class RetailerMessageBean
implements javax.ejb.MessageDrivenBean, javax.jms.MessageListener {
```

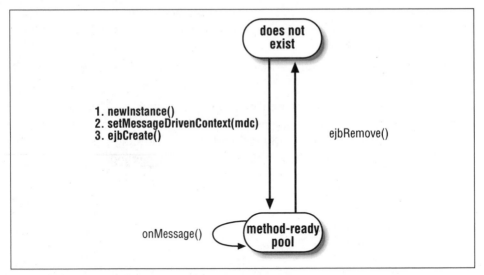

Figure 8-3. Lifecycle of a message-driven bean

```
private javax.jms.QueueConnection connect = null;
private javax.jms.QueueSession session = null;
private javax.jms.QueueSender sender = null;
private javax.jms.Queue buyQueue = null;


public void setMessageDrivenContext(MessageDrivenContext mdc){
}

public void ejbCreate(){
    try {
        InitialContext jndiEnc = new InitialContext();

        QueueConnectionFactory factory = (QueueConnectionFactory)
          jndiEnc.lookup("java:comp/env/jms/broker");

        connect = factory.createQueueConnection();

        session = connect.createQueueSession
                            (false,Session.AUTO_ACKNOWLEDGE);

        buyQueue = (Queue)
          jndiEnc.lookup("java:comp/env/jms/BuyQueue");

        sender  = session.createSender(buyQueue);
        connect.start();

    } catch (javax.jms.JMSException jmse){
        throw new javax.ejb.EJBException();
```

```
            } catch (javax.naming.NamingException jne){
                throw new javax.ejb.EJBException();
            }
    }
    public void ejbRemove( ){
        try {
            connect.close();
        } catch (javax.jms.JMSException jmse){
            throw new javax.ejb.EJBException();
        }
    }
    public void onMessage(javax.jms.Message aMessage){
        try{
            autoBuy(aMessage);
        } catch (java.lang.RuntimeException rte){
            throw new javax.ejb.EJBException();
        }
    }


    private void autoBuy (javax.jms.Message message){
        int count = 1000;
        try{
            StreamMessage strmMsg = (StreamMessage)message;
            String dealDesc = strmMsg.readString();
            String itemDesc = strmMsg.readString();
            float oldPrice = strmMsg.readFloat();
            float newPrice = strmMsg.readFloat();
            System.out.println("Received Hot Buy :"+dealDesc);

            // If price reduction is greater than 10 percent, buy
            if (newPrice == 0 || oldPrice / newPrice > 1.1){
                System.out.println
                ("\nBuying " + count + " " + itemDesc);

                TextMessage textMsg = session.createTextMessage();
                textMsg.setText(count + " " + itemdesc );

                sender.send(
                    textMsg,
                    javax.jms.DeliveryMode.PERSISTENT,
                    javax.jms.Message.DEFAULT_PRIORITY,
                    1800000);
            } else {
                System.out.println ("\nBad Deal.  Not buying");
            }
        } catch (javax.jms.JMSException jmse){
            jmse.printStackTrace();
        }
    }
}
```

The `RetailerMessageBean` uses the `BuyQueue` to publish buy orders. The `QueueConnectionFactory` and `BuyQueue` destination are obtained from the JNDI ENC. The `RetailerMessageBean` uses the factory and queue to create a `QueueSender`, but how does the bean subscribe to the `HotDeals` topic? Where is the code to set up the `HotDeals` subscription?

A message-driven bean is, by definition, a JMS consumer. The EJB container in which the bean is deployed takes care of subscribing the bean to the desired topic or connecting it to the desired queue, based on JMS configuration information provided by the deployer. Like any other enterprise bean, message-driven beans have an XML deployment descriptor, which is used as a reference by the deployer. The deployment descriptor includes elements for describing the type of destination (topic or queue), whether to use durable or nondurable subscriptions with topics, the acknowledgment mode, and even the message selector used. In addition, the message-driven bean's deployment descriptor contains elements common to all beans, like those for specifying environment entries, bean references, resource connections, etc. This makes the beans very portable across vendors, as well as simplifying configuration.

With the message-driven bean, it is important to understand that messages do not have to be produced by other beans in order for them to consumed by a message-driven bean. Message-driven beans can consume messages from any topic or queue administered by a JMS provider.* Messages consumed by message-driven beans may have come from other beans (session, entity, or message-driven beans), web components, application client components, normal non-J2EE JMS clients, or even legacy messaging systems supported by a JMS provider. A legacy application might, for example, use IBM's MQSeries to deliver messages to a queue, which is consumed by other legacy applications as well as message-driven beans.

The `MessageDrivenBean` interface is not specific to JMS-based messaging. While EJB 2.0 requires support for JMS-based messaging, the specification also allows vendors to support other protocols and messaging systems (e.g., HTTP, ebXML, SMTP) using proprietary message-driven beans. And this is why the message-driven bean in EJB 2.0 implements both the `MessageDrivenBean` interface, as well as the `MessageListener` interface, to distinguish it as a message-driven bean. message-driven beans

---

* In most cases the EJB vendor will also be the JMS provider, but it's possible some EJB vendors will provide hooks that allow third-party JMS providers to manage delivery of messages to an EJB container's message-driven beans.

9

JMS Providers

This chapter provides an overview of the top six JMS providers today (IBM's MQSeries, Progress's SonicMQ, Fiorano's FioranoMQ, Softwired's iBus, Sun's JMQ, BEA's Weblogic), as well as one open source JMS provider (OpenJMS). It is important to note that not all enterprise messaging systems support JMS. Some of the largest MOM products still do not support JMS, namely Microsoft Message Queue (MSMQ) and Tibco. While the authors expect that Tibco will eventually support JMS, MSMQ is not expected to do so—Microsoft has never supported Java enterprise APIs.

Each product summary addresses the following five topics:

- Product history
- JMS version and operating systems supported
- Architecture (centralized or distributed) and administration tools
- Persistence mechanism and transactional support
- Security (firewall tunneling, authentication, access control)

We have attempted to provide the version number for each product we discussed. Since new releases of these products will have additional features, we have also included a section on features expected for new versions along with all the product summaries.

NOTE   The term "JMS-compliant" is used throughout this chapter to indi-
              cate which version of JMS specification each provider claims to
              implement. It is important to note that Sun does not have any
              compatibility tests for JMS at this time, so there is no standard for
              verifying vendor's claims of compatibility.

              Most vendors do not support two-phase commit. This is understand-
              able, since support for the JMS XA interfaces and two-phase commit
              is purely optional.

IBM: MQSeries

Version 5.1

IBM's MQSeries leads the enterprise messaging market. It was introduced in 1993,
so it predates JMS and even Java as we know it. MQSeries was originally based on a
point-to-point model, and recently introduced support for the publish-and-
subscribe messaging in Version 5.

MQSeries provides a JMS 1.0.2-compliant provider that supports both the pub/sub
and p2p JMS messaging models. The MQSeries JMS provider is supported on AIX,
HP-UX, Windows 95, 98, 2000, NT, and Sun Solaris.

The server, MQSeries Queue Manager, is supported on a cornucopia of IBM platforms including AIX, MVS/ESA, OS/2 Warp, OS/390, AS/400 (IMPI & RISC),
and VSE/ESA. It's also supported on a large number of Compaq platforms,
including Tru64 UNIX, OpenVMS AXP, OpenVMS VAX, and Non-Stop Kernel. In
addition, its server is supported on Linux (technology release), Microsoft Windows 2000 and NT, NCR (AT&T GIS) Unix, Siemens Nixdorf SINIX and DC/OSx,
SCO OpenServer & UnixWare, SGI, Solaris, and HP-UX.

The MQSeries architecture is both centralized and distributed. It includes a hub-
and-spoke model. A network can be made up of numerous interconnected
MQSeries servers. It supports several network protocols in addition to TCP/IP,
including LU 6.2, NetBIOS, and SPX. MQSeries provides a clustering architecture
with fault-tolerance, fail-over, and load-balancing among servers in the cluster
across different platforms. MQSeries provides a command-line tool and an administrative API for configuring and managing administered objects.

Persistence in MQSeries is based on a proprietary mechanism using the actual
MQSeries queues. This allows messages to be exchanged directly with other
MQSeries applications, without the need for a bridge program. Only local transactions are supported by MQSeries' JMS provider, so the JMS provider cannot participate as a resource in a two-phase commit.

MQSeries provides support for HTTP firewall tunneling through both client and server-side firewalls. It controls access to queues and topics via access control lists, based on operating system principals (on Windows NT this includes the Windows SID). Sender identification is included in MQSeries messages. Secure communications can be provided by user-written exit code, or third-party security products. Code to interface with the Entrust PKI is available.

Next Version

Future plans for IBM's JMS implementation include further integration with IBM's WebSphere software platform, an ASF and XA capability, enhanced performance, and a route to coexistence of messaging and object technologies.

Progress: SonicMQ

Version 3.0

SonicMQ is compliant with JMS 1.0.2 specification and provides support for both the publish-and-subscribe and the point-to-point JMS messaging models. The server and clients are written in Java and are therefore supported on any platform with a Java Virtual Machine (JDK 1.1.8 and above).

SonicMQ uses a centralized architecture based on the hub-and-spoke model. It provides GUI and command-line tools for configuring and monitoring administered objects.

Persistence uses a high performance file-based solution for optimized throughput of messages in-transit, and uses JDBC to an embedded, pure Java relational database for longer-term storage. This can be replaced with JDBC connections to Oracle or SQL Server.

The most important new feature in Version 3.0 is SonicMQ's Dynamic Routing Architecture (DRA), which is targeted at large-scale B2B infrastructures. DRA provides fault-tolerant shared queues within a cluster, allowing parallel queue access, load balancing and failover, and the ability to share queues across application domains.

An XML message type extends the `TextMessage`, allowing a message to be dealt with as either straight text or as a DOM tree. *Lazy parsing* means the built-in XML parser is only invoked if you ask for the message in DOM format.

SonicMQ provides support for HTTP firewall tunneling ans SSL. The HTTP tunneling supports client-side proxy servers as well as server-side reverse-proxy servers. HTTP 1.1, HTTP 1.0 Keep-Alive, and vanilla HTTP 1.0 connections are automatically negotiated at connection time based on the best available protocol. Authentication is supported with simple usernames and passwords; PKI server authentication using digital certificates is also supported. Access control for administered objects is also provided. Using hierarchical topic trees, ACLs may be administratively defined at any level of the topic tree. Both positive and negative permissions may be granted for groups of users and individual users. SonicMQ also includes a unique Message-level payload encryption.

Clustered message servers are configured through centralized management tools. Message traffic is routed across geographically dispersed message servers using TCP, SSL, or HTTP.

Automatic Flow Control allows for smooth delivery of messages under heavy load. There are also client APIs for C/C++ and ActiveX/COM+ for integration with non-Java systems.

Also available is a multiclient performance and scalability test harness, which allows you to do your own vendor-to-vendor comparisons. Currently SonicMQ is the only JMS vendor offering a performance comparison tool that scales beyond a handful of clients.

Next Version

The next version will include the JMS XA interfaces and two-phase commit, and a new deployment option based on an IP multicast architecture. In addition, the next version of SonicMQ will include support for the EJB message-driven bean discussed in Chapter 8, *J2EE, EJB, and JMS.* As always, each new version will include continued performance and scalability enhancements.

Fiorano: FioranoMQ

Fiorano's product was originally the Fiorano Middleware Platform. It was completely rewritten in Java and renamed FioranoMQ, which first shipped in 1998. Fiorano now offers two different JMS products: FioranoMQ Multicast and FioranoMQ Enterprise.

FioranoMQ Multicast 4.5

FioranoMQ Multicast is compliant with JMS 1.0.2 and supports the pub/sub JMS messaging model. The server and clients are written in Java and therefore run on any platform with a JDK 1.1 or higher Virtual Machine.

The FioranoMQ Multicast product offers a distributed architecture based on IP multicast. As a distributed architecture, it doesn't require clustering. FioranoMQ

Multicast provides a command-line tool for configuring administered objects as well as a administration and monitoring API.

FioranoMQ Multicast does not provide any persistence mechanism for its JMS clients (IP multicast products frequently do not). Only local transactions are supported, so FioranoMQ Multicast cannot participate as a resource in a two-phase commit.

FioranoMQ Enterprise 4.5

FioranoMQ Enterprise is compliant with JMS 1.0.2 and supports both p2p and the pub/sub JMS messaging models. The server and clients are written in Java and therefore run on any platform with a JDK 1.1 or higher Virtual Machine.

FioranoMQ Enterprise is based on a centralized messaging architecture that uses the hub-and-spoke model. FioranoMQ Enterprise provides a clustering architecture with fault-tolerance, fail-over, and load balancing among servers in the cluster. FioranoMQ Enterprise provides command-line and GUI tools for configuring administered objects as well as an API for administration and monitoring.

Persistence in FioranoMQ is achieved using a proprietary file-based storage system. Only local transactions are supported, so FioranoMQ Enterprise cannot participate as a resource in a two-phase commit.

FioranoMQ products provide HTTP firewall tunneling via SOCKS or HTTP proxies. SSL is supported, including support for client certificates. Additionally, FioranoMQ provides access control for destinations, users, and servers.

Next Version

The next versions of FioranoMQ products will support the JMS XA interfaces and two-phase commit, XML content-based routing, failover via replicated databases, integration with MSMQ and IBM's MQSeries, and support for Microsoft's SOAP standard.

Softwired: iBus

SoftWired AG offers three JMS products: iBus//MessageBus, iBus//Message-Server, and iBus//Mobile. These products can be used separately or in combination.

iBus//MessageBus 3.1

iBus//MessageBus is based on a distributed architecture. It predates JMS and was originally shipped with a proprietary Java API. After JMS was introduced, iBus//MessageBus changed to support the JMS publish-and-subscribe messaging model.

iBus//MessageBus is compliant with the JMS 1.0.1 specification. The JMS clients for iBus//MessageBus are written in Java and can be run on any platform with a JDK 1.1 or 1.2 (Java 2) Virtual Machine.

iBus//MessageBus uses IP multicast, so clustering is not applicable; JMS clients in iBus//MessageBus are peer-to-peer. iBus//MessageBus also provides a protocol composition framework that allows other protocols to be implemented and integrated by third parties. iBus//MessageBus doesn't provide any administration or configuration tools—configuration for each JMS client is based on a local text file conforming to the `java.util.Properties` format.

iBus//MessageBus doesn't provide persistence. Only local transactions are supported, so iBus//MessageBus can't participate as a resource in a two-phase commit.

iBus//MessageBus provides support for HTTP tunneling, but only between two dedicated JMS clients. Client authorization (access control) is supported by a plug-in, which can be replaced by the customer to integrate the JMS application into existing systems. SSL is supported, including authorization using certificates, which can be made available to the authorization plug-in.

iBus//MessageServer 4.1

The iBus//MessageServer product is based on a centralized message server that uses a hub-and-spoke model. It was developed for JMS and supports both the pub/sub and p2p messaging models.

iBus//MessageServer is compliant with the JMS 1.0.2 specification. The JMS clients for iBus//MessageServer are written in Java and can be run on JDK 1.1 or 1.2 (Java 2) Virtual Machines. The iBus//MessageServer is also written in Java and can be run on any platform with a JDK 1.2 (Java 2) Virtual Machine.

iBus//MessageServer does not support clustering or fail-over, although it is fault tolerant, allowing the client to reconnect transparently after a timeout is reached. It supports firewall tunnelling using SSL and HTTP. iBus//MessageServer is also built on top of a protocol composition framework that allows other protocols to be implemented and integrated by third parties. The iBus//MessageServer provides a proprietary `XMLMessage` type that takes either XML text or a DOM tree as a payload. It offers an administration API as well as command-line and GUI administration and configuration tools.

This product uses a proprietary file-based storage or, optionally, JDBC for persistence. Only local transactions are supported, so iBus//MessageServer cannot participate as a resource in a two-phase commit.

iBus//MessageServer provides HTTP 1.0 and HTTPS client- and server-side fire-wall tunneling. Access control and SSL are supported.

iBus//Mobile 1.0

Softwired AG also offers support for wireless JMS clients with its iBus//Mobile product. iBus//Mobile is used by JMS clients on hand-held devices like cell phones and pocket organizers that work with iBus//MessageServer. iBus//Mobile can run on wireless devices running PalmOS, EPOC, Symbian, or Windows CE.

The iBus//Mobile product uses a Java API for its client that is similar to JMS, but much lighter to accommodate smaller palm and mobile phone platforms. iBus//Mobile also supports nonprogrammable mobile devices, such as current genera-tion pagers and cellular phones.

iBus//Mobile supports several protocols, including the WAP protocol stack (nota-bly WAP-Push, WDP, and WTLS), IrDA, Bluetooth, SMS, GPRS, TCP/IP, and HTTP. The Mobile product is specially designed to handle frequent disconnec-tion, which is the norm in a wireless environment.

The iBus//Mobile clients connect to an iBus//MessageServer via a special proxy that translates between WAP and SMS (used by the clients) and the native proto-col used by iBus//MessageServer.

Next Versions

The next versions of the SoftWired JMS providers will support JMS 1.0.2, includ-ing the JMS XA interfaces for two-phase commit. In addition, the next versions will support hierarchical topics and clustering (MessageServer). SoftWired products will be offered in Standard, Business, and Enterprise editions.

Sun Microsystems: Java Message Queue

Although Sun is primarily responsible for defining the JMS API, it also provides a JMS product.

Version 1.1

Version 1.1 of the Java Message Queue product is based on InterAgent, a product that was initially developed by Modulus Inc., which was later acquired by Enron Corp. InterAgent is written in C and originally had a proprietary Java API. This proprietary API was replaced with the JMS API. Sun licensed InterAgent from Enron to create the Java Message Queue (JMQ) 1.1 product.

JMQ is compliant with the JMS 1.0.2 specification. The JMS clients are written in Java and can be run on JDK 1.1.8 and JDK 1.2.2 Virtual Machines. The server is written in C and is supported on Solaris-Sparc and WinNT/Win2000-Intel machines.

JMQ uses a centralized architecture base on the hub-and-spoke model and the TCP/IP. Although clustering is not supported, message routing to other servers is supported. This allows clients to consume messages from and produce messages to destinations connected to another server while maintaining a connection to a single server. The servers (called routers) must be connected together to support this kind of forwarding. JMQ offers both a GUI console and command-line utilities for administration and configuration.

Persistence is achieved using a proprietary file-based storage system. Only local transactions are supported, so JMS clients cannot participate as a resource in a two-phase commit.

JMQ does not support firewall tunneling. JMQ provides a username/password authentication support, but doesn't provide any authorization (access control) for administered objects.

Next Version

Version 2.0 of JMQ will be a complete rewrite and will no longer be based on Enron's InterAgent product. JMQ will be written in Java, which will increase the number of platforms the server can run on. JMQ 2.0 will support the optional JMS Application Server Facilities, JDBC for persistence, JMS XA interfaces for two-phase commit, server clustering, HTTP/HTTPS firewall tunneling, authentication, some access control, and improved Admin GUI console.

BEA: WebLogic Server

BEA was one of the first (and most important) companies to introduce a full-fledged EJB container. Their approach to JMS has been to add a JMS server to their existing product, WebLogic Server.

Version 5.1

WebLogic Server is an application server that includes an EJB container, servlet, and JSP container and other facilities. In addition, WebLogic includes a JMS service provider that was introduced in version 4.5.1. In earlier versions, WebLogic provided a proprietary messaging system called WebLogic Events, which is still supported but is not the basis of their JMS implementation.

WebLogic's JMS service is compliant with JMS 1.0 and provides support for both the pub/sub and the p2p JMS messaging models. The server and clients are written in Java and therefore run on any platform with a Java Virtual Machine (JDK 1.1 or higher).

WebLogic uses a centralized architecture based on the hub-and-spoke model. Clustering of JMS services is not currently supported, so load balancing and scalability are limited to a single server instance. The WebLogic server provides administrators with a GUI console that includes support for configuring JMS administered objects.

Persistent messages are supported through any relational database that can be accessed with JDBC. WebLogic does not support 2PC, but it does support coordinated transactions between their EJB container and JMS clients, provided that the database used for JMS persistence is the same database used by the enterprise beans.

WebLogic supports HTTP 1.1 tunneling (as well as HTTPS) which can be used to tunnel through both client-side and server-side firewalls. Support for tunneling is one of the core services provided by the WebLogic server. For authentication and access control, WebLogic supplies a pluggable "realm" Service-Provider Interface and a set of default realms (LDAP, NT, Unix, and a simple file-based realm). WebLogic supports SSL, including client-side certificates. WebLogic also supports access control lists on topics and queues; access lists control who may send or receive messages to a particular destination. Access control is used on message delivery, and when establishing consumers. It can also be used in their JNDI naming service to prevent access to administered objects.

Next Version

The next version of WebLogic server will support JMS 1.0.2, clustering of JMS services, a web console based on the Java Management Extension (JMX), and 2PC. In addition, the next version of WebLogic will include support for the EJB message-driven bean discussed in Chapter 7, *Deployment Considerations*. The next version requires that JMS clients run on the JDK 1.2 or JDK 1.3 Virtual Machine, while the servers must run on the JDK 1.3 Virtual Machine.

ExoLab: OpenJMS

The ExoLab Group is a major contributor of open source J2EE servers. OpenJMS is their JMS server.

Beta Version 0.4

The OpenJMS project was started by Jim Alateras and Jim Mourikis. It is sponsored by The ExoLab Group. OpenJMS was developed to the JMS 1.0.2 specification and supports both the pub/sub and p2p JMS messaging models. OpenJMS is currently in development but its source code is freely available and can be used in testing and learning about JMS. Obviously, the final version will be more complete. The server and clients are written in Java and can run on any platform with a Java 2 Virtual Machine. OpenJMS is based on a centralized hub-and-spoke messaging architecture. Clustering is not currently supported, so scalability and load balancing are limited to a single server instance.

Persistent messages are supported through any relational database that can be accessed with JDBC. Only local transactions are supported, so OpenJMS cannot participate as a resource in a two-phase commit. OpenJMS does not currently support firewall tunneling or any level of authentication or access control.

Version 1.0

In the final release, clustering will be supported through a server-to-server communication protocol. OpenJMS will also support IP multicast and the HTTP 1.1 protocol, two-phase commit (as a XA resource), firewall tunneling, and security services such as authentication and access control.

A

The Java Message Service API

This appendix is a quick reference guide to the Java Message Service API. It is organized into three sections: common facilities, publish-and-subscribe, and point-to-point. Each section provides a summary of its interfaces and is organized alphabetically. The "Common Facilities" section covers all the common base interfaces of the p2p and pub/sub programming APIs, as well as the six message types. The "Point-to-Point API" section covers the queue-based API, and the "Publish-and-Subscribe API" section covers the topic-based API.

The XA-compliant interfaces are not included in this section because they are essentially the same as their non-XA interfaces. In addition, the Application Server API (ConnectionConsumer, ServerSession, and ServerSessionPool) is not covered because this API is not supported by most vendors and therefore is not covered in this book.

Common Facilities

This section covers all the common base interfaces of the p2p and pub/sub programming APIs, as well as the six message types.

BytesMessage

This Message type carries an array of primitive bytes as its payload. It's useful for exchanging data in an application's native format, which may not be compatible with other existing Message types. It is also useful where JMS is used purely as a transport between two systems, and the message payload is opaque to the JMS client:

```
public interface BytesMessage extends Message {

    public byte readByte() throws JMSException;
```

```
    public void writeByte(byte value) throws JMSException;
    public int readUnsignedByte() throws JMSException;
    public int readBytes(byte[] value) throws JMSException;
    public void writeBytes(byte[] value) throws JMSException;
    public int readBytes(byte[] value, int length)
        throws JMSException;
    public void writeBytes(byte[] value, int offset, int length)
        throws JMSException;
    public boolean readBoolean() throws JMSException;
    public void writeBoolean(boolean value) throws JMSException;
    public char readChar() throws JMSException;
    public void writeChar(char value) throws JMSException;
    public short readShort() throws JMSException;
    public void writeShort(short value) throws JMSException;
    public int readUnsignedShort() throws JMSException;
    public void writeInt(int value) throws JMSException;
    public int readInt() throws JMSException;
    public void writeLong(long value) throws JMSException;
    public long readLong() throws JMSException;
    public float readFloat() throws JMSException;
    public void writeFloat(float value) throws JMSException;
    public double readDouble() throws JMSException;
    public void writeDouble(double value) throws JMSException;
    public String readUTF() throws JMSException;
    public void writeUTF(String value) throws JMSException;
    public void writeObject(Object value) throws JMSException;
    public void reset() throws JMSException;
}
```

Connection

The `Connection` is the base interface for the `TopicConnection` and the
`QueueConnection`. It defines several general-purpose methods used by clients of
the messaging system in managing a JMS connection. Among these methods are
the `getMetaData()`, `start()`, `stop()`, and `close()` methods:

```
public interface Connection {
    public void close() throws JMSException;
    public String getClientID() throws JMSException;
    public ExceptionListener getExceptionListener() throws JMSException;
    public ConnectionMetaData getMetaData() throws JMSException;
    public void setClientID(java.lang.String clientID)
        throws JMSException;
    public void setExceptionListener(ExceptionListener listener)
        throws JMSException;
    public void start() throws JMSException;
    public void stop() throws JMSException;
}
```

A Connection object represents a physical connection to a JMS provider for either point-to-point (QueueConnection) or publish-and-subscribe (TopicConnection) messaging. A JMS client might choose to create multiple connections from the same connection factory, but this is rare as connections are relatively expensive (each connection requires a network socket, I/O streams, memory, etc.). Creating multiple Session objects from the same Connection object is considered more efficient, because sessions share access to the same connection.

ConnectionFactory

The ConnectionFactory is the base type for the TopicConnectionFactory and the QueueConnectionFactory, which are used in the publish-and-subscribe and point-to-point messaging models, respectively.

The ConnectionFactory is implemented differently by each vendor, so configuration options available vary from product to product. A connection factory might, for example, be configured to manufacture connections that use a particular protocol, security scheme, clustering strategy, etc.:

```
public interface ConnectionFactory {
}
```

ConnectionMetaData

This type of object is obtained from a Connection object (TopicConnection or QueueConnection). It provides information describing the JMS connection and the JMS provider. Information available includes the identity of the JMS provider, the JMS version supported by the provider, JMS provider version numbers, and the JMS properties supported:

```
public interface ConnectionMetaData {
    public int getJMSMajorVersion() throws JMSException;
    public int getJMSMinorVersion() throws JMSException;
    public String getJMSProviderName() throws JMSException;
    public String getJMSVersion() throws JMSException;
    public Enumeration getJMSXPropertyNames() throws JMSException;
    public int getProviderMajorVersion() throws JMSException;
    public int getProviderMinorVersion() throws JMSException;
    public String getProviderVersion() throws JMSException;
}
```

DeliveryMode

This class contains two final static variables, PERSISTENT and NON_PERSISTENT. These variables are used when establishing the delivery mode of a Message-Producer (TopicPublisher or QueueSender).

There are two types of delivery modes in JMS: persistent and nonpersistent. A persistent message should be delivered *once-and-only-once*, which means that a message is not lost if the JMS provider fails; it will be delivered after the server recovers. A nonpersistent message is delivered *at-most-once*, which means that it can be lost and never delivered if the JMS provider fails:

```
public interface DeliveryMode {
public static final int NON_PERSISTENT = 1;
public static final int PERSISTENT = 2;
}
```

Destination

This interface is the base interface for the Topic and Queue interfaces, which represent destinations in the pub/sub and p2p domains respectively.

In all modern enterprise messaging systems, applications exchange messages through virtual channels called *destinations*. When sending a message, the message is addressed to a destination, not a specific application. Any application that subscribes or registers an interest in that destination may receive that message. In this way, the applications that receive messages and those that send messages are decoupled. Senders and receivers are not bound to each other in any way and may send and receive messages as they see fit:

```
public interface Destination {
}
```

ExceptionListener

JMS provides an ExceptionListener interface for trapping a lost connection and notifying the client of this condition. The ExceptionListener is bound to the connection. The ExceptionListener is very useful to JMS clients that wait passively for messages to be delivered and otherwise have no way of knowing that a connection has been lost.

It is the responsibility of the JMS provider to call the onException() method of all registered ExceptionListeners after making reasonable attempts to reestablish the connection automatically. The JMS client can implement the ExceptionListener so that it can be alerted to a lost connection, and possibly attempt to reestablish the connection manually:

```
public interface ExceptionListener {
    public void onException(JMSException exception);
}
```

JMSException

The JMSException is the base exception type for all exceptions thrown by the JMS API. It may provide an error message describing the cause of the exception, a provider-specific error code, and possibly a reference to the exception that caused the JMS exception:

```
public class JMSException extends java.lang.Exception {
    public JMSException(java.lang.String reason) { .. }
    public JMSException(java.lang.String reason,
                        java.lang.String errorCode) { .. }
    public String getErrorCode() { .. }
    public Exception getLinkedException() { .. }
    public void setLinkedException(java.lang.Exception ex) { .. }
}
```

While the JMSException is usually declared as the exception type thrown from methods in the JMS API, the actual exception thrown may be one of a dozen subtypes, which are enumerated below. The descriptions of these exception types are derived from Sun Microsystems' JMS API documentation and they implement the methods defined by the JMSException super type:

IllegalStateException

> Thrown when a method is invoked illegally or inappropriately, or if the provider is not in an appropriate state when the method is called. For example, this exception should be thrown if Session.commit() is called on a nontransacted session.

InvalidClientIDException

> Thrown when a client attempts to set a connection's client ID to a value that the provider rejects.

InvalidDestinationException

> Thrown when the provider doesn't understand the destination, or the destination is no longer valid.

InvalidSelectorException

> Thrown when the syntax of a message selector is invalid.

JMSSecurityException

> Thrown when a provider rejects a username/password. Also thrown when a security restriction prevents a method from completing.

MessageEOFException

> Thrown if a stream ends unexpectedly when a StreamMessage or BytesMessage is being read.

MessageFormatException

> Thrown when a JMS client attempts to use a data type not supported by a message, or attempts to read data in a message as the wrong type. Also thrown when type errors are made with message property values. Note that this exception should not be thrown when attempting to read improperly formatted `String` data as numeric values. `java.lang.NumberFormatException` should be used in this case.

MessageNotReadableException

> Thrown when a JMS client tries to read a write-only message.

MessageNotWriteableException

> Thrown when a JMS client tries to write to a read-only message.

ResourceAllocationException

> Thrown when a provider is unable to allocate the resources required by a method. This exception should be thrown when a call to `createTopicConnection()` fails because the JMS provider has insufficient resources.

TransactionInProgressException

> Thrown when an operation is invalid because a transaction is in progress. For instance, it should be thrown if you call `Session.commit()` when a session is part of a distributed transaction.

TransactionRolledBackException

> Thrown when calling `Session.commit()` results in a transaction rollback.

MapMessage

This `Message` type carries a set of name-value pairs as its payload. The payload is similar to a `java.util.Properties` object, except the values must be Java primitives or their wrappers. The `MapMessage` is useful for delivering keyed data:

```java
public interface MapMessage extends Message {

    public boolean getBoolean(String name) throws JMSException;
    public void setBoolean(String name, boolean value)
        throws JMSException;
    public byte getByte(String name) throws JMSException;
    public void setByte(String name, byte value) throws JMSException;
    public byte[] getBytes(String name) throws JMSException;
    public void setBytes(String name, byte[] value)
        throws JMSException;
    public void setBytes(String name, byte[] value,
                         int offset, int length)
        throws JMSException;
    public short getShort(String name) throws JMSException;
```

```
        public void setShort(String name, short value) throws JMSException;
        public char getChar(String name) throws JMSException;
        public void setChar(String name, char value) throws JMSException;
        public int getInt(String name) throws JMSException;
        public void setInt(String name, int value)throws JMSException;
        public long getLong(String name) throws JMSException;
        public void setLong(String name, long value) throws JMSException;
        public float getFloat(String name) throws JMSException;
        public void setFloat(String name, float value)
            throws JMSException;
        public double getDouble(String name) throws JMSException;
        public void setDouble(String name, double value)
            throws JMSException;
        public String getString(String name) throws JMSException;
        public void setString(String name, String value)
            throws JMSException;
        public Object getObject(String name) throws JMSException;
        public void setObject(String name, Object value)
            throws JMSException;
        public Enumeration getMapNames() throws JMSException;
        public boolean itemExists(String name) throws JMSException;
    }
```

Message

The Message interface is the super interface for all message types. There are six messages types including: Message, TextMessage, ObjectMessage, Stream-Message, BytesMessage, and MapMessage. The Message type has no payload. It is useful for simple event notification.

A message basically has two parts: a *header* and *payload*. The header is comprised of special fields that are used to identify the message, declare attributes of the message, and provide information for routing. The difference between message types is determined largely by their payload, which determines the type of application data the message contains:

```
    public interface Message {
        public void acknowledge() throws JMSException;
        public void clearBody() throws JMSException;

        public Destination getJMSDestination() throws JMSException;
        public void setJMSDestination(Destination destination)
            throws JMSException;
        public int getJMSDeliveryMode() throws JMSException;
        public void setJMSDeliveryMode(int deliveryMode)
            throws JMSException;
        public String getJMSMessageID() throws JMSException;
        public void setJMSMessageID(String id) throws JMSException;
```

```java
public long getJMSTimestamp() throws JMSException;
public void setJMSTimestamp(long timestamp) throws JMSException
public long getJMSExpiration() throws JMSException;
public void setJMSExpiration(long expiration) throws JMSException;
public boolean getJMSRedelivered() throws JMSException;
public void setJMSRedelivered(boolean redelivered)
    throws JMSException;
public int getJMSPriority() throws JMSException;
public void setJMSPriority(int priority) throws JMSException;
public Destination getJMSReplyTo() throws JMSException;
public void setJMSReplyTo(Destination replyTo) throws JMSException;
public String getJMSCorrelationID() throws JMSException;
public void setJMSCorrelationID(String correlationID)
    throws JMSException;
public byte[] getJMSCorrelationIDAsBytes() throws JMSException;
public void setJMSCorrelationIDAsBytes(byte[] correlationID)
    throws JMSException;
public String getJMSType() throws JMSException;
public void setJMSType(String type) throws JMSException;

public String getStringProperty(String name)
    throws JMSException, MessageFormatException;
public void setStringProperty(String name, String value)
    throws JMSException, MessageNotWriteableException;
public int getIntProperty(String name)
    throws JMSException, MessageFormatException;
public void setIntProperty(String name, int value)
    throws JMSException, MessageNotWriteableException;
public boolean getBooleanProperty(String name)
    throws JMSException, MessageFormatException;
public void setBooleanProperty(String name, boolean value)
    throws JMSException, MessageNotWriteableException;
public double getDoubleProperty(String name)
    throws JMSException, MessageFormatException;
public void setDoubleProperty(String name, double value)
    throws JMSException, MessageNotWriteableException;
public float getFloatProperty(String name)
    throws JMSException, MessageFormatException;
public void setFloatProperty(String name, float value)
    throws JMSException, MessageNotWriteableException;
public byte getByteProperty(String name)
    throws JMSException, MessageFormatException;
public void setByteProperty(String name, byte value)
    throws JMSException, MessageNotWriteableException;
public long getLongProperty(String name)
    throws JMSException, MessageFormatException;
public void setLongPreperty(String name, long value)
    throws JMSException, MessageNotWriteableException;
```

```
    public short getShortProperty(String name)
        throws JMSException, MessageFormatException;
    public void setShortProperty(String name, short value)
        throws JMSException, MessageNotWriteableException;
    public Object getObjectProperty(String name)
        throws JMSException, MessageFormatException;
    public void setObjectProperty(String name, Object value)
        throws JMSException, MessageNotWriteableException;
    public void clearProperties()
        throws JMSException;
    public Enumeration getPropertyNames()
        throws JMSException;
    public boolean propertyExists(String name)
        throws JMSException;
}
```

MessageConsumer

The MessageConsumer is the base interface for the TopicSubscriber and the QueueReceiver. It defines several general-purpose methods used by clients when using a consumer. Among these methods are the setMessageListener()and close() methods, and three types of receive() methods.

MessageConsumer can consume messages asynchronously or synchronously. To consume messages asynchronously, the JMS client must provide the Message-Consumer with a MessageListener object, which will then receive the messages as they arrive. To consume messages synchronously, the JMS client may call one of three receive methods: receive(), receive(long timeout), and receiveNoWait():

```
public interface MessageConsumer {
    public void close() throws JMSException;
    public MessageListener getMessageListener() throws JMSException;
    public String getMessageSelector() throws JMSException;
    public Message receive() throws JMSException;
    public Message receive(long timeout) throws JMSException;
    public Message receiveNoWait() throws JMSException;
    public void setMessageListener(MessageListener listener)
        throws JMSException;
}
```

MessageListener

The MessageListener is implemented by the JMS client. It receives messages asynchronously from one or more Consumers (TopicSubscriber or QueueReceiver).

The `Session` (`TopicSession` or `QueueSession`) must ensure that messages are passed to the `MessageListener` serially, so that the messages can be processed separately. A `MessageListener` object may be registered with many consumers, but serial delivery is only guaranteed if all of its consumers were created by the same session:

```
public interface MessageListener {
    public void onMessage(Message message);
}
```

MessageProducer

The `MessageProducer` is the base interface for the `TopicPublisher` and the `QueueSender`. It defines several general-purpose methods used by clients. Among these methods are `setDeliveryMode()`, `close()`, `setPriority()`, and `set-TimeToLive(long timeToLive)`.

`MessageProducer` sends messages to a specified destination (`Topic` or `Queue`). The default destination can be determined when the `MessageProducer` is created by its session, or the destination can be set each time a message is sent—in this case there is no default destination:

```
public interface MessageProducer {
    public void setDisableMessageID(boolean value) throws JMSException;
    public boolean getDisableMessageID() throws JMSException;
    public void setDisableMessageTimestamp(boolean value)
        throws JMSException;
    public boolean getDisableMessageTimestamp() throws JMSException;
    public void setDeliveryMode(int deliveryMode) throws JMSException;
    public void setPriority(int defaultPriority) int getDeliveryMode()
        throws JMSException;
    public int getPriority() throws JMSException;
    public void setTimeToLive(long timeToLive) throws JMSException;
    public long getTimeToLive() throws JMSException;
    public void close() throws JMSException;
}
```

ObjectMessage

This `Message` type carries a serializable Java object as its payload. It is useful for exchanging Java objects:

```
public interface ObjectMessage extends Message {
    public java.io.Serializable getObject()
        throws JMSException;
    public void setObject(java.io.Serializable payload)
        throws JMSException, MessageNotWriteableException;
}
```

Session

The Session is the base interface for the TopicSession and the QueueSession. It defines several general-purpose methods used by JMS clients for managing a JMS Session. Among these methods are the six createMessage() methods (one for each type of Message object), setMessageListener(), close(), and transaction methods.

A Session is a single-threaded context for producing and consuming messages. It creates message consumers, producers, and messages for a specific JMS provider. The Session manages the scope of transactions across send and receive operations, tracks message acknowledgment for consumers, and serializes delivery of messages to MessageListener objects:

```
public interface Session extends java.lang.Runnable {
    public static final int AUTO_ACKNOWLEDGE = 1;
    public static final int CLIENT_ACKNOWLEDGE = 2;
    public static final int DUPS_OK_ACKNOWLEDGE = 3;

    public BytesMessage createBytesMessage() throws JMSException;
    public MapMessage createMapMessage() throws JMSException;
    public Message createMessage() throws JMSException;
    public ObjectMessage createObjectMessage() throws JMSException;
    public ObjectMessage createObjectMessage(Serializable object)
        throws JMSException;
    public StreamMessage createStreamMessage() throws JMSException;
    public TextMessage createTextMessage() throws JMSException;
    public TextMessage createTextMessage(java.lang.String text)
        throws JMSException;
    public boolean getTransacted() throws JMSException;
    public void commit() throws JMSException;
    public void rollback() throws JMSException;
    public void close() throws JMSException;
    public void recover() throws JMSException;
    public MessageListener getMessageListener() throws JMSException;
    public void setMessageListener(MessageListener listener)
        throws JMSException;
    public void run();
}
```

StreamMessage

This Message type carries a stream of primitive Java types (int, double, char, etc.) as its payload. It provides a set of convenience methods for mapping a formatted stream of bytes to Java primitives. It provides an easy programming model for exchanging primitive application data in a fixed order:

```
public interface StreamMessage extends Message {
```

```
    public boolean readBoolean() throws JMSException;
    public void writeBoolean(boolean value) throws JMSException;
    public byte readByte() throws JMSException;
    public int readBytes(byte[] value) throws JMSException;
    public void  writeByte(byte value) throws JMSException;
    public void writeBytes(byte[] value) throws JMSException;
    public void writeBytes(byte[] value, int offset, int length)
        throws JMSException;
    public short readShort() throws JMSException;
    public void writeShort(short value) throws JMSException;
    public char readChar() throws JMSException;
    public void writeChar(char value) throws JMSException;
    public int readInt() throws JMSException;
    public void writeInt(int value) throws JMSException;
    public long readLong() throws JMSException;
    public void writeLong(long value) throws JMSException;
    public float readFloat() throws JMSException;
    public void writeFloat(float value) throws JMSException;
    public double readDouble() throws JMSException;
    public void  writeDouble(double value) throws JMSException;
    public String  readString() throws JMSException;
    public void writeString(String value) throws JMSException;
    public Object readObject() throws JMSException;
    public void writeObject(Object value) throws JMSException;
    public void reset() throws JMSException;
}
```

TextMessage

This Message type carries a java.lang.String as its payload. It is useful for
exchanging simple text messages and for more complex character data, such as
XML documents:

```
public interface TextMessage extends Message {
    public String getText()
        throws JMSException;
    public void setText(String payload)
        throws JMSException, MessageNotWriteableException;
}
```

Point-to-Point API

This section covers the queue-based API.

Queue

The Queue is an administered object that acts as a handle or identifier for an
actual queue, called a *physical queue,* on the messaging server. A physical queue is a

channel through which many clients can receive and send messages. The Queue is a subtype of the Destination interface.

Multiple receivers may connect to a queue, but each message in the queue may only be consumed by one of the queue's receivers. Messages in the queue are ordered so that consumers receive messages in the order the message server placed them in the queue:

```
public interface Queue extends Destination {
    public String getQueueName() throws JMSException;
    public String toString();
}
```

QueueBrowser

A QueueBrowser is a specialized object that allows you to peek ahead at pending messages on a Queue without actually consuming them. This feature is unique to point-to-point messaging. Queue browsing can be useful for monitoring the contents of a queue from an administration tool, or for browsing through multiple messages to locate a message that is more important than the one that is at the head of the queue:

```
public interface QueueBrowser {
    public Queue getQueue() throws JMSException;
    public String getMessageSelector() throws JMSException;
    public Enumeration getEnumeration() throws JMSException;
    public void close() throws JMSException;
}
```

QueueConnection

The QueueConnection is created by the QueueConnectionFactory. Each QueueConnection represents a unique connection to the server.* The QueueConnection is a subtype of the Connection interface:

```
public interface QueueConnection extends Connection {
    public QueueSession createQueueSession(boolean transacted,
                                           int acknowledgeMode)
        throws JMSException;
    public ConnectionConsumer createConnectionConsumer
                        (Queue queue,
                         String messageSelector,
                         ServerSessionPool sessionPool,
                         int maxMessages)
```

---

* The actual physical network connection may or may not be unique, depending on the vendor. However, the connection is considered to be logically unique so authentication and connection control can be managed separately from other connections.

```
        throws JMSException;
    }
```

QueueConnectionFactory

The QueueConnectionFactory is an administered object that is used to manufacture QueueConnectionFactory objects. The QueueConnection is a subtype of
the ConnectionFactory interface:

```
    public interface QueueConnectionFactory extends ConnectionFactory {
        public QueueConnection createQueueConnection() throws JMSException;
        public QueueConnection createQueueConnection(String username, String password)
            throws JMSException;
    }
```

QueueReceiver

The QueueReceiver is created by a QueueSession for a specific queue. The JMS
client uses the QueueReceiver to receive messages delivered to its assigned
queue. The QueueReceiver is a subtype of the MessageConsumer interface.

Each message in a queue is delivered to only one QueueReceiver. Multiple
receivers may connect to a queue, but each message in the queue may only be consumed by one of the queue's receivers:

```
    public interface QueueReceiver extends MessageConsumer {
        public Queue getQueue() throws JMSException;
    }
```

QueueSender

A QueueSender is created by a QueueSession, usually for a specific queue.
Messages sent by the QueueSender to a queue are delivered to a client connected
to that queue. The QueueSender is a subtype of the MessageProducer interface:

```
    public interface QueueSender extends MessageProducer {
        public Queue getQueue() throws JMSException;
        public void send(Message message) throws JMSException;
        public void send(Message message, int deliveryMode, int priority,
                        long timeToLive)
            throws JMSException;
        public void send(Queue queue, Message message) throws JMSException;
        public void send(Queue queue, Message message,int deliveryMode,
                        int priority,long timeToLive)
            throws JMSException;
    }
```

QueueSession

The QueueSession is created by the QueueConnection. A QueueSession object is a factory for creating Message, QueueSender, and QueueReceiver objects. A client can create multiple QueueSession objects to provide more granular control over senders, receivers, and their associated transactions. The QueueSession is a subtype of the Session interface:

```
public interface QueueSession extends Session {
    public Queue createQueue(java.lang.String queueName)
        throws JMSException;
    public QueueReceiver createReceiver(Queue queue)
        throws JMSException;
    public QueueReceiver createReceiver(Queue queue, String messageSelector)
        throws JMSException;
    public QueueSender createSender(Queue queue) throws JMSException;
    public QueueBrowser createBrowser(Queue queue) throws JMSException;
    public QueueBrowser createBrowser(Queue queue, String messageSelector)
        throws JMSException;
    public TemporaryQueue createTemporaryQueue() throws JMSException;
}
```

TemporaryQueue

A TemporaryQueue is created by a QueueSession. A temporary queue is associated with the connection that belongs to the QueueSession that created it. It is only active for the duration of the session's connection, and is guaranteed to be unique across all connections. It lasts only as long as its associated client connection is active. In all other respects, a temporary queue is just like a "regular" queue. The TemporaryQueue is a subtype of the Queue interface.

Since a temporary queue is created by a JMS client, it is unavailable to other JMS clients unless the queue identity is transferred using the JMSReplyTo header. While any client may send messages on another client's temporary queue, only the sessions that are associated with the JMS client connection that created the temporary queue may receive messages from it. JMS clients can also, of course, send messages to their own temporary queues:

```
public interface TemporaryQueue extends Queue {
    public void delete() throws JMSException;
}
```

Publish-and-Subscribe API

This section covers the topic-based API.

TemporaryTopic

A `TemporaryTopic` is created by a `TopicSession`. A temporary topic is associated with the connection that belongs to the `TopicSession` that created it. It is only active for the duration of the session's connection, and it is guaranteed to be unique across all connections. Since it is temporary it can't be durable—it lasts only as long as its associated client connection is active. In all other respects it is just like a "regular" topic. The `TemporaryTopic` is a subtype of the `Topic` interface.

Since a temporary topic is created by a JMS client, it is unavailable to other JMS clients unless the topic identity is transferred using the `JMSReplyTo` header. While any client may publish messages on another client's temporary topic, only the sessions that are associated with the JMS client connection that created the temporary topic may subscribe to it. JMS clients can also, of course, publish messages to their own temporary topics:

```
public interface TemporaryTopic extends Topic {
    public void delete() throws JMSException;
}
```

Topic

The `Topic` is an administered object that acts as a handle or identifier for an actual topic, called a *physical topic,* on the messaging server. A physical topic is a channel to which many clients can subscribe and publish. When a JMS client delivers a `Message` object to a topic, all the clients subscribed to that topic receive the `Message`. The `Topic` is a subtype of the `Destination` interface:

```
public interface Topic extends Destination {
    public String getTopicName() throws JMSException;
    public String toString();
}
```

TopicConnection

The `TopicConnection` is created by the `TopicConnectionFactory`. The `TopicConnection` represents a connection to the message server. Each `TopicConnection` created from a `TopicConnectionFactory` is a unique connection to the server.[*] The `TopicConnection` is a subtype of the `Connection` interface:

```
public interface TopicConnection extends Connection {
```

---

[*] The actual physical network connection may or may not be unique, depending on the vendor. However, the connection is considered to be logically unique so authentication and connection control can be managed separately from other connections.

```
      public TopicSession createTopicSession(boolean transacted,
                                             int acknowledgeMode)
         throws JMSException;
      public ConnectionConsumer createConnectionConsumer
                              (Topic topic, String messageSelector,
                               ServerSessionPool sessionPool,
                               int maxMessages)
         throws JMSException;
      public ConnectionConsumer createDurableConnectionConsumer
                              (Topic topic, String subscriptionName,
                               String messageSelector,
                               ServerSessionPool sessionPool,
                               int maxMessages)
         throws JMSException;
   }
```

TopicConnectionFactory

The TopicConnectionFactory is an administered object that is used to manufacture TopicConnection objects. The TopicConnectionFactory is a subtype of
the ConnectionFactory interface:

```
   public interface TopicConnectionFactory extends ConnectionFactory {
      public TopicConnection createTopicConnection() throws JMSException;
      public TopicConnection createTopicConnection(String username,
                                                   String password)
         throws JMSException;
   }
```

TopicPublisher

A TopicPublisher is created by a TopicSession, usually for a specific Topic.
Messages that are sent by the TopicPublisher are copied and delivered to each
client subscribed to that topic. The TopicPublisher is a subtype of the
MessageProducer interface:

```
   public interface TopicPublisher extends MessageProducer {
      public Topic getTopic() throws JMSException;
      public void publish(Message message) throws JMSException;
      public void publish(Message message, int deliveryMode,int priority,
                          long timeToLive)
         throws JMSException;
      public void publish(Topic topic,Message message)
         throws JMSException;
      public void publish(Topic topic, Message message, int deliveryMode,
                          int priority,long timeToLive)
         throws JMSException;
   }
```

TopicSession

The TopicSession is created by the TopicConnection. A TopicSession object is a factory for creating Message, TopicPublisher, and TopicSubscriber objects. A client can create multiple TopicSession objects to provide more granular control over publishers, subscribers, and their associated transactions. The TopicSession is a subtype of the Session interface:

```
public interface TopicSession extends Session {
    public Topic createTopic(java.lang.String topicName)
        throws JMSException;
    public TopicSubscriber createSubscriber(Topic topic)
        throws JMSException;
    public TopicSubscriber createSubscriber(Topic topic,
                                            String messageSelector,
                                            boolean noLocal)
        throws JMSException;
    public TopicSubscriber createDurableSubscriber(Topic topic,
                                            String name)
        throws JMSException;
    public TopicSubscriber createDurableSubscriber
                                    (Topic topic,
                                     String name,
                                     String messageSelector,
                                     boolean noLocal)
        throws JMSException;
    public TopicPublisher createPublisher(Topic topic)
        throws JMSException;
    public TemporaryTopic createTemporaryTopic() throws JMSException;
    public void unsubscribe(java.lang.String name) throws JMSException;
}
```

TopicSubscriber

The TopicSubscriber is created by a TopicSession for a specific topic. The messages are delivered to the TopicSubscriber as they become available, avoiding the need to poll the topic for new messages. The TopicSubscriber is a subtype of the MessageConsumer interface:

```
public interface TopicSubscriber extends MessageConsumer
    public Topic getTopic() throws JMSException;
    public boolean getNoLocal() throws JMSException;
}
```

B

Message Headers

The message headers provide metadata describing who or what created the message, when it was created, how long its data is valid, etc. The headers also contain routing information that describes the destination of the message (topic or queue), how a message should be acknowledged, and a lot more.

The `Message` interface provides mutator ("set") methods for each of the JMS headers, but only the `JMSReplyTo`, `JMSCorrelationID`, and `JMSType` headers can be modified using these methods. Calls to the mutator methods for any of the other JMS headers will be ignored when the message is sent. According to the authors of the specification, the mutator methods were left in the `Message` interface for "general orthogonality"; to balance the accessor methods—a fairly strange but well-established justification.

The accessor ("get") methods always provide the JMS client with information about the JMS headers. However, some JMS headers (i.e., `JMSTimestamp`, `JMSRedelivered`, etc.) are not available until after the message is sent or even received.

JMSDestination

Purpose: Routing

Message objects are always sent to some kind of destination. In the pub/sub model, `Message` objects are delivered to a topic, identified by a `Topic` object. In Chapter 2, *Developing a Simple Example*, you learned that the destination of a `Message` object is established when the `TopicPublisher` is created:

```
Topic chatTopic = (Topic)jndi.lookup(topicName);
TopicPublisher publisher = session.createPublisher(chatTopic);
```

```
...
TextMessage message = session.createTextMessage();
message.setText(username+" : "+text);
publisher.publish(message);
```

The JMSDestination header identifies the destination of a Message object using a javax.jms.Destination object. The Destination class is the superclass of both Topic (pub/sub) and Queue (p2p). The JMSDestination header is obtained using the Message.getJMSDestination() method.

Identifying the destination to which a message was delivered is valuable to JMS clients that consume messages from more than one topic or queue. MessageListener objects might, for example, listen to multiple consumers (TopicSubscriber or QueueReceiver types) so that they receive messages from more than one topic or queue. For example, the Chat client from Chapter 2 could be modified to subscribe to more than one chat topic at a time. In this scenario, the onMessage() method of the MessageListener would use the JMS-Destination header to identify which chat topic a message came from:

```
public void onMessage(Message message){
    try {
        TextMessage textMessage = (TextMessage)message;
        String text = textMessage.getText();
        Topic topic = (Topic)textMessage.getJMSDestination();
        System.out.println(topic.getTopicName()+" : "+text);
    } catch (JMSException jmse){jmse.printStackTrace();}
}
```

The JMSDestination header is set automatically by the JMS provider when the message is delivered. The Destination used in the JMSDestination is typically specified when the publisher is created, as shown here:

```
Queue queue = (Queue)jndi.lookup(queueName);
QueueSender queueSender = session.createSender(queue);
Message message = session.createMessage();
queueSender.send(message);
...
Topic topic = (Topic)jndi.lookup(topicName);
TopicPublisher topicPublisher = session.createPublisher(topic);
Message message = session.createMessage();
topicPublisher.publish(message);
```

An unspecified message producer—one created without a Destination—will require that a Destination be supplied with each send() operation:

```
QueueSender queueSender = session.createSender(null);
Message message = session.createMessage();

Queue queue = (Queue)jndi.lookup(queueName);
```

```
queueSender.send(queue, message);
...
TopicPublisher topicPublisher = session.createPublisher(null);
Message message = session.createMessage();

Topic topic = (Topic)jndi.lookup(topicName);
topicPublisher.publish(topic, message);
```

In this case, the JMSDestination header becomes the Destination used in the send() operation.

JMSDeliveryMode

Purpose: Routing

There are two types of delivery modes in JMS: persistent and nonpersistent. A persistent message should be delivered once-and-only-once, which means that a message is not lost if the JMS provider fails; it will be delivered after the server recovers. A nonpersistent message is delivered at-most-once, which means that it can be lost and never delivered if the JMS provider fails. In both persistent and nonpersistent delivery modes the message server should not send a message to the same consumer more than once, but it is possible; see the section on JMSRedelivered for more details.

NOTE   The vendor-supplied client runtime and the server functionality are collectively referred to as the JMS provider. A "provider failure" generically describes any failure condition that is outside of the domain of the application code. It could mean a hardware failure that occurs while the provider is entrusted with the processing of a message, or it could mean an unexpected exception or halting of a process due to a software defect. It could also mean a network failure that occurs between two processes that are part of the JMS vendor's internal architecture.

Persistent messages are intended to survive system failures of the JMS provider (the message server). Persistent messages are written to disk as soon as the message server receives them from the JMS client. After the message is persisted to disk the message server can then attempt to deliver the message to its intended consumer. As the messaging server delivers the message to the consumers it keeps track of which consumers successfully receive the message. If the JMS provider fails while delivering the message, the message server will pick up where it left off following a recovery. Persistent messages are delivered once-and-only-once. The mechanics of this are covered in greater detail in Chapter 6, *Guaranteed Messaging, Transactions, Acknowledgments, and Failures.*

Nonpersistent messages are not written to disk when they are received by the message server, so if the JMS provider fails, the message will be lost. In general nonpersistent messages perform better than persistent messages. They are delivered more quickly and require less system resources on the message server. However, nonpersistent messages should only be used when a loss of messages due to a JMS provider failures is not an issue. The chat example used in Chapter 2 is a good example of a system that doesn't require persistent delivery. It's not critical that every message be delivered to all consumers in a chat application. In most business systems, however, messages are delivered using the persistent mode, because it's important that they be successfully delivered.

The delivery mode can be set using the `setDeliveryMode()` method defined in both the `TopicPublisher` and `QueueSender` message producers. The `javax.jms.DeliveryMode` class defines the two constants used to declare the delivery mode: `PERSISTENT` and `NON_PERSISTENT`:

```
// Publish-and-subscribe
TopicPublisher topicPublisher = topicSession.createPublisher(topic);
topicPublisher.setDeliveryMode(DeliveryMode.NON_PERSISTENT);

// Point-to-point
QueueSender queueSender = queueSession.createSender(queue);
queueSender.setDeliverMode(DeliveryMode.PERSISTENT);
```

Once the delivery mode has been set on the message producer, it will be applied to all the messages delivered by that producer. The delivery mode can be changed at any time using the `setDeliveryMode()` method; the new mode will be applied to subsequent messages. The default delivery mode of a message producer is always `PERSISTENT`.

The delivery mode of a message producer can be overridden for an individual message during the send operation, which allows a message producer to deliver a mixture of persistent and nonpersistent messages to the same destination (topic or queue):

```
// Publish-and-subscribe
Message message = topicSession.createMessage();
topicPublisher.publish(message, DeliveryMode.PERSISTENT, 5, 0);

// Point-to-point
Message message = queueSession.createMessage();
queueSender.send(message, DeliveryMode.NON_PERSISTENT, 5, 0);
```

The JMSDeliveryMode can be obtained from the Message object using the getJMSDeliveryMode() method:

```
public void onMessage(Message message){
    try {
    if (message.getJMSDeliveryMode() == DeliveryMode.PERSISTENT){
        // Do something
    } else {
        // Do something else
    }
    } catch (JMSException jmse){jmse.printStackTrace();}
}
```

JMSMessageID

Purpose: Routing

The JMSMessageID is a String value that uniquely identifies a message. How unique the identifier is depends on the vendor. It may only be unique for that installation of the message server, or it may be universally unique.

The JMSMessageID can be useful for historical repositories in applications where messages need to be uniquely indexed. The JMSMessageID is also useful for correlating messages, which is done using the JMSCorrelationID header.

The message provider generates the JMSMessageID automatically when the message is received from a JMS client. The JMSMessageID must start with ID:, but the rest of JMSMessageID can be any collection of characters that uniquely identifies the message to the JMS provider. Here is an example of a JMSMessageID generated by Progress' SonicMQ:

```
// JMSMessageID generated by SonicMQ
ID:6c867f96:20001:DF59525514
```

If a unique message ID is not needed by the JMS application, the JMS client can provide a hint to the message server that an ID is not necessary by using the setDisableMessageID() method (as shown in the following code). Vendors that heed this hint can reduce message processing time by not generating unique IDs for each message. If a JMSMessageID is not generated, the getJMSMessageID() method returns null:

```
// Publish-and-subscribe
TopicPublisher topicPublisher = topicSession.createPublisher(topic);
topicPublisher.setDisableMessageID(true);

// Point-to-point
```

```
QueueSender queueSender = queueSession.createSender(topic);
queueSender.setDisableMessageID(true);
```

JMSTimestamp

Purpose: Identification

The JMSTimestamp is set automatically by the message producer when the send
operation is invoked. The value of the JMSTimestamp is the *approximate* time that
the send operation was invoked. Sometimes messages are not transmitted to the
message server immediately. A message can be delayed for many reasons, depending on the JMS provider and configuration of the message producer: whether it's a
transacted session, the acknowledgement mode, etc. When the send() operation
returns, the message object will have its timestamp:

```
Message message = topicSession.createMessage();
topicPublisher.publish(message);
long time = message.getJMSTimestamp();
```

The timestamp is set automatically, thus any value set explicitly by the JMS client
will be ignored and discarded when the send() operation is invoked. The value of
the timestamp is the amount of time, measured in milliseconds, that has elapsed
since midnight, January 1, 1970, UTC (see the "UTC" sidebar later in this chapter
for more information).

Timestamps can be used by message consumers as indicators of the approximate
time that the message was delivered by the message producer. The timestamp can
be useful when ordering messages or for historical repositories.

The JMSTimestamp is set during the send operation and may be calculated locally
by the producer (TopicPublisher or QueueSender) on the client or it may be
obtained from the message server. In the first case, when the producer calculates
the timestamp, the timestamps can vary from JMS client to client. This is because
the timestamp is obtained from the JMS client's local system clock, which may not
be synchronized with other JMS client machines. Timestamps acquired from the
message server are more consistent across JMS clients using the same JMS provider, since all the times are acquired from the same source, the common message server. It's possible to disable timestamps—or at least hint that they are not
needed—by invoking the setDisableMessageTimestamp() method, available
on both TopicPublisher and QueueSender objects:

```
// Publish-and-subscribe
TopicPublisher topicPublisher = topicSession.createPublisher(topic);
topicPublisher.setDisableMessageTimestamp(true);
```

```
// Point-to-point
QueueSender queueSender = queueSession.createSender(topic);
queueSender.setDisableMessageTimestamp(true);
```

If the JMS provider heeds the hint to disable the timestamp, the JMSTimestamp is set to 0, indicating that no timestamp was set. Disabling the timestamp can reduce the workload for JMS providers that use the message server to generate timestamps (instead of the JMS client), and can reduce the size of a message by at least 8 bytes (the size of a long value), which reduces the amount of network traffic. Support for disabling the timestamp is optional, which means that some vendors will set the timestamp whether you need it or not.

JMSExpiration

Purpose: Routing

A Message object can have an expiration date, the same as on a carton of milk. The expiration date is useful for messages that are only relevant for a fixed amount of time. For example, the B2B example developed in Chapter 4, *Publish-and-Subscribe Messaging*, and Chapter 5, *Point-to-Point Messaging*, might use expiration dates on messages representing "Hot Deals" that a wholesaler extends to retailers. The "Hot Deal" is only valid for a short time, so the Message that represents a deal expires after that deadline.

The expiration time for messages is set in milliseconds by the producer using the setTimeToLive() method on either the QueueSender or TopicPublisher as shown below:

```
// Publish-and-subscribe
TopicPublisher topicPublisher = topicSession.createPublisher(topic);
// Set time to live as 1 hour (1000 millis x 60 sec x 60 min)
topicPublisher.setTimeToLive(3600000);

// Point-to-point
QueueSender queueSender = queueSession.createSender(topic);
// Set time to live as 2 days (1000 millis x 60 sec x 60 min x 48 hours)
queueSender.setTimeToLive(172800000);
```

By default the timeToLive is zero, which indicates that the message doesn't expire. Calling setTimeToLive() with a zero value as the argument ensures that message is created without an expiration date.

The JMSExpiration date itself is calculated as:

```
JMSExpiration = currenttime + timeToLive.
```

The value of the `currenttime` is the amount of time, measured in milliseconds, that has elapsed since the Java epoch (midnight, January 1, 1970, UTC).

The JMS specification doesn't state whether the current time is calculated by the client computer or the message server, so consistency is dependent on either the accuracy of every client machine or the message server. We can certainly empathize with the JMS spec producers for remaining agnostic on this issue. Whether or not timestamps are synchronized across clients depends on the application. There is nothing preventing a JMS vendor from providing a configuration setting to control this behavior.

The `JMSExpiration` is the date and time that the message will expire. JMS clients should be written to discard any unprocessed messages that have expired, because the data and event communicated by the message is no longer valid. Message providers (servers) are also expected to discard any undelivered messages that expire while in their queues and topics. Even persistent messages are supposed to be discarded if they expire before being delivered.

UTC

UTC (Universal Time Coordinated, a.k.a. Coordinated Universal Time) is an internationally accepted official standard time based on the coordination of hundreds of atomic clocks worldwide. The JMS specification states that the time used to calculate the `JMSExpiration` and `JMSTimestamp` are based on UTC time, but in reality this is rarely the case. Ordinarily, there is a discrepancy between the current time reported by the Java Virtual Machine and the true UTC. This is because the system clocks on desktop computers and business servers are usually not synchronized with UTC, and are not accurate enough to keep UTC time. System clocks can be coordinated with the UTC through an Internet protocol called NTP (Network Time Protocol), which periodically queries for the actual UTC from a network time service and resynchronizes the system clock with the UTC.

You can get the system clock's time from any Java Virtual Machine using the `System` class as shown here:

```
long currentTime = System.currentTimeMillis();
```

The system clock's time, as reported by the JVM, is calculated as the number of milliseconds (1000 milliseconds = 1 second) that have elapsed since January 1st, 1970, assuming that the system clock is reasonably accurate.

JMSRedelivered

Purpose: Routing

The JMSRedelivered header indicates if the message was redelivered to the consumer. The JMSRedelivered header is true if the message has been redelivered, and false if has not. A message may be marked as redelivered if a consumer failed to acknowledge delivery, or if the JMS provider is otherwise uncertain whether the consumer received the message.

When a message is delivered to a consumer, the consumer must acknowledge receipt of the message. If it doesn't, the message server may attempt to redeliver the message. Consumers can acknowledge messages automatically or manually, depending on how the consumer was created. A consumer created with an acknowledgment mode of AUTO_ACKNOWLEDGE or DUPS_OK_ACKNOWLEDGE automatically informs the message server that the message was received. When the consumer is created with CLIENT_ACKNOWLEDGE mode, the JMS client must manually acknowledge the messages.

In general, when a message has a JMSRedelivered value of false, the consumer should assume that there is no chance it has seen this message before. If the redelivered flag is true, the client may have been given this message before so it may need to take some precautions it would not otherwise take. Redelivery can occur under a variety of conditions, and a JMS provider may mark a message as redelivered when it's in doubt due to failures, error conditions, and other anomalous conditions.

Message acknowledgment and redelivery are covered in detail in Chapter 6. Durable subscribers are addressed in Chapter 4.

JMSPriority

Purpose: Routing

Messages may be assigned a priority by the message producer when they are delivered. The message servers may use message's priority to order delivery of messages to consumers; messages with a higher priority are delivered ahead of lower priority messages.

The message's priority is contained in the JMSPriority header, which is set automatically by the JMS provider. The priority of messages can be declared by the JMS client using the `setPriority()` method on the producer. The following code shows how this method is used by both the p2p and pub/sub message models:

```
// p2p setting the message priority to 9
QueueSender queueSender = QueueSession.createSender(someQueue);
queueSender.setPriority(9);

//pub/sub setting the message priority to 9
TopicPublisher topicPublisher = TopicSession.createPublisher(someTopic);
topicPublisher.setPriority(9);
```

Once a priority is established on a producer (`QueueSender` or `TopicPublisher`), that priority will be used for all messages delivered from that producer, unless it is explicitly overridden. The priority of a specific message can be overridden during the send operation. The following code shows how to override the priority of a message during the send operation. In both cases, the priority is set to 3:

```
// p2p setting the priority on the send operation
QueueSender queueSender = QueueSession.createSender(someQueue);

queueSender.send(message,DeliveryMode.PERSISTENT, 3, 0);

// pub/sub setting the priority on the send operation
TopicPublisher topicPublisher = TopicSession.createPublisher(someTopic);

topicPublisher.publish(message,DeliveryMode.PERSISTENT, 3, 0);
```

There are two basic categories of message priorities: levels 0–4 are gradations of normal priority; levels 5–9 are gradations of expedited priority. Message servers are not required to enforce message ordering based on the `JMSPriority` header, but they should attempt to deliver expedited messages before normal messages.

The `JMSPriority` header is set automatically when the message is delivered. It can be read by JMS clients using the `Message.getJMSPriority()` method, but it is mostly used by message servers when routing messages.

JMSReplyTo

Purpose: Routing

In some cases, a message producer may want the consumers to reply to a message. The `JMSReplyTo` header indicates which address, if any, a JMS consumer should reply to. The `JMSReplyTo` header is set explicitly by the JMS client; its contents will be a `javax.jms.Destination` object (either `Topic` or `Queue`).

In some cases the JMS client will want the message consumers to reply to a temporary topic or queue set up by the JMS client. Here is an example of a pub/sub JMS client that creates a temporary topic and uses its `Topic` object identifier as a `JMSReplyTo` header:

```
TopicSession session =
connection.createTopicSession(false, Session.AUTO_ACKNOWLEDGE);
...
Topic tempTopic = session.createTemporaryTopic();
...

TextMessage message = session.createTextMessage();
message.setText(text);
message.setJMSReplyTo(tempTopic);
publisher.publish(message);
```

When a JMS message consumer receives a message that includes a `JMSReplyTo` destination, it can reply using that destination. A JMS consumer is not required to send a reply, but in some JMS applications clients are programmed to do so. Here is an example of a JMS consumer that uses the `JMSReplyTo` header on a received message to send a reply. In this case, the reply is a simple empty `Message` object:

```
Topic chatTopic = ... get topic from somewhere
...
// Publisher is created without a specified Topic
TopicPublisher publisher = session.createPublisher(null);
...

public void onMessage(Message message){
    try {
        TextMessage textMessage = (TextMessage)message;
        Topic replyTopic = (Topic)textMessage.getJMSReplyTo();
        Message replyMessage = session.createMessage();
        publisher.publish(replyTopic, replyMessage);
    } catch (JMSException jmse){jmse.printStackTrace();}
}
```

The `JMSReplyTo` destination set by the message producer can be any destination in the messaging system. Using other established topics or queues allows the message producer to express routing preferences for the message itself or for replies to that message. Typically, this kind of routing is used in workflow applications. In a workflow application, a message represents some task that is processed one step at a time by several JMS clients—possibly over days. For example, an order message might be processed by sales first, then inventory, then shipping, and finally accounts receivable. When each JMS client (sales, inventory, shipping, or accounts receivable) is finished processing the order data, it could use the `JMSReplyTo` address to deliver the message to the next step.

JMSCorrelationID

Purpose: Routing

The JMSCorrelationID provides a header for associating the current message with some previous message or application-specific ID. In most cases, the JMSCorrelationID will be used to tag a message as a reply to a previous message. The following code shows how the JMSCorrelationID is set and used along with the JMSReplyTo and JMSMessageID headers to send a reply to a message:

```
public void onMessage(Message message){
    try {
        TextMessage textMessage = (TextMessage)message;
        Topic replyTopic = (Topic)textMessage.getJMSReplyTo();
        Message replyMessage = session.createMessage();
        String messageID = textMessage.getJMSMessageID();
        replyMessage.setJMSCorrelationID(messageID);
        publisher.publish(replyTopic, replyMessage);
    } catch (JMSException jmse){jmse.printStackTrace();}
}
```

When the JMS client receives the reply message, it can match the JMSCorrelationID of the new message with the corresponding JMSMessageID of the message it sent, so that it knows which message received a reply. The JMSCorrelationID can be any value, not just a JMSMessageID. The JMSCorrelationID header is often used with application-specific identifiers. Our example in Chapter 4 uses the JMSCorrelationID as a way of identifying the sender. The important thing to remember, however, is that the JMSCorrelationID does not have to be a JMSMessageID, although it frequently is. If you decide to use your own ID, be aware that an application-specific JMSCorrelationID must not start with ID:. That prefix is reserved for ID generated by JMS providers.

The methods for accessing and mutating the JMSCorrelationID come in two forms: a String form and an AsBytes form. The String-based header is the most common and must be supported by JMS providers. The AsBytes method, which is based on a byte array, is an optional feature that JMS providers do not have to support. It's used for setting the JMSCorrelationID to some native JMS provider correlation ID:

```
Message message = topicSession.createMessage();
byte [] byteArray = ... set to some JMS specific byte array
...
message.setJMSCorrelationIDAsBytes(byteArray);
publisher.publish(message);
```

If the JMS provider supports messaging exchanges with a legacy messaging system that uses a native form of the correlation ID, the `AsBytes` method will be useful. If the `AsBytes` form is not supported, `setJMSCorrelationIDAsBytes()` throws a `java.lang.UnsupportedOperationException`.

JMSType

Purpose: Identification

`JMSType` is an optional header set by the JMS client. Its name is somewhat misleading because it has nothing to do with the type of message being sent (`BytesMessage`, `MapMessage`, etc.). Its main purpose is to identify the message structure and type of payload; it is only supported by a couple of vendors.

Some MOM systems (e.g., IBM's MQSeries) treat the message body as uninterpreted bytes and provide applications with a simple way of labeling the body (the message type). So the message type header can be useful when exchanging messages with non-JMS clients that require this type of information to process the payload.

Other MOM systems (such as Sun's JMQ) and EAI systems (such as SagaVista and MQIntegrator) directly tie each message to some form of external message schema, and the message type is the link. These MOM systems require the message type because they provide metadata services bound to it.

In addition, the `JMSType` might be used on a application level. For example, a B2B application that uses XML as its message payload might use the `JMSType` to keep track of which XML DTD the message payload conforms to.

C

Message Properties

Message properties are additional headers that can be assigned to a message. They provide the application developer or JMS vendor with the ability to attach more information to a message. The `Message` interface provides several accessor and mutator methods for reading and writing properties. Properties can have a `String` value, or one of several primitive (`boolean`, `byte`, `short`, `int`, `long`, `float`, `double`) values. The naming of properties, together with their values and conversion rules, are strictly defined by JMS.

Property Names

Properties are name-value pairs. The name, called the identifier, can be just about any `String` that is a valid identifier in the Java language. With a couple of exceptions, the rules that apply to naming a property are the same as those that apply to the naming of variables. One difference between a JMS property name and a Java variable name is that a property name can be any length. In addition, property names are prohibited from using one of the message selector reserved words. These words include: NOT, AND, OR, BETWEEN, LIKE, IN, IS, NULL, TRUE, and FALSE.

The property names used in JMS-defined properties and provider-specific properties use predefined prefixes. These prefixes (`JMSX` and `JMS_`) may not be used for application property names.

Property Values

Property values can be any `boolean`, `byte`, `short`, `int`, `long`, `float`, `double`, or `String`. The `javax.jms.Message` interface provides accessor and mutator methods for each of these property value types. Here is the portion of the Message interface definition that shows these methods:

```
package javax.jms;

public interface Message {

    public String getStringProperty(String name)
        throws JMSException, MessageFormatException;
    public void setStringProperty(String name, String value)
        throws JMSException, MessageNotWriteableException;
    public int getIntProperty(String name)
        throws JMSException, MessageFormatException;
    public void setIntProperty(String name, int value)
        throws JMSException, MessageNotWriteableException;
    public boolean getBooleanProperty(String name)
        throws JMSException, MessageFormatException;
    public void setBooleanProperty(String name, boolean value)
        throws JMSException, MessageNotWriteableException;
    public double getDoubleProperty(String name)
        throws JMSException, MessageFormatException;
    public void setDoubleProperty(String name, double value)
        throws JMSException, MessageNotWriteableException;
    public float getFloatProperty(String name)
        throws JMSException, MessageFormatException;
    public void setFloatProperty(String name, float value)
        throws JMSException, MessageNotWriteableException;
    public byte getByteProperty(String name)
        throws JMSException, MessageFormatException;
    public void setByteProperty(String name, byte value)
        throws JMSException, MessageNotWriteableException;
    public long getLongProperty(String name)
        throws JMSException, MessageFormatException;
    public void setLongPreperty(String name, long value)
        throws JMSException, MessageNotWriteableException;
    public short getShortProperty(String name)
        throws JMSException, MessageFormatException;
    public void setShortProperty(String name, short value)
        throws JMSException, MessageNotWriteableException;
    public Object getObjectProperty(String name)
        throws JMSException, MessageFormatException;
    public void setObjectProperty(String name, Object value)
        throws JMSException, MessageNotWriteableException;

    public void clearProperties()
        throws JMSException;
    public Enumeration getPropertyNames()
        throws JMSException;
    public boolean propertyExists(String name)
```

```
        throws JMSException;
    ...

    }
```

The following code shows how a JMS client might produce and consume messages with properties that have primitive values:

```
// A message producer writes the properties
message.setStringProperty("username","William");
message.setDoubleProperty("Limit", 33456.72);
message.setBooleanProperty("IsApproved",true);
publisher.publish(message);
...
// A message consumer reads the properties
String name = message.getStringProperty("username");
double limit = message.getDoubleProperty("Limit");
boolean isApproved = message.getBooleanProperty("IsApproved");
```

The `Object` property methods that are defined in the `Message` interface (`setObjectProperty()` and `getObjectProperty()`) are also used for properties, but they don't give you as much functionality as their names suggest. Only the primitive wrappers that correspond to the allowed primitive types and the `String` type can be used by the `Object` property methods. Attempting to use any other `Object` type will result in a `javax.jms.MessageFormatException`.

Given that the `Object` methods don't really let you do anything new, why do they exist? The `Object` property methods provide more flexibility, letting you write clients that don't hard-code the property types into the application. JMS publishers can decide at runtime what form properties should take, and JMS consumers can read the properties and use reflection to determine the value types at runtime. Here is an example of how the `Object` property methods are used to set and access properties in a message:

```
// A message producer writes the properties
String username = "William";
Double limit = new Double(33456.72);
Boolean isApproved = new Boolean(true);
...
message.setObjectProperty("username",username);
message.setObjectProperty("Limit", limit);
message.setObjectProperty("IsApproved",isApproved);
publisher.publish(message);
...
// A message consumer reads the properties
String name = (String)message.getObjectProperty("username");
Double limit = (Double)message.setObjectProperty("Limit");
Boolean isApproved = (Boolean)message.setObjectProperty("IsApproved");
```

Read-Only Properties

Once a message is produced (sent), its properties become read-only; the properties cannot be changed. While consumers can read the properties using the property accessor methods (get<TYPE>Property()), they cannot modify the properties using any of the mutator methods (set<TYPE>Property()). If the consumer attempts to set a property, the mutator method throws a javax.jms. MessageNotWriteableException.

Once a message is received, the only way its properties can be changed is by clearing out all the properties using the clearProperties() method. This removes all the properties from the message so that new ones can be added. Individual properties cannot be modified or removed once a message is sent.

Property Value Conversion

The JMS specification defines rules for conversion of property values, so that, for example, a property value of type int can be read as a long:

```
Message message = topicSession.createMessage();
// Set the property "Age" as an int value
message.setIntProperty("Age", 72);
...
// Read the property "Age" as a long is legal
long age = message.getLongProperty("Age");
```

The conversion rules are fairly simple, as shown in Table C-1. A property value can be set as one primitive type or String, and read as one of the other value types.

Table C-1. Property Type Conversions

Message.set<TYPE>Property( )	Message.get<TYPE>Property( )
boolean	boolean, String
byte	byte, short, int, long, String
short	short, int, long, String
int	int, long, String
long	long, String
float	float, double, String
double	double, String
String	String, boolean, byte, short, int, long, float, double

Each of the accessor methods (get<TYPE>Property()) can throw the MessageFormatException. The MessageFormatException is thrown by the accessor methods in order to indicate that the original type could not be converted to the type requested. The `MessageFormatException` might be thrown if, for example, a JMS client attempted to read a `float` property as an `int`.

`String` values can be converted to any primitive type, provided the `String` is formatted correctly:

```
Message message = topicSession.createMessage();

// Set the property "Weight" as a String value
message.setStringProperty("Weight","240.00");

// Set the property "IsProgrammer" as a String value
message.setStringProperty("IsProgrammer", "true");
...


// Read the property "Weight" as a flaot type
float weight = message.getFloatProperty("Weight");
// Read the property "IsProgrammer" as a boolean type
boolean isProgrammer = message.getBooleanProperty("IsProgrammer");
```

If the `String` value cannot be converted to the primitive type requested, a `java.lang.NumberFormatException` is thrown. Any property can be accessed as a `String` using the `getStringProperty()` method; all the primitive types can be converted to a `String` value.

The `getObjectProperty()` returns the appropriate object wrapper for that property. For example, an `int` can be retrieved by the message consumer as a `java.lang.Integer` object. Any property that is set using the `setObjectProperty()` method can also be accessed using the primitive property accessors; the conversion rules outlined in Table C-1 apply. The following code shows two properties (`Age` and `Weight`) that are set using primitive and `Object` property methods. The properties are later accessed using the `Object`, primitive, and `String` accessors:

```
Message message = topicSession.createMessage();

// Set the property "Weight" as a float value
message.setFloatProperty("Weight",240.00);

// Set the property "Age" as an Integer value
Integer age = new Integer(72);
message.setObjectProperty("Age", age);
...


// Read the property "Weight" as a java.lang.Float type
Float weight1 = (Float)message.getObjectProperty("Weight");
// Read the property "Weight" as a float type
float weight2 = message.getFloatProperty("Weight");
```

```
// Read the property "Age" as an Object type
Integer age1 = (Integer)message.getObjectProperty("Age");
// Read the property "Age" as a long is legal
long age2 = message.getLongProperty("Age");
```

Nonexistent Properties

If a JMS client attempts to access a nonexistent property using
getObjectProperty(), null is returned. The rest of the property methods
attempt to convert the null value to the requested type using the valueOf()
operations. This results in some interesting behavior. The getStringProperty()
returns a null or possibly an empty String ("") depending on the implementation. The getBooleanProperty() method returns false for null values, while
the other primitive property methods throw the java.lang.Number-
FormatException.

The propertyExists() method can be used to avoid erroneous values or exceptions for properties that have not been set on the message. Here is an example of
how it's used:

```
if (message.propertyExists("Age"))
    age = message.getIntProperty("Age");
}
```

Property Iteration

The getPropertyNames() method in the Message interface can be used to
obtain an Enumeration of all the property names contained in the message.
These names can then be used to obtain the property values using the property
accessor methods. The following code shows how you might use this Enumeration
to print all the property values:

```
public void onMessage(Message message) {
    Enumeration propertyNames = message.getPropertyNames();
    while(propertyNames.hasMoreElements()){
        String name = (String)propertyNames.nextElement();
        Object value = getObjectProperty(name);
        System.out.println("\nname+" = "+value);
    }
}
```

JMS-Defined Properties

JMS-defined properties have the same characteristics as application properties,
except that most of them are set automatically by the JMS provider when the message is sent. JMS-defined properties are basically optional JMS headers; vendors

can choose to support none, some, or all of them. There are nine JMS-defined properties, each of which starts with "JMSX" in the property name.

Optional JMS-Defined Properties

Here are the optional JMS-defined properties and their descriptions:

JMSXUserID

> This property is a String that is set automatically by the JMS provider when the message is sent. Some JMS providers can assign a client a user ID, which is the value associated with this property.

JMSXAppID

> This property is a String that is set automatically by the JMS provider when the message is sent. Some JMS providers can assign an identifier to a specific JMS application, which is a set of consumers and subscribers that communicate using a set of destinations.

JMSXProducerTXID *and* JMSXConsumerTXID

> Messages can be produced and consumed within a transaction. Every transaction in a system has a unique identity that can be obtained from the producer or consumer using these properties. The JMSXProducerTXID is set by the JMS provider when the message is sent, and the JMSXConsumerTXID is set by the JMS provider when the message is received.

JMSXRcvTimestamp

> This property is a primitive long value that is set automatically by the JMS provider when the message is received. It represents the UTC time (see the "UTC" sidebar in Appendix B, *Message Headers*) that the message was received by the consumer.

JMSXDeliveryCount

> This property is an int that is set automatically by the JMS provider when the message is received. If a message is not properly acknowledged by a consumer it may be redelivered. This property keeps a tally of the number of times the message server attempts to deliver the message to that particular consumer.

JMSXState

> This property is an int that is set automatically by the JMS provider. The property is for use by repositories and JMS provider tools and is not available to either the consumer or producer—as a developer, you will never have access to this property. The property provides a standard way for a JMS provider to annotate the state of a message. States can be one of the following: 1 (waiting), 2 (ready), 3 (expired), or 4 (retained). This property can be safely ignored by most JMS developers, but an explanation of its purpose is provided for completeness.

The JMS-defined properties that are assigned when the message is received (JMSXConsumerTXID, JMSXRcvTimestamp, and JMSXDeliveryCount) are not available to the message's producer, but only available to the message consumer.

Group JMS-Defined Properties

While the bulk of JMSX properties are optional, the group properties are not optional; they must be supported by the JMS provider. The group properties allow a JMS client to group messages together and assign each message in the group with a sequence ID. Here are the group properties:

JMSXGroupID

> This property is a String that is set by the JMS client before the message is sent. It is the identity of the group to which the message belongs.

JMSXGroupSeq

> This property is a primitive int type that is set by the JMS client before the message is sent. It is the sequence number of the message within a group of messages.

Provider-Specific Properties

Every JMS provider can define a set of proprietary properties of any type. These properties can be set by the client or the provider automatically. Provider-specific properties must start with the prefix "JMS_" followed by the property name (JMS_ <vendor-property-name>). The purpose of the provider-specific properties is to support proprietary vendor features.

D

Message Selectors

Message selectors allow a JMS consumer to be more selective about the messages it receives from a particular topic or queue. Message selectors use `Message` properties and headers as criteria in conditional expressions. These conditional expressions use boolean logic to declare which messages should be delivered to a client.

The message selectors are based on a subset of the SQL-92 conditional expression syntax that is used in the `WHERE` clauses of SQL statements. This section is a detailed exploration of the message selector syntax.

To illustrate how message selectors are applied, we will consider a hypothetical message that contains three application properties: `Age`, `Weight`, and `LName`. `Age` is an `int`, `Weight` is a `double`, and `LName` is a `String` property. The values of these properties depend on the message. The message selector is used to obtain only those messages with property values of interest to the consumer.

Identifiers

An identifier is the part of the expression that is being compared. For example, the identifiers in the following expression are `Age`, `Weight`, and `LName`:

```
Age < 30 AND Weight >= 100.00 AND LName = 'Smith'
```

Identifiers can be any application-defined, JMS-defined, or provider-specific property, or one of several JMS headers. Identifiers must match the property or JMS header name exactly; identifiers are case sensitive. Identifiers have the same naming restrictions as property names (see Appendix C, *Message Properties*).

The JMS headers that can be used as identifiers include `JMSDeliveryMode`, `JMSPriority`, `JMSMessageID`, `JMSTimestamp`, `JMSCorrelationID`, and `JMS-Type`. The `JMSDestination` and `JMSReplyTo` headers cannot be used as identifiers because their corresponding values are Destination objects whose underlying value is proprietary and therefore undefined.

The JMSRedelivered value may be changed during delivery. If a consumer uses a message selector where "JMSRedelivered = FALSE", and there was a failure delivering a message, the JMSRedelivered flag might be set to TRUE. JMSExpiration is not supported as an identifier because JMS providers may choose to implement this value differently. Some may store it with the message, while others calculate it as needed.

Literals

Literals are expression values that are hard-coded into the message selector. In the message selector shown here, 30, 100.00, and 'Smith' are all literals:

```
Age < 30 AND Weight >= 100.00 AND LName = 'Smith'
```

String literals are enclosed in single quotes. An apostrophe or single quote can be included in a String literal by using two single quotes (e.g., 'Smith''s').

Numeric literals are expressed using exact numerical (+22, 30, -52134), approximate numerical with decimal (-33.22, 100.00, +7.0), or scientific (-9E4, 3.5E6) notation.

Boolean literals are expressed as TRUE or FALSE.

Comparison Operators

Comparison operators compare identifiers to literals in a boolean expression that evaluates to either TRUE or FALSE. Comparison operations can be combined into more complex expressions using the logical operators AND and OR. Expressions are evaluated from left to right:

```
Age < 30 AND Weight >= 100.00 OR LName = 'Smith'
```

In this example, the expression would be evaluated as if it had parentheses placed as follows (parentheses can be used to group expressions and can change the precedence of evaluation):

```
(Age < 30 AND Weight >= 100.00)  OR  (LName = 'Smith')
```

Either the LName must be equal to 'Smith' or the LName can be any value as long as the Age is less than 30 and the Weight is greater than or equal to 100. Evaluating these kinds of expressions should be second nature for most programmers.

The following message selector uses three of the six algebraic comparison operators, which are =, >, >=, <, <=, and <> (not equal):

```
Age < 30 AND Weight >= 100.00 OR LName = 'Smith'
```

These algebraic comparison operators can be used on any of the primitive property types except for `boolean`. The `boolean` and `String` property types are restricted to the = or the <> algebraic operators.

String types can be compared using the `LIKE` comparison operator. For example:

```
Age < 30 AND Weight >= 100.00 OR LName LIKE 'Sm%th'
```

The `LIKE` comparison operator attempts to match each character in the literal with characters of the property value. Two special wildcard characters, underscore (_) and percent (%), can be used with the `LIKE` comparison. The underscore stands for any single character. The percent symbol stands for any sequence of characters. All other characters stand for themselves and are case sensitive. Table D-1 provides some examples of successful and unsuccessful comparisons using the `LIKE` operator.

Table D-1. Comparisons Using the LIKE Operator

Expression	True for Values	False for Values
LName LIKE 'Sm_th'	Smith, Smeth, Sm4th	Smooth, Smth, Smiths
LName LIKE 'Smit_'	Smith, Smitt, Smit4	Smoth, Smiths
LName LIKE 'Sm%th'	Smith, Smoo3th, Smth	Smott, Rmith, Smiths
LName LIKE '%ith'	Smith, Synoonith, ith	Smoth, Smiths

The `BETWEEN` operator can be used to specify a range (inclusive). For example:

```
Age BETWEEN 20 and 30
```

This expression is the same as:

```
(Age >= 20) AND (Age <=30)
```

The `IN` operator can be used to specify membership in a set:

```
LName IN ('Smith', 'Jones', 'Brown')
```

This expression is the same as:

```
(LName = 'Smith') OR (LName = 'Jones') OR (LName = 'Brown')
```

The `NOT` logical operator can be used in combination with the `LIKE`, `BETWEEN`, `IN`, and `IS NULL` (discussed later) operators to reverse their evaluation. If the expression would have evaluated to `TRUE`, it becomes `FALSE`, and vice versa.

When no property or header exists to match an identifier in a message selector, the value of the identifier is assigned a `null` value. Nonexistent properties evaluating to `null` present some problems with message selectors. In some cases, the `null` value of the property cannot be evaluated in a conditional expression. The result is an *unknown* evaluation—a nice way of saying the result is not predictable across JMS providers. If, for example, a particular message contains the `Age = 20` and `Weight = 90.00` properties but does not have an `LName` property, then the message selector following would evaluate as shown:

```
Age < 30 AND Weight >= 100.00 OR LName = 'Smith'
 ____          _____                 _____
 TRUE    AND    FALSE     OR         UNKNOWN
```

The results of evaluating `unknown` expressions with logical operators (`AND`, `OR`, `NOT`) are shown in Table D-2, Table D-3, and Table D-4.

Table D-2. Definition of the AND Operator

Expression	Result
TRUE AND TRUE	TRUE
TRUE AND FALSE	FALSE
TRUE AND Unknown	Unknown
FALSE AND Unknown	FALSE
Unknown AND Unknown	Unknown

Table D-3. Definition of the OR Operator

Expression	Result
TRUE OR TRUE	TRUE
TRUE OR FALSE	TRUE
TRUE OR Unknown	TRUE
FALSE OR Unknown	Unknown
Unknown OR Unknown	Unknown

Table D-4. Definition of the NOT Operator

Expression	Result
NOT TRUE	FALSE
NOT FALSE	TRUE
NOT Unknown	Unknown

To avoid problems, the `IS NULL` or `IS NOT NULL` comparison can be used to check for the existence of a property:

```
Age IS NULL AND Weight IS NOT NULL
```

The previous expression selects messages that do not have an `Age` property but do have a `Weight` property.

Arithmetic Operators

In addition to normal comparison operators, message selectors can use arithmetic operators to calculate values for evaluation dynamically at runtime. Table D-5 shows the arithmetic operators in their order of precedence.

Table D-5. Arithmetic Operators

Type	Symbol
Unary	+, −
Multiplication and division	*, /
Addition and subtraction	+, −

For example, the following expression applies arithmetic operations to the Age, Height, and Weight properties to select people who have a weight outside a certain range:

```
Weight NOT BETWEEN (Age * 5) AND (Height/Age * 2.23)
```

Declaring a Message Selector

When a consumer is created with a message selector, the JMS provider must validate that the selector statement is syntactically correct. If the selector is not correct, the operation throws a `javax.jms.InvalidSelectorException`. Here are the session methods used to specify a message selector when creating a consumer:

```
// P2P Session's Message Consumer Methods
public QueueSession extends Session{
   QueueBrowser createBrowser(Queue queue, String messageSelector)
   throws JMSException, InvalidSelectorException,
        InvalidDestinationException;
   QueueReciever createReceiver(Queue queue, String messageSelector)
   throws JMSException, InvalidSelectorException,
        InvalidDestinationException;
   ...
}
```

The QueueBrowser and QueueReceiver types of the QueueSession interface are explored in Chapter 5, *Point-to-Point Messaging*. The durable subscriber (shown here) is covered in Chapter 4, *Publish-and-Subscribe Messaging*:

```
// Pub/Sub Session's Message Consumer Methods
public TopicSession extends Session {
   TopicSubscriber createSubscriber(Topic topic,
                                    String messageSelector,
                                    boolean noLocal)
```

```
                        throws JMSException,
                              InvalidSelectorException,
                              InvalidDestinationException;

     TopicSubscriber createDurableSubscriber(Queue queue,
                                    String name,
                                    String messageSelector,
                                    boolean noLocal)
                        throws JMSException,
                              InvalidSelectorException,
                              InvalidDestinationException;

     ...
     }
```

The message selector used for a consumer can always be obtained by calling the `getMessageSelector()` method on a `QueueReceiver`, `QueueBrowser`, or `TopicSubscriber`. The `getMessageSelector()` method returns the message selector for that consumer as a `String`.

Once a consumer's message selector has been established, it cannot be changed. The consumer must be closed or deleted (durable subscriber) and a new consumer created with a new message selector.

Not Delivered Semantics

What happens to messages that are not selected for delivery to the consumer by its message selector? This depends on the message model used.

For the publish-and-subscribe model, the messages are not delivered to that consumer; they are, however, delivered to other pub/sub consumers. This is true for both nondurable and durable subscriptions.

For the p2p model, any messages that are not selected by the consumer are not visible to that consumer. They are, however, visible to other p2p consumers.

Index

About the Authors

Richard Monson-Haefel is a leading expert in Enterprise Java development. He is the architect of OpenEJB, an open source EJB server, and has consulted as an architect on Enterprise JavaBeans, CORBA, Java RMI, and other distributed computing projects over the past several years.

Mr. Monson-Haefel is also the author of O'Reilly's *Enterprise JavaBeans*, which was awarded the JDJ Editor's Choice Award (1999) and has been on Amazon.com's list of best-selling Java books for over 18 months. In addition, Mr. Monson-Haefel has authored numerous magazine articles and was a contributing author to the book *Special Edition: Using JavaBeans* (Macmillan 1997).

Mr. Monson-Haefel maintains *jMiddleware.com*, a web site with resources and articles dedicated to the discussion of JMS, EJB, J2EE, and other Java middleware technologies.

David A. Chappell is Vice President and SonicMQ Chief Technology Evangelist at Progress Software Corp. Dave has over 18 years of industry experience building software tools and infrastructure for application developers, spanning all aspects of R&D, sales, marketing, and support services. Dave has also been published in *Network World* magazine and has presented technical topics at numerous speaking engagements including JavaOne and XMLOne.

As Director of Engineering for SonicMQ, Progress Software's award-winning JMS Internet Commerce Messaging System, Dave oversaw the design and development of the fastest, most scalable, reliable, and robust implementation of JMS in the marketplace.

Dave has under his belt a broad cross-platform background in designing and developing Internet-based middleware and distributed object systems across a broad range of technologies including C++, Java, DCOM, CORBA, and EJB. Dave's experience also includes development of client/server infrastructure, graphical user interfaces, language interpreters, and various utility libraries.

Colophon

Our look is the result of reader comments, our own experimentation, and feedback from distribution channels. Distinctive covers complement our distinctive approach to technical topics, breathing personality and life into potentially dry subjects. The image on the cover of *Java Message Service* is a passenger pigeon.

Colleen Gorman was the production editor and the copyeditor, and Clairemarie Fisher O'Leary was the proofreader, for *Java Message Service*. Catherine Morris and Rachel Wheeler provided quality control. Matt Hutchinson and Rachel Wheeler provided production support. John Bickelhaupt wrote the index.

The animal on the cover of *Java Message Service* is a passenger pigeon. Hanna Dyer designed the cover of this book, based on a series design by Edie Freedman. The cover image is a 19th-century engraving from the Dover Pictorial Archive. Emma Colby produced the cover layout with QuarkXPress 4.1 using Adobe's ITC Garamond font.

Melanie Wang designed the interior layout based on a series design by Nancy Priest. Mike Sierra implemented the design in FrameMaker 5.5.6. The heading font is Bodoni BT, the text font is New Baskerville, and the code font is Constant Willison. The illustrations that appear in the book were produced by Robert Romano using Macromedia FreeHand 8 and Adobe Photoshop 5.

Whenever possible, our books use a durable and flexible lay-flat binding. If the page count exceeds this binding's limit, perfect binding is used.

How to stay in touch with O'Reilly

1. Visit Our Award-Winning Web Site

http://www.oreilly.com/

★"Top 100 Sites on the Web" —*PC Magazine*
★"Top 5% Web sites" —*Point Communications*
★"3-Star site" —*The McKinley Group*

Our web site contains a library of comprehensive product information (including book excerpts and tables of contents), downloadable software, background articles, interviews with technology leaders, links to relevant sites, book cover art, and more. File us in your Bookmarks or Hotlist!

2. Join Our Email Mailing Lists

New Product Releases
To receive automatic email with brief descriptions of all new O'Reilly products as they are released, send email to:
ora-news-subscribe@lists.oreilly.com
Put the following information in the first line of your message (*not* in the Subject field):
subscribe ora-news

O'Reilly Events
If you'd also like us to send information about trade show events, special promotions, and other O'Reilly events, send email to:
ora-news-subscribe@lists.oreilly.com
Put the following information in the first line of your message (*not* in the Subject field):
subscribe ora-events

3. Get Examples from Our Books via FTP

There are two ways to access an archive of example files from our books:

Regular FTP
- ftp to:
  ftp.oreilly.com
  (login: anonymous
  password: your email address)
- Point your web browser to:
  ftp://ftp.oreilly.com/

FTPMAIL
- Send an email message to:
  ftpmail@online.oreilly.com
  (Write "help" in the message body)

4. Contact Us via Email

order@oreilly.com
To place a book or software order online. Good for North American and international customers.

subscriptions@oreilly.com
To place an order for any of our newsletters or periodicals.

books@oreilly.com
General questions about any of our books.

software@oreilly.com
For general questions and product information about our software. Check out O'Reilly Software Online at **http://software.oreilly.com/** for software and technical support information. Registered O'Reilly software users send your questions to: **website-support@oreilly.com**

cs@oreilly.com
For answers to problems regarding your order or our products.

booktech@oreilly.com
For book content technical questions or corrections.

proposals@oreilly.com
To submit new book or software proposals to our editors and product managers.

international@oreilly.com
For information about our international distributors or translation queries. For a list of our distributors outside of North America check out:
http://www.oreilly.com/distributors.html

5. Work with Us

Check out our website for current employment opportunites:
http://jobs.oreilly.com/

O'Reilly & Associates, Inc.
101 Morris Street, Sebastopol, CA 95472 USA
TEL   707-829-0515 or 800-998-9938
          (6am to 5pm PST)
FAX   707-829-0104

O'REILLY®

International Distributors

http://international.oreilly.com/distributors.html • international@oreilly.com

UK, EUROPE, MIDDLE EAST AND AFRICA (EXCEPT FRANCE, GERMANY, AUSTRIA, SWITZERLAND, LUXEMBOURG, AND LIECHTENSTEIN)

INQUIRIES
O'Reilly UK Limited
4 Castle Street
Farnham
Surrey, GU9 7HS
United Kingdom
Telephone: 44-1252-711776
Fax: 44-1252-734211
Email: information@oreilly.co.uk

ORDERS
Wiley Distribution Services Ltd.
1 Oldlands Way
Bognor Regis
West Sussex PO22 9SA
United Kingdom
Telephone: 44-1243-843294
UK Freephone: 0800-243207
Fax: 44-1243-843302 (Europe/EU orders)
or 44-1243-843274 (Middle East/Africa)
Email: cs-books@wiley.co.uk

FRANCE

INQUIRIES & ORDERS
Éditions O'Reilly
18 rue Séguier
75006 Paris, France
Tel: 33-1-40-51-71-89
Fax: 33-1-40-51-72-26
Email: france@oreilly.fr

GERMANY, SWITZERLAND, AUSTRIA, LUXEMBOURG, AND LIECHTENSTEIN

INQUIRIES & ORDERS
O'Reilly Verlag
Balthasarstr. 81
D-50670 Köln, Germany
Telephone: 49-221-973160-91
Fax: 49-221-973160-8
Email: anfragen@oreilly.de (inquiries)
Email: order@oreilly.de (orders)

CANADA (FRENCH LANGUAGE BOOKS)

Les Éditions Flammarion ltée
375, Avenue Laurier Ouest
Montréal (Québec) H2V 2K3
Tel: 1-514-277-8807
Fax: 1-514-278-2085
Email: info@flammarion.qc.ca

HONG KONG

City Discount Subscription Service, Ltd.
Unit A, 6th Floor, Yan's Tower
27 Wong Chuk Hang Road
Aberdeen, Hong Kong
Tel: 852-2580-3539
Fax: 852-2580-6463
Email: citydis@ppn.com.hk

KOREA

Hanbit Media, Inc.
Chungmu Bldg. 210
Yonnam-dong 568-33
Mapo-gu
Seoul, Korea
Tel: 822-325-0397
Fax: 822-325-9697
Email: hant93@chollian.dacom.co.kr

PHILIPPINES

Global Publishing
G/F Benavides Garden
1186 Benavides Street
Manila, Philippines
Tel: 632-254-8949/632-252-2582
Fax: 632-734-5060/632-252-2733
Email: globalp@pacific.net.ph

TAIWAN

O'Reilly Taiwan
1st Floor, No. 21, Lane 295
Section 1, Fu-Shing South Road
Taipei, 106 Taiwan
Tel: 886-2-27099669
Fax: 886-2-27038802
Email: mori@oreilly.com

INDIA

Shroff Publishers & Distributors Pvt. Ltd.
12, "Roseland", 2nd Floor
180, Waterfield Road, Bandra (West)
Mumbai 400 050
Tel: 91-22-641-1800/643-9910
Fax: 91-22-643-2422
Email: spd@vsnl.com

CHINA

O'Reilly Beijing
SIGMA Building, Suite B809
No. 49 Zhichun Road
Haidian District
Beijing, China PR 100080
Tel: 86-10-8809-7475
Fax: 86-10-8809-7463
Email: beijing@oreilly.com

JAPAN

O'Reilly Japan, Inc.
Yotsuya Y's Building
7 Banch 6, Honshio-cho
Shinjuku-ku
Tokyo 160-0003 Japan
Tel: 81-3-3356-5227
Fax: 81-3-3356-5261
Email: japan@oreilly.com

SINGAPORE, INDONESIA, MALAYSIA AND THAILAND

TransQuest Publishers Pte Ltd
30 Old Toh Tuck Road #05-02
Sembawang Kimtrans Logistics Centre
Singapore 597654
Tel: 65-4623112
Fax: 65-4625761
Email: wendiw@transquest.com.sg

ALL OTHER COUNTRIES

O'Reilly & Associates, Inc.
101 Morris Street
Sebastopol, CA 95472 USA
Tel: 707-829-0515
Fax: 707-829-0104
Email: order@oreilly.com

AUSTRALIA

Woodslane Pty., Ltd.
7/5 Vuko Place
Warriewood NSW 2102
Australia
Tel: 61-2-9970-5111
Fax: 61-2-9970-5002
Email: info@woodslane.com.au

NEW ZEALAND

Woodslane New Zealand, Ltd.
21 Cooks Street (P.O. Box 575)
Waganui, New Zealand
Tel: 64-6-347-6543
Fax: 64-6-345-4840
Email: info@woodslane.com.au

ARGENTINA

Distribuidora Cuspide
Suipacha 764
1008 Buenos Aires
Argentina
Phone: 54-11-4322-8868
Fax: 54-11-4322-3456
Email: libros@cuspide.com

O'REILLY®

TO ORDER: **800-998-9938** • **order@oreilly.com** • **http://www.oreilly.com/**
OUR PRODUCTS ARE AVAILABLE AT A BOOKSTORE OR SOFTWARE STORE NEAR YOU.
FOR INFORMATION: **800-998-9938** • **707-829-0515** • **info@oreilly.com**